HELEN FRANKENTHALER
A PAINTINGS RETROSPECTIVE

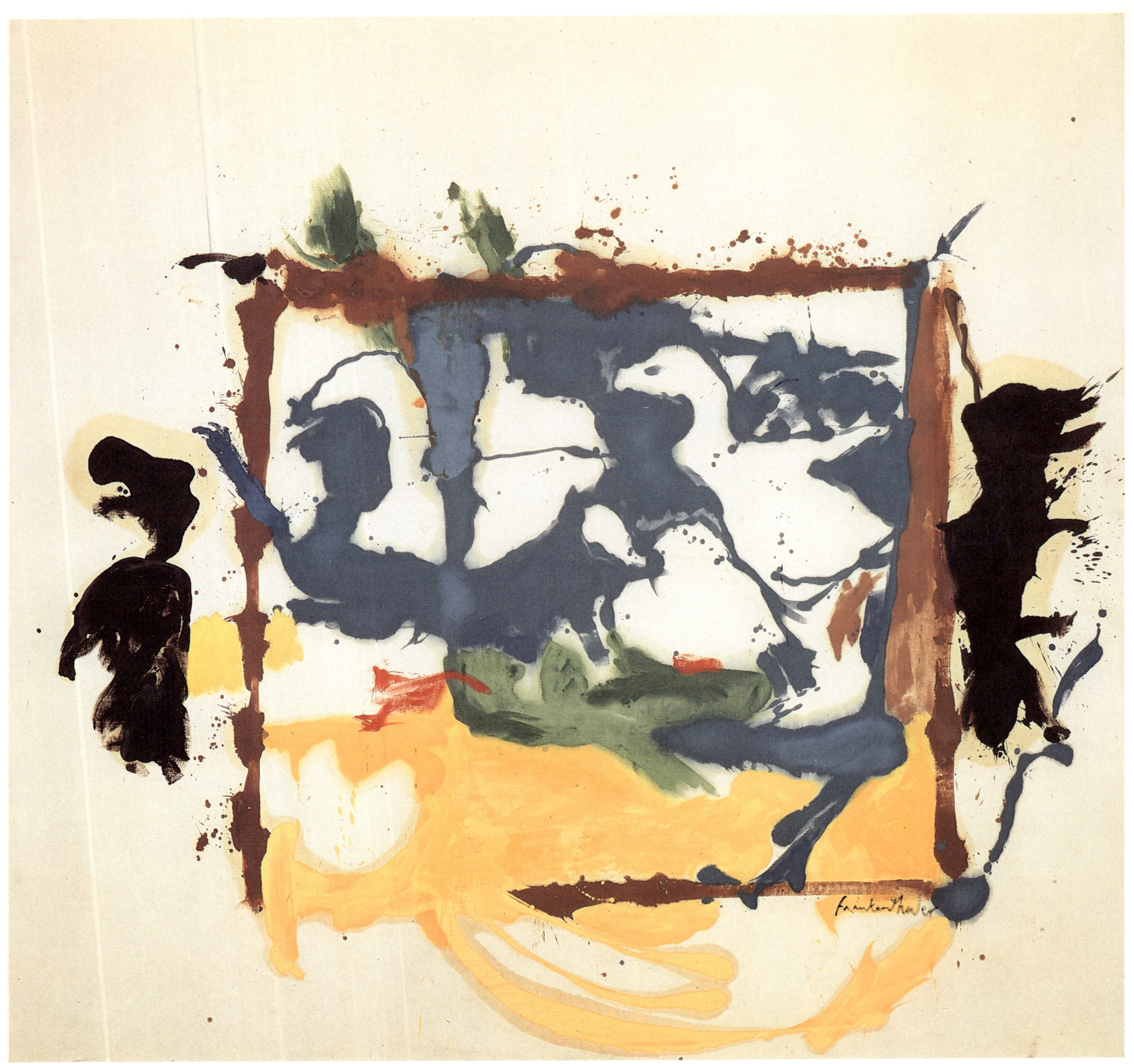

HELEN FRANKENTHALER
A PAINTINGS RETROSPECTIVE

E.A. CARMEAN, JR.

Harry N. Abrams, Inc., Publishers, New York, in association with the Modern Art Museum of Fort Worth

Project Director: Robert Morton
Editor: Harriet Whelchel
Designer: Vicki Whistler

Cover: *For E. M.* 1981. Acrylic on canvas, 5'11" x 9'7."
Private Collection

Back: *Las Mayas.* 1958. Oil on canvas, 8'4" x 3'7¾."
Collection Norman and Irma Braman

Frontispiece: *Swan Lake I.* 1961. Oil on canvas, 7'5⅛" x 7'9¾."
Private Collection

Library of Congress Cataloging-in-Publication Data

Carmean, E.A.
    Helen Frankenthaler: a paintings retrospective / E.A. Carmean, Jr.
        p. cm.
    Catalogue of a traveling exhibition, The Museum of Modern Art,
        New York, 6/89, Modern Art Museum of Fort Worth, 11/89, and
        Los Angeles County Museum of Art, 2/90, The Detroit Institute
        of Arts, 6/90
    Bibliography:
    Includes index.
    ISBN 0–8109–1179–5
    ISBN 0–929865–01–4 (pbk. : Modern Art Museum of Fort Worth)
        1. Frankenthaler, Helen, 1928–   .   — Exhibitions.
    I. Frankenthaler, Helen, 1928–   .   II. The Museum of Modern Art
    (New York, N.Y.) III. Title.
    ND237.F675A4   1989
    759.13–dc19   88–39301

Modern Art Museum of Fort Worth
© The Board of Trustees
The Fort Worth Art Association, 1989

Published in 1989 by Harry N. Abrams, Incorporated, New York.
All rights reserved. No part of the contents of this book may be
reproduced without the written permission of the publisher

A Times Mirror Company

Printed and bound in Japan

Photograph Credits:

The author and publisher wish to thank the museums, galleries, and
private collectors for supplying the necessary photographs. Other
photograph credits are listed below.

Geoffrey Clements: pp. ii, 29; courtesy André Emmerich Gallery,
    New York: p. 69
Gamma One Conversions, Inc.: pp. 23, 85, 91; courtesy André
    Emmerich Gallery, New York: p. 87
Paul Hester: p. 53
Los Angeles County Museum of Art, copyright © 1986 Museum
    Associates: p. 21
T. E. Moore, courtesy former David Mirvish Gallery, Toronto: p. 61
Otto Nelson: p. 17
Douglas M. Parker ©: p. 31
David Preston: p. 45
Steven Sloman ©: front cover, pp. 55, 59, 65, 73, 75, 79, 81, 93;
    courtesy André Emmerich Gallery, New York: p. 63; courtesy John
    Berggruen Gallery, San Francisco: p. 89
Roland Unruh: back cover, pp. 6, 25

Exhibition Itinerary:

The Museum of Modern Art
June 5–August 20, 1989

Modern Art Museum of Fort Worth
November 5, 1989–January 7, 1990

Los Angeles County Museum of Art
February 8–April 22, 1990

The Detroit Institute of Arts
June 11–September 2, 1990

Small's Paradise (cat. no. 13) and *Flood* (cat. no. 19) will not exhibit at
The Detroit Institute of Arts. *Buddha's Court* (cat. no. 14) and *Chairman
of the Board* (cat. no. 22) exhibit only at The Museum of Modern Art,
New York.

Contents

Acknowledgments 1

Lenders to the Exhibition 3

Introduction 5
  by E.A. Carmean, Jr.

Catalogue of the Exhibition 11

Selected Chronology 95

Selected Exhibition History 101

Selected Bibliography 107

Museum Board of Trustees 113

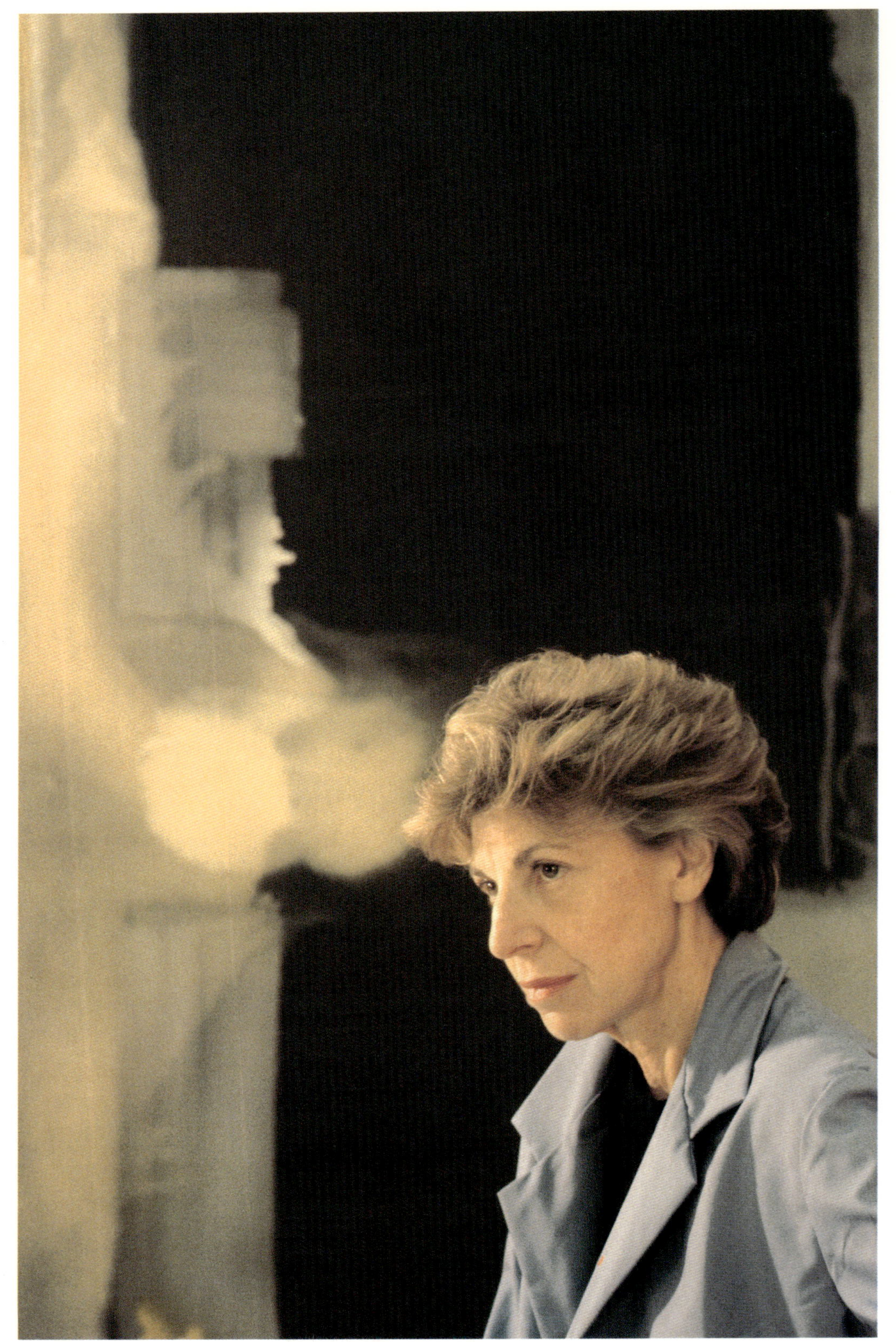

Acknowledgments

For Becky

This exhibition, *Helen Frankenthaler: A Paintings Retrospective,* required the time and efforts of a number of individuals and, on behalf of the Board of Trustees, I wish to acknowledge them here. At Frankenthaler's studio, Maureen St. Onge, the artist's majordomo, assisted in many phases of the exhibition. Our colleagues at Harry N. Abrams, Inc. in New York—particularly Robert Morton, director of special projects, and Harriet Whelchel, editor—created this publication. Also in New York, André Emmerich, of André Emmerich Gallery Inc., gave great encouragement and advice to this project.

At the Museum, Ruth Hazel, curatorial associate, prepared the catalogue entries, exhibition history, and bibliography; Cathy Craft, museum intern, prepared the chronology; Vicki Whistler designed this publication. The many details of organization were ably handled by James L. Fisher, assistant to the director for exhibitions, and Rachael Blackburn Wright, registrar. The installation here in Fort Worth was designed and executed by Tony Wright, head of design and installation, and Bill LeSueur. Susan Colegrove, secretary to the director, assisted throughout all phases of the project.

I also wish to thank our colleagues who will share this exhibition: The Museum of Modern Art, Richard E. Oldenburg, director; Los Angeles County Museum of Art, Dr. Earl A. Powell III, director; Detroit Institute of Arts, Samuel Sachs II, director.

No exhibition is possible without the generosity of its lenders, and we thank them here for their participation in this retrospective.

Finally, we must thank Helen Frankenthaler for her time and efforts in the long process of assembling this exhibition. The catalogue that follows records her insights into her paintings. The same conversations that generated these words also held much laughter and somber reflection as well as exuberance for the past, present, and future.

E.A. Carmean, Jr.
Director
Modern Art Museum of Fort Worth

Helen Frankenthaler in her New York studio, November 1988
Photograph: Alexander Liberman

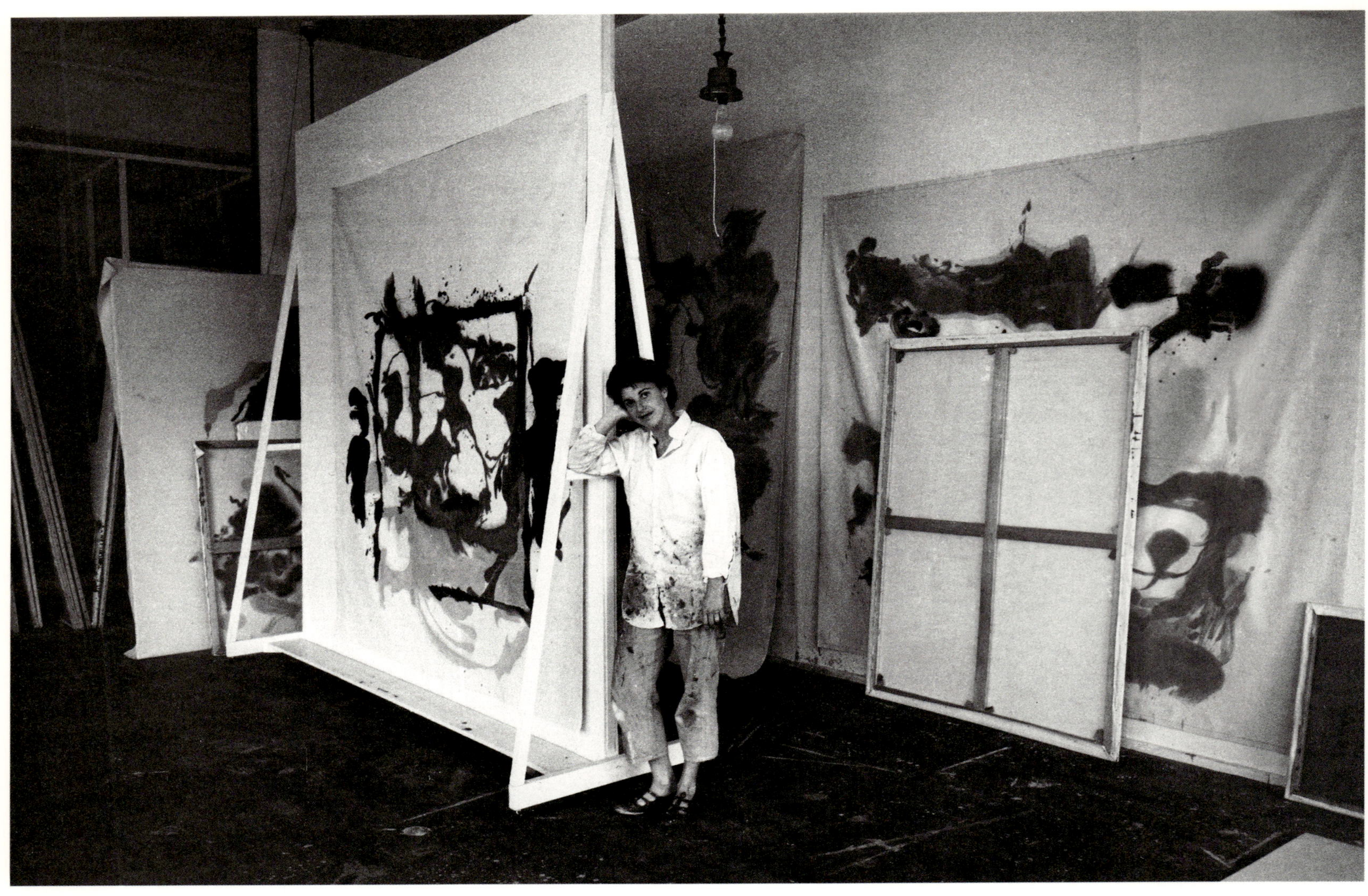

Helen Frankenthaler in her New York studio, spring 1961. To the artist's
immediate right is *Swan Lake I* (cat. no. 8).
Photograph: André Emmerich

Lenders to the Exhibition

Albright-Knox Art Gallery, Buffalo, New York
Art Gallery of Ontario, Canada
The artist
Norman and Irma Braman
The Eli and Edythe L. Broad Collection
Nina and Gordon Bunshaft Collection, New York
Lois and Georges de Menil
The Detroit Institute of Arts, Michigan
Everson Museum of Art, Syracuse, New York
Grey Art Gallery and Study Center, New York University
    Art Collection
Mr. and Mrs. Ellwood M. Haynes, San Francisco,
    California
Mr. and Mrs. Robert Hoffman, Texas
Los Angeles County Museum of Art, California
Mr. and Mrs. David Mirvish, Toronto, Canada
Museum moderner Kunst, Vienna, Austria
The Museum of Modern Art, New York
National Museum of American Art, Smithsonian
    Institution, Washington, D.C.
Phoenix Art Museum, Arizona
Private Collections
San Francisco Museum of Modern Art, California
Mr. and Mrs. Fayez Sarofim, Houston, Texas
Robert and Linda Schmier
Virginia Museum of Fine Arts, Richmond
Whitney Museum of American Art, New York

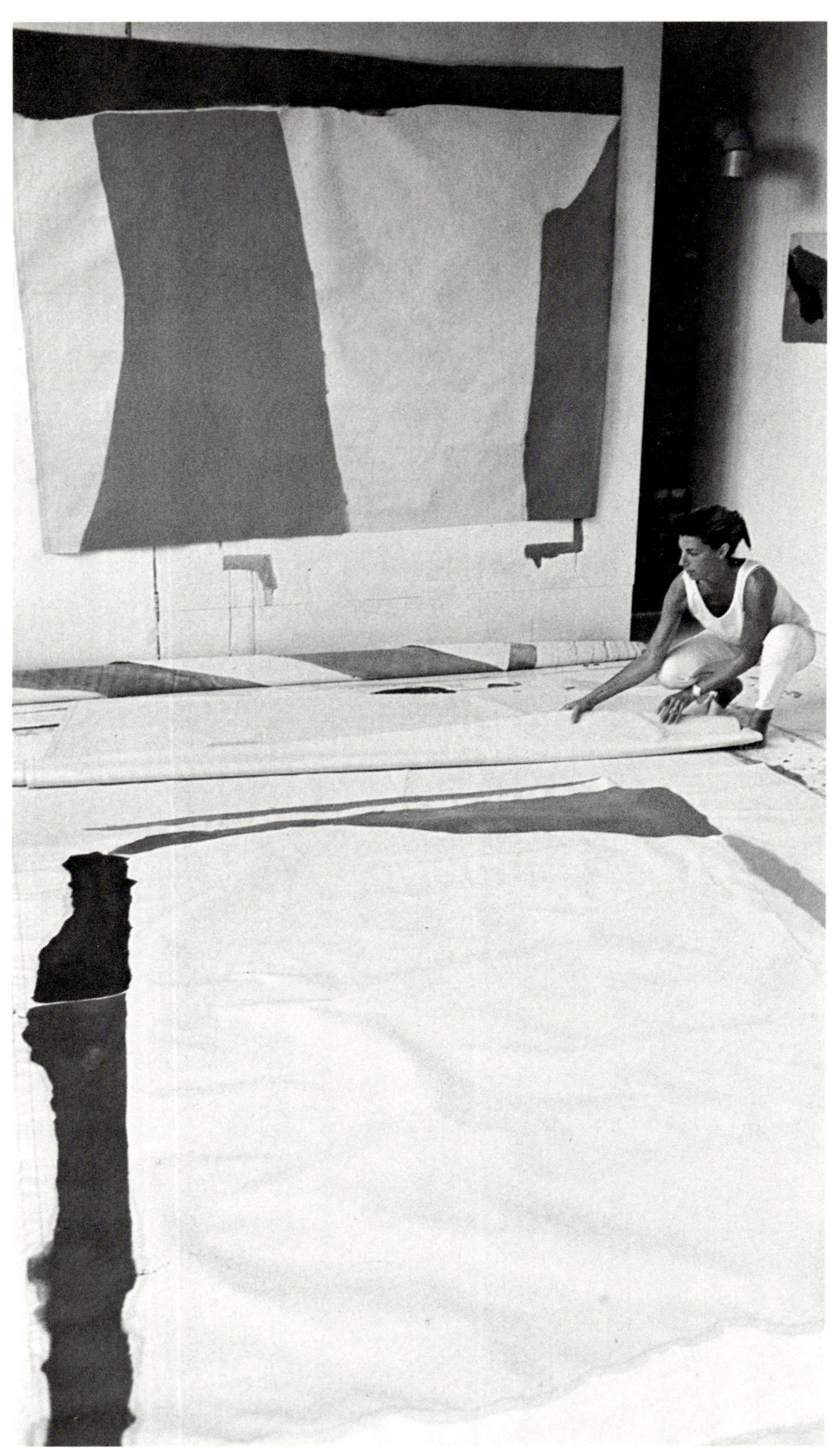

Helen Frankenthaler in
her Provincetown, Massa-
chusetts studio in summer 1968.
Behind the artist is *Summer Banner* (cat. no. 20),
seen on the wall as it was
hung initially (see p. 52).
Photograph: Alexander
Liberman

Introduction

"It is an order familiar and new at the same time."

Helen Frankenthaler

The selection of forty paintings by Helen Frankenthaler in this exhibition and the corresponding individual commentaries that follow in this publication largely grew out of a host of extended conversations between the artist and myself. We began in 1984 by talking in general about her career, her work, and the idea of this show; we ended in 1988 by discussing each picture in particular, each painting seen in virtual isolation from any other work.

The idea of moving from the general to the specific is certainly not odd or novel in preparing a retrospective of an artist's work. What makes it telling for this exhibition is that our conclusion was to select the show on a picture-by-picture basis. Each work is the subject of its own catalogue entry rather than being treated as a representative player in a broader historical treatise. Thus this exhibition is a considered study of specific Frankenthaler paintings rather than a general survey of her career as a painter.

The impulse behind this approach was broached in our initial conversation about selecting the exhibition. "When one gets within the work, into my career," she remarked, "one sees the paintings are not the same, in that each canvas is essentially its own breakthrough and development, not always the result of a serial theme and variation. One sees a basic signature that develops over the decades."[1]

As viewers of this exhibition will see and readers of this volume discover, the visual diversity of Frankenthaler's painting from picture to picture is extreme. This is especially so for an artist whose work was initially made (and seen in 1952–60) in the context of Abstract Expressionism with its repeated subjects, such as De Kooning's Women, Gottlieb's Bursts, and Motherwell's Spanish Elegies. This visual diversity was even more telling—and to critics, perhaps disturbing—in the company of the aesthetic of her own generation, where serialism was paramount—for example, Louis's Unfurleds, Noland's Targets, or Stella's Stripes.

The perception of this diversity in the artist's painting is not recent, although it is important to recognize that it has continued to the present as an essential aesthetic characteristic. As early as 1961 E. C. Goossen, one of her most insightful critics, observed that "most of our younger artists, instead of addressing themselves to the problems of art, search desperately for a trademark. . . . This is hardly Frankenthaler's problem . . . she has kept the door open by painting pictures rather than variations on a theme. Her pictures tend to be so dedicated to themselves. . . ."[2]

In coordination with the exhibition, this publication discusses the works as individual paintings and thus consists of separate entries. This introduction serves to clarify certain issues rather than offering an art-historical essay: Such

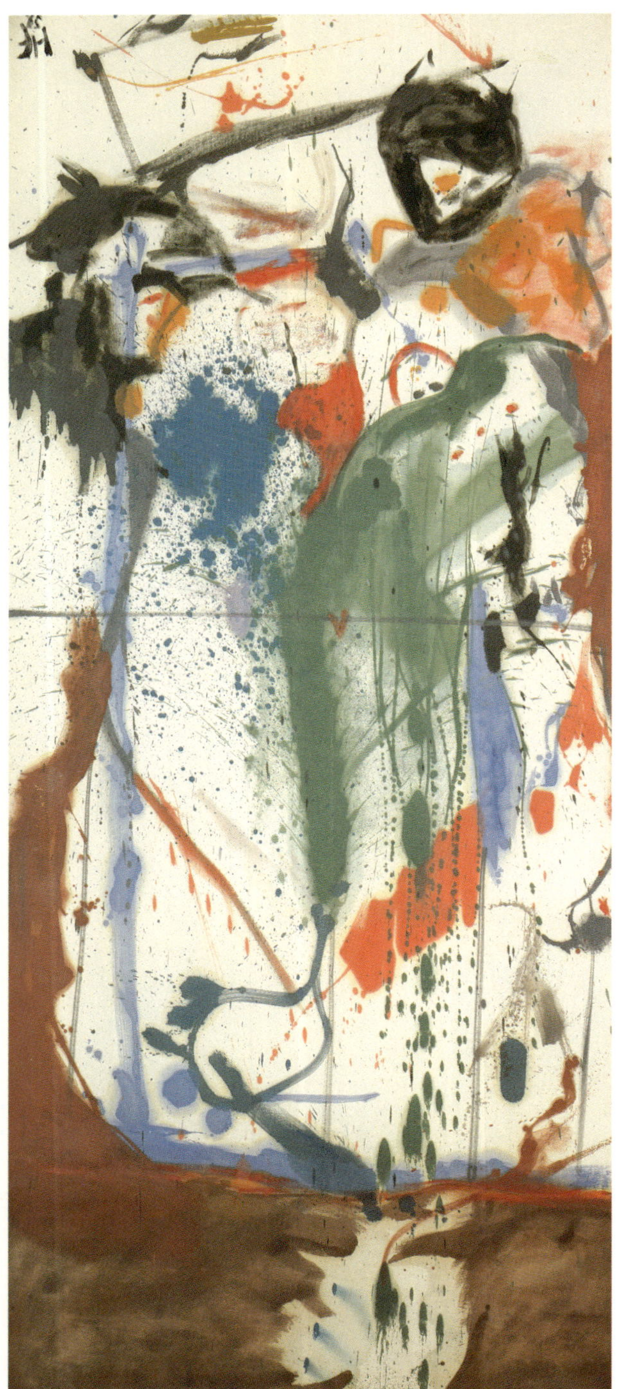

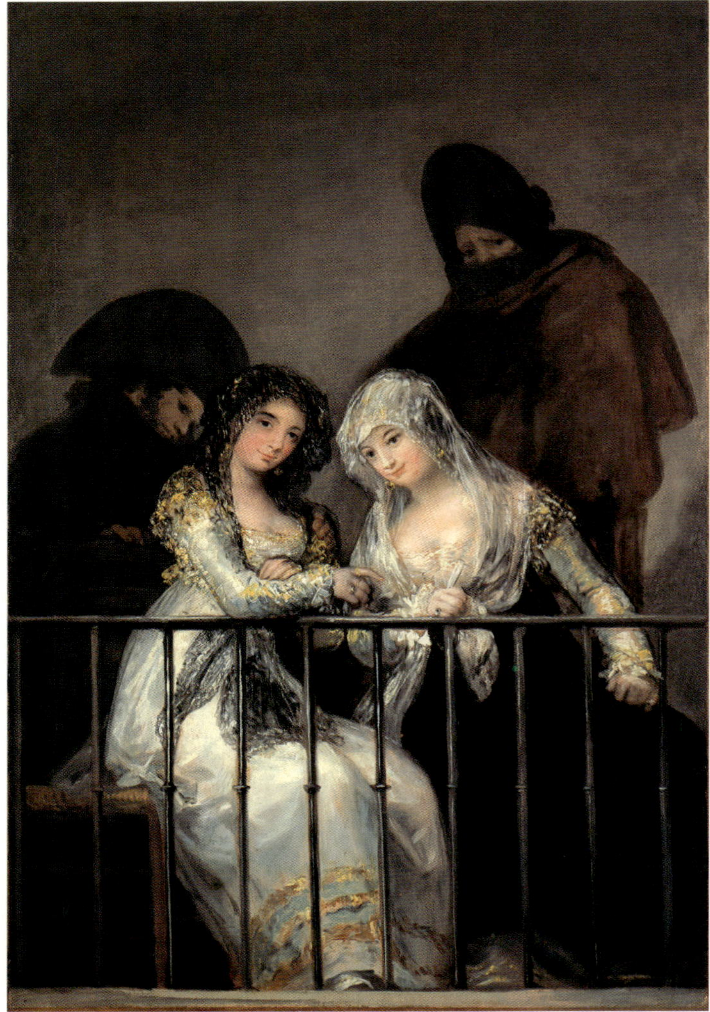

Fig. 2   Francisco José de Goya y Lucientes
Majas on a Balcony. c. 1800–14
Oil on canvas
76¾ x 49½" (195 x 125.7 cm.)
The Metropolitan Museum of Art, Bequest of Mrs. H. O. Havemeyer,
1929. The H. O. Havemeyer Collection, 29.100.10

Fig. 1   Helen Frankenthaler
Las Mayas. 1958 (cat. no. 6)
Reproduced upside down to illustrate the compositional
development of the painting (see p. 24)

a broader perspective was initiated by Barbara Rose in her 1972 study of Frankenthaler and continues in John Elderfield's 1989 monograph on the artist.[3]

The entries in this catalogue consist of factual information on the work, including provenance, exhibitions, and selected references, as well as commentary on that specific painting. In addition to my own observations, these brief essays include Frankenthaler's remarks on the particular picture, either from earlier interviews (and thus cited) or made in our conversations about this exhibition (and thus uncited). These essays also survey the work's "history and critical fortune" (as the French say), recording the significant critical comments often made when the picture was first exhibited as well as those subsequent discussions that appear in its historical literature.

This "critical fortune" may also serve to correct what is perhaps a widely held view, namely that the literature on Frankenthaler is largely formalist, or even Greenbergian, in nature, given to endless discussions of "flatness" or "opticality."[4] It is surprising to see how undoctrinaire this literature is and, even more unexpected, how attentive it is to the individuality of each picture. With a perspective of nearly four decades, one senses that the particulars of each picture evoked a corresponding (even if negative), very picture-directed response by the various authors.

Neither the commentaries nor this introduction discusses at any length the aesthetic and historic role of Frankenthaler's invention of stain painting, a subject dealt with at length by Rose and by Elderfield. To be sure, physical properties of many pictures are remarked upon with regard to that particular painting. Given the exceptional range of her picture-making techniques, such focus is essential, for as she remarked during our first conversation, "I am an artist of paint, making discoveries." In a similar manner, the entries discuss color within the context of the particular work; again, her palette is so wide and yet so localized in the individual work that it precludes any synthesizing conclusion.

Other formal traits do reoccur. The majority of works in this exhibition reveal a tendency in her art toward the symmetrical and the asymmetrical, a composition that suggests as well as denies a side-to-side equivalence. Almost all are informed by her use of the Cubist compositional device of blocking out space, with its attendant ambiguities of surface and depth and its counterbalancing elements. This often occurs in the dialogue she establishes between color shapes and color drawing, "where shape and drawing become one" in what she calls her "well-ordered collisions." We also see in four works in the exhibition examples of her periodic return to Old Master paintings for inspiration in color and in composition.

The entries in this catalogue follow the chronological order of the paintings. Within this arrangement Frankenthaler's broad themes of landscape and figuration as well as that of pure abstraction weave in and out. For many paintings, given their complexity and ever-present abstraction, any verbal equivalent of even a general theme is impossible, while others are only barely suggestive of conventional subject matter. Thus no overall consensus is reached in the commentaries.

The titles of the paintings are sometimes helpful in identifying a general theme and sometimes not. Nevertheless, titles are discussed at length in the commentaries due to their large role in the Frankenthaler literature. Many critics have seen her titles as handles for the pictures' themes and by using their references have proceeded to read into abstracted passages all kinds of images and associations. The aptness of each historical interpretation is dealt with in the particular entry. Asked to comment if these associations are correct overall, Frankenthaler replies, "Yes, no, and sometimes maybe."

The idea that the artist herself remarks "maybe" to the presence of certain abstract themes in her work—that is to say, has questions about if they are there or not—derives from the intersection of two different kinds of *place* in her art. (When we talked initially about this exhibition, I asked her what she hoped viewers would learn from this show about her work. She replied that the exhibition should convey the sense that "in my art I've moved and have been able to grow. I've been someplace. Hopefully, others should be similarly moved.")

The first kind of place is the physical painting itself. One has the feeling that her pictures are an environment *into* which we look and, in a similar way, that it is an environment, a place, where she has been. This aspect may also account for the very separateness of the individual pictures.

More incidentally, the second kind of place is that of her real world, not only physical places like New York City or the seashore or Arizona but also places of personal and artistic interests, from her family to Old Master pictures.

As this selection of paintings shows, Frankenthaler, like all of us in varying degrees, is clearly affected by where she is, from Cape Cod to the European painting galleries of The Metropolitan Museum of Art. It is this effect of place that merges with the abstract-picture place to create the underlying, sometimes irretractable sense of place — and thus feeling, mood, and emotion — in her art.

I believe that, given the abstract character of her work, it is important to realize that even if specific kinds of space cannot be accurately described, general traits of location can be. Of the pictures in this exhibition, a great many can be grouped together by the kinds of place they suggest in their titles. There are places of water, summer, and nature: *Mountains and Sea, Yellow Caterpillar, Seascape with Dunes, The Bay, Flood, Summer Banner, Ocean Drive West #1, Grey Fireworks, Nature Abhors a Vacuum, Lush Spring, Tulip Tint,* and *Natural Answer*; titles that suggest religious or mythological places: *Eden, Arden, Buddha's Court, Small's Paradise, Salome*; as well as those of worlds that are imaginary: *Winter Hunt, Mother Goose Melody, Swan Lake I, Interior Landscape, Mauve District,* and *Snow Queen*. There are titles that reflect travel to a place: *Round Trip* and *Into the West*; and titles that indicate the place of the world of art: *Las Mayas, Nude, The*

Human Edge, Hint from Bassano, Burnt Norton, Portrait of a Lady in White, For E. M., and *Casanova*.

Frankenthaler does not depict these places in her art in any conventional way, and she is cautious of her titles leading to a belief that she does. During our conversations in the summer of 1988, we talked about the painting *Ocean Drive West #1*, a picture made only a short distance away from where we sat by the ocean off the Connecticut coast. Being there, one could easily make a connection between the blue grays of the water and the long horizontals of Long Island and the blue-gray tone and horizontal forms found in the picture. Frankenthaler allowed the relationship between the two *places* — an ocean view and the abstract picture, and said: "But one is always someplace. On Ocean Drive West you are always staring at horizon lines — horizon lines that vary."

Perhaps because we were at the conjunction of the two *places* — the picture and seascape — Frankenthaler and I talked longer about this work than any other. Her comments about this painting, its metaphorical theme, and its places can be extended to the usage of them in her work in general.

"I'm not protesting the association," she commented, "but the painting as a painting has no more to do with nature . . . than the greatest Pollocks or Monets have to do with nature. Even the apples in a Cézanne primarily have little to do with apples. Yes, of course, references are there, but they are probably there in the best late Mondrians as well. Anything that has beauty and provides order (rather than chaos or shock alone), anything resolved in a picture (as in nature) gives pleasure — a sense of rightness, as in being one with nature. Once you are beyond the pain and effort, finally there is something uplifting and pleasing in what you are being given. It is an order familiar and new at the same time. Any successful picture — an abstract work or a landscape — has a place and rightness and an ability to last and grow. It is not merely a matter of painting a tree, but of making a picture that works."

Notes:

1. Unless cited, all quotations by Helen Frankenthaler are from conversations with the author.

2. E. C. Goossen, "Helen Frankenthaler," *Art International* 5 (20 October 1961): 79.

3. Barbara Rose, *Frankenthaler* (New York: Harry N. Abrams, 1972), and John Elderfield, *Frankenthaler* (New York: Harry N. Abrams, 1989).

4. On this point, see Michael Fried, *Morris Louis* (New York: Harry N. Abrams, 1970).

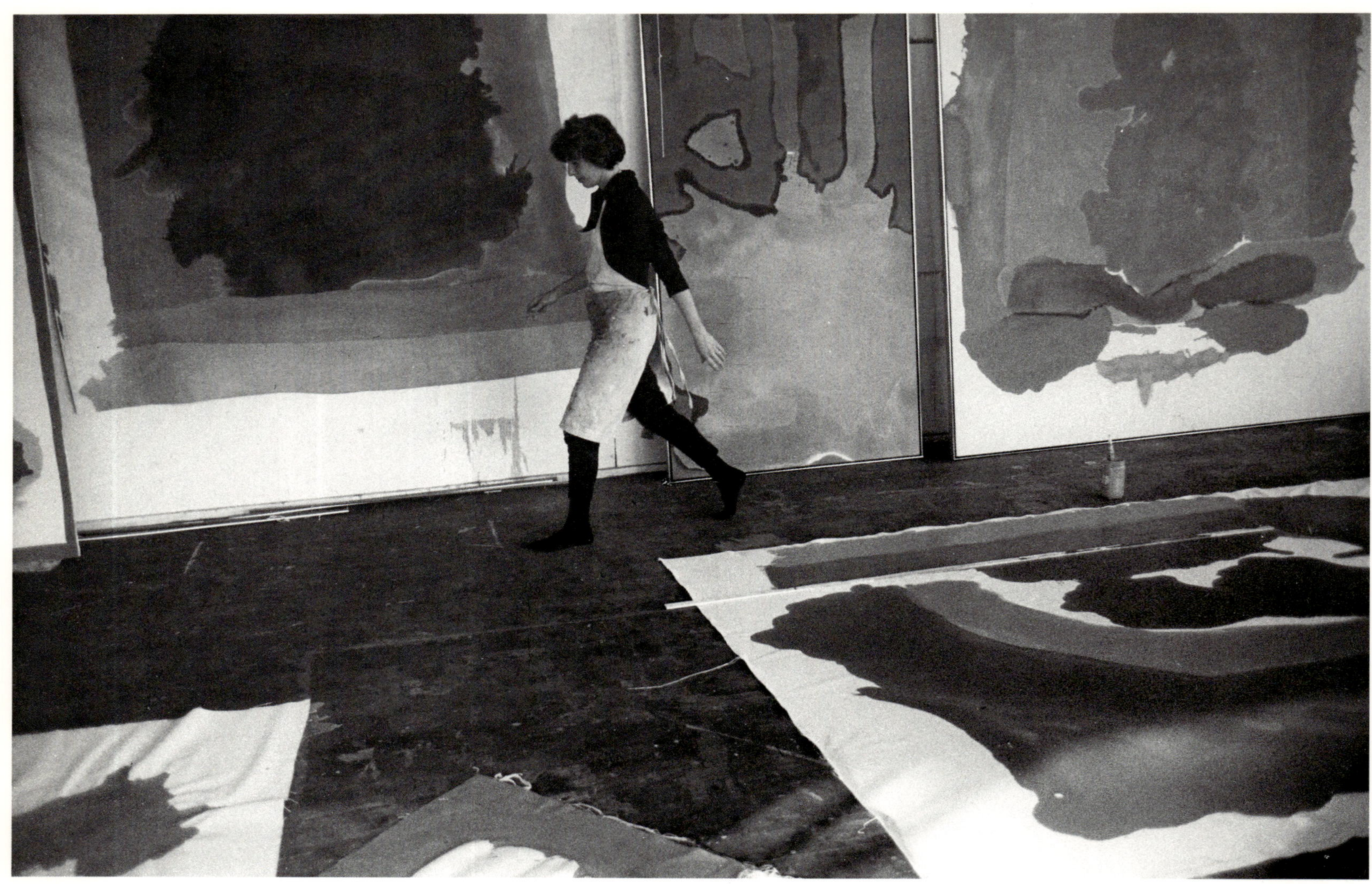

Helen Frankenthaler in her New York studio in 1964. On the wall to the
right is *Small's Paradise* (cat. no. 13) in an unfinished state.
Photograph: Alexander Liberman

Catalogue of the Exhibition

1. *Mountains and Sea.* 1952*
Oil on canvas
7'2⅝" x 9'9¼" (220.1 x 297.8 cm.)
Inscribed, l.r.: 10/26/52
Collection the artist, on extended loan to the National Gallery
    of Art, Washington, D.C.

Mountains and Sea is, in historical terms, the most famous of Helen Frankenthaler's works. Curiously, it has received the greatest attention not for what the artist painted, but rather for *how* she painted and for how this process, ultimately called "stain painting," influenced — some might even say gave genesis to — the works of Kenneth Noland and Morris Louis. Indeed, as Hilton Kramer later observed of *Mountains and Sea*, "The reputation it has acquired [makes it] a sort of 'Demoiselles d'Avignon' of the Color-field [sic] school. . . ."[1]

Certainly the making of *Mountains and Sea* was radical.[2] Frankenthaler had just returned from a painting trip in Nova Scotia to her studio in New York, which she shared with Friedel Dzubas. Dzubas later recalled that "Helen just walked in, painted the picture, and then asked me to come over and look at it."[3]

Later that day, art critic Clement Greenberg arrived at the studio to see the painting, and she asked the questions she would continue to ask herself when judging her works: "Is it finished? Is it a complete picture?" Eventually that evening Frankenthaler decided that it was, and she dated *Mountains and Sea* "10/26/52" in large numbers. "I usually don't, but I remember wanting to do so with the picture that day," the artist has recalled.[4]

Shortly thereafter Louis and Noland learned of the painting from Greenberg, and on April 3, 1953, the two Washington artists made a special trip to New York to see it, thus beginning the "legend." Louis and Noland were stunned by the picture; Noland recalled that it "showed us a way to think about and use color," while Louis is remembered as proclaiming *Mountains and Sea* a "revelation." Noland's later observation of the picture's effect was that "it was as if Morris had been waiting all his life for [this] information."[5] Then, apparently, from this viewing emerged the Color Field painting of the 1960s.

This profile of *Mountains and Sea* has been building since 1960, when Greenberg wrote that "his first sight of . . . an extraordinary painting done in 1952 by Helen Frankenthaler, called 'Moun-

tains and Sea,' led Louis to change his direction abruptly."[6] But with this "historic role" held uppermost in art-historical writings, the making and the appearance of as well as the actual reception to the painting have been obscured. One has the sense that *Mountains and Sea* was somehow always hidden away, accessible only to these few artists.

In fact, *Mountains and Sea* had been exhibited in New York at the Tibor de Nagy Gallery in January and February of 1953, fully two months before the famous Louis-Noland studio viewing. Indeed, its first appearance in the literature on Frankenthaler is in a brief review of the show in the February 15, 1953, issue of *Art Digest*, which called the painting "lyric, washy, a composition of fluid spontaneities."[7] The general reception, however, was less than enthusiastic, and Frankenthaler remembers that "at the time, the painting looked to many people like a large paint rag, casually accidental and incomplete."[8] Priced at around a hundred dollars, it did not sell. Shortly thereafter it was rolled up and kept in storage, reappearing twice in exhibitions during the 1950s.

Even so, it was not until 1961 — interestingly concurrent with the emergence of the "legend" — that E. C. Goossen would write of the continuing misfortune "that Frankenthaler's *Mountains and Sea* (1952) and *Eden* (1957) should have to wait for the recognition they deserve as major paintings of the 1950s. . . ."[9]

Frankenthaler later recalled of making the work: "In 1952 on a trip to Nova Scotia I did landscapes with folding easel equipment. I came back and did the *Mountains and Sea* painting and I know the landscapes were in my arms as I did it."[10] Despite this observation made by the artist, until recently little critical comment had been made on the picture's theme, aside from general references to its being an abstract "landscape."[11]

Andrew Hudson, writing in 1975, would make a connection, however, noting that the composition offered "a suggestion of landscape, of mountain boulders looming on the edge of a blue sea."[12] While Hudson's "boulders" may be too specific for the abstraction of the picture, nevertheless the image does convey a sense of mass (the center) adjacent to a major horizontal passage of blue (at the right). Indeed, Frankenthaler later observed of the relationship between Nova Scotia and the painting: "One of the things that struck me was the unique contrast between the great wooded peaks and the horizontal ocean—the mountains and the sea of its title."[13]

*For all entries refer to "Notes to the catalogue" on page 112.

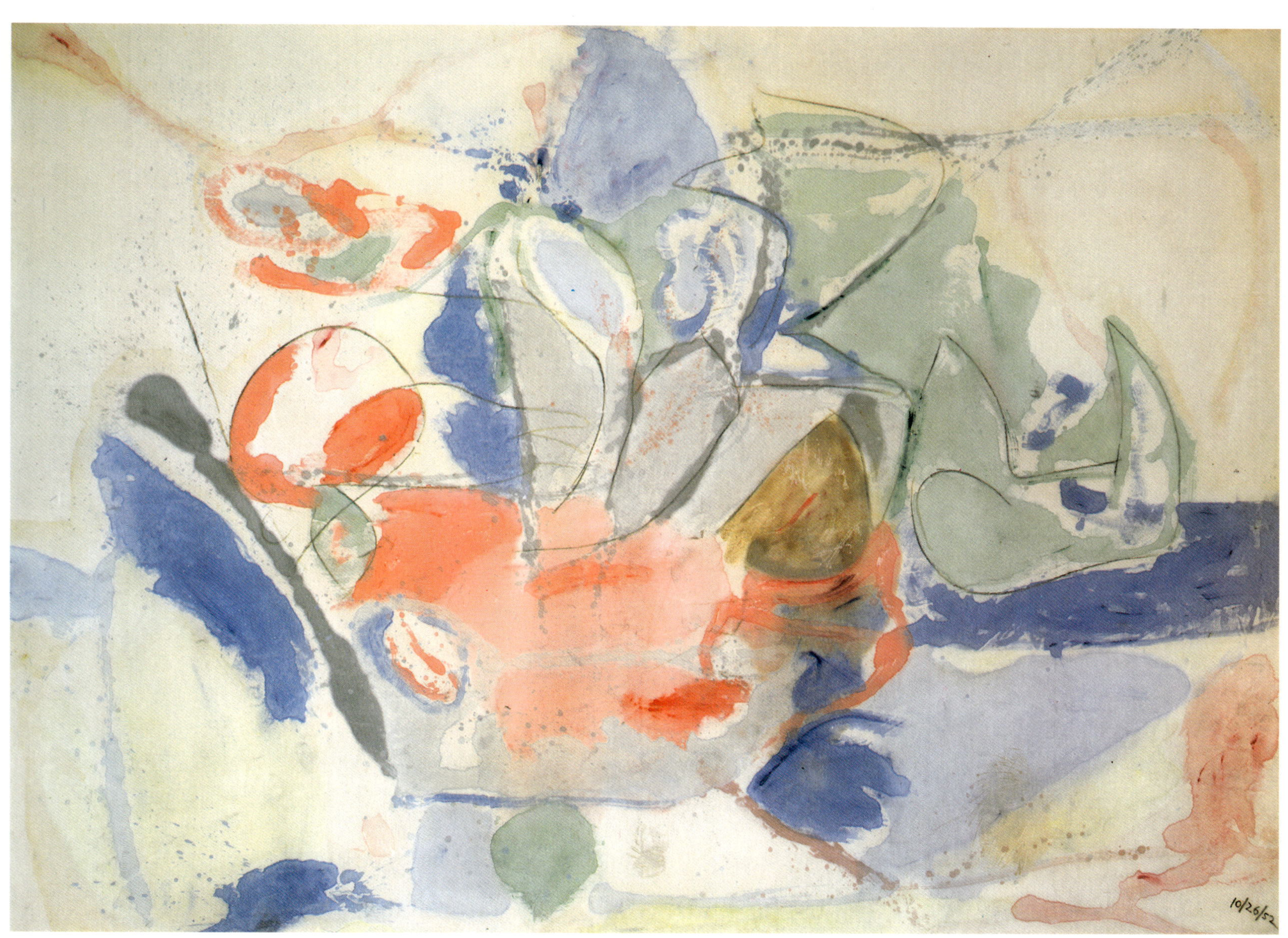
10/26/52

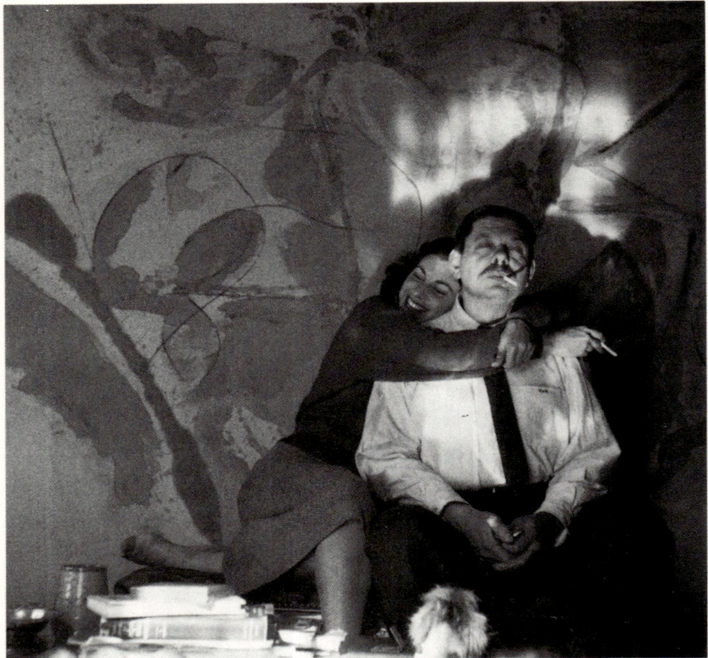

Fig. 3   Helen Frankenthaler with David Smith in front of
Mountains and Sea (cat. no. 1)
at her West End Avenue apartment, 1956.
Photograph: Burt Glinn © 1970 Magnum Photos

Especially referential, albeit more abstractly, is the palette of the picture, which recalls "the colors and images of the trip—the oranges and grays of the rocky landscape and the blues and greens of the Nova Scotia seacoast."[14] The color in *Mountains and Sea* is low-key and washy, perhaps in connection with the watercolors the artist had just made during the trip. The palette, which is almost Cézannesque in its pale tone, has been little remarked upon, again a curious aspect of a work placed art historically as the genesis of 1960s color painting. Even more ignored to this point is the drawing in the picture, which loops through the entire composition. Indeed, this linear element determined much of the somewhat symmetrical compositional layout, for as the artist recalls: "I put in the charcoal gestures first because I wanted to *draw* in with color and shape the totally abstract memory of the landscape . . . the charcoal lines were original guideposts that eventually became unnecessary."[15]

In *Mountains and Sea* Frankenthaler established numerous formal traits—washes of color, line in dialogue with painting, symmetry and asymmetry, even, "Is it finished?"—as well as a general theme of "place," that inform much of her art to the present. In that sense, the most lasting impact of the painting has not been on the "legend" of Color Field painting but on her own career.

Notes:
1. Hilton Kramer, "Helen Frankenthaler's Art in the 50's," *The New York Times*, 7 June 1981, p. D31.
2. April Kingsley, "James Brooks: Stain into Image," *Artnews* (December 1972): 48.
3. E.A. Carmean, Jr., "Celebrating the Birth of Stain Painting," *The Washington Post,* 26 October 1982, p. B7.
4. Ibid.
5. Ibid.
6. Clement Greenberg, "Louis and Noland," *Art International* 4 (May 1960): 28.
7. S[am] F[einstein], "Helen Frankenthaler," *Art Digest* 27 (15 February 1953): 20.
8. Carl Belz, *Helen Frankenthaler and the 1950s* (Waltham, Massachusetts: Rose Art Museum, Brandeis University, 1981), 11.
9. E. C. Goossen, "Helen Frankenthaler," *Art International* 5 (20 October 1961): 79.

10. Henry Geldzahler, "An Interview with Helen Frankenthaler," *Artforum* 4 (October 1965): 36.

11. *Mountains and Sea* is discussed at length in John Elderfield's monograph on the artist (New York: Harry N. Abrams, Inc., 1989).

12. Andrew Hudson, "Washington Letter," *Art International* 6 (15 June 1975): 98.

13. Carmean, "Celebrating the Birth," p. B7.

14. Ibid.

15. Gene Baro, "The Achievement of Helen Frankenthaler," *Art International* 11 (September 1967): 36. At length again, these aspects will be discussed in Elderfield.

Exhibition History:
New York: Tibor de Nagy Gallery, 1953
New York: Stable Gallery (checklist), 1955
Kassel, West Germany: *Documenta II* (cat. no. 1), 1959
New York: The Jewish Museum (cat. no. 2, ill. p. 14), 1960
Bennington, Vermont: Bennington College (checklist no. 1), 1962
Venice: XXXIII Venice Biennale (traveling exhibition, cat. color ill. p. 11), 1966
New York: The Metropolitan Museum of Art, on extended loan, 1967–74
New York: Whitney Museum of American Art (traveling exhibition, cat. no. 2, color ill. p. 19), 1969

Selected Critical References:
Feinstein, *Art Digest* (15 February 1953), comm. p. 20
Greenberg, *Art International* (May 1960), comm. p. 28
Goossen, *Art International* (20 October 1961), comm. p. 79
Fried, *Artforum* (February 1965), comm. pp. 36–37
Berkson, *Arts Magazine* (May–June 1965), comm. p. 49
Geldzahler, *Artforum* (October 1965), comm. p. 36
Friedman, *Artnews* (Summer 1966), comm. pp. 31, 67
Baro, *Art and Artists* (June 1966), comm. p. 59
Geldzahler, *Artforum* (June 1966), comm. p. 38, color ill. p. 32
Lynton, *Art International* (September 1966), comm. p. 80
Hudson, *The Washington Post,* 4 December 1966, comm. p. G1
Rose, 1967, comm. pp. 224–26
Baro, *Art International* (September 1967), comm. and ill. p. 36
Gold, *The Sun,* 8 October 1967, comm. p. D20
Bowles, *Arts Magazine* (March 1969), comm. p. 22

Rosenstein, *Artnews* (March 1969), comm. p. 30
Gold, *The Sun,* 23 March 1969, comm. p. D22
Time (28 March 1969), comm. p. 69
Rose, *Artforum* (April 1969), comm. p. 29, ill. p. 31
Battcock, *Art and Artists* (May 1969), ill. p. 53
Grinke, *The Spectator,* 16 May 1969, comm.
Fried, 1970, comm. pp. 21–22, color ill. p. 21
Lucie-Smith and White, 1970, comm. p. 52
Heinz Ohff Galerie der neuen Kunste, 1971, color ill. p. 274
Leymarie, 1971, ill. p. 69
Alloway, *Artnews* (November 1971), comm. pp. 89–90
Rose, 1972, comm. pp. 54, 56–58, 60, 66; colorpl. 18
Kingsley, *Artnews* (December 1972), comm. p. 48
O'Hara, 1975, comm. and ill. p. 122
Forgey, *Washington Star-News,* 15 January 1975, ill. p. E3
Richard, *The Washington Post,* 16 January 1975, comm. and ill. p. C1
Guest, *Arts Magazine* (April 1975), comm. p. 59
Baro, *Vogue* (June 1975), comm. p. 144
Hudson, *Art International* (15 June 1975), comm. p. 98
Kagan, *Arts Magazine* (September 1975), comm. p. 89
Carmean, *Arts Magazine* (September 1976), comm. p. 71
———, 1977, ill. fig. 1
Elderfield, *Art International* (May–June 1977), comm. p. 24
Sandler, 1978, comm. p. 60, ill. p. 61
Carmean, *Art International* (April–May 1978), comm. pp. 28–30, ill. p. 29
Forge, *Art International* (April–May 1978), comm. p. 24
Rose, 1980, comm. p. 103
Belz, 1981, comm. pp. 9, 11
Russell, 1981, ill. p. 358
Kramer, *The New York Times,* 7 June 1981, comm. p. D31
Rubinstein, 1982, comm. p. 328
Fenton, *Arts Magazine* (September 1982), comm. p. 66
Carmean, *The Washington Post,* 26 October 1982, comm. p. B7
Hunter and Jacobus, 1985, comm. p. 315, color ill. p. 314
Upright, 1985, comm. pp. 12, 21
Elderfield, 1986, comm. pp. 12–16, ill. p. 13
———, 1989, comm. pp. 17, 65–69, 70, 74–75, 76, 80–81, 83, 85, 86, 89, 92, 98, 120, 125, 126, 139, 172, 218, 246, 337, 352; color ill. p. 64

2. *Eden.* 1956
Oil on canvas
8'7" x 9'9" (261.6 x 297.2 cm.)
Inscribed, verso, stretcher: "Eden" 1956 103 x 117" oil
   on canvas
Private Collection

"*Eden,*" reflects Frankenthaler, "represents the frequent need to sometimes paint out ideas on a large format. As I was making it I thought it was a major picture, a big expression. It just came out and made its own order."

Just as *Mountains and Sea* occupies a central place in the Frankenthaler literature for its formal attributes, *Eden* has been the subject of extensive commentary for its supposed thematic content. As early as 1957, when *Eden* was first shown at the Tibor de Nagy Gallery in New York, it was described by E. C. Goossen as "a provocative but abandoned landscape."[1] Elizabeth Pollet, reviewing the same exhibition, went much further, identifying the central red oval and its surrounding olive-tan verticals on the basis of its title and commenting, "The apple is as huge and unsubstantial as the two trees, which could never have produced it."[2] In 1961 Goossen would extend this Biblical association, writing of "the snake in 'Eden,' not to mention the house of God,"[3] the latter presumably in reference to the red form at the upper center. By 1966 this particular passage in *Eden* had become more specifically interpreted in B. H. Friedman's reference to "the large, witty red hand of God, saying STOP."[4]

In 1981 Carl Belz would add two more identifications, seeing the yellow shape at the upper left as "the glowing sun" and suggesting the two 100s—already identified with the apple by Pollet—as "emblems of some perfect score?"[5] Finally, in 1982 John Elderfield would summarize these interpretations, calling the painting "an ideal world of sensuous delight," and noting, "Hoisted into the trees in *Eden*, the winning 100 scores of prelapsarian perfection are marvelously witty inventions that also carry extraordinary visual force."[6]

These readings raise some curious theological and iconographic questions, foremost being why the artist would identify perfection —the winning 100s—with the forbidden fruit, the apple. But more importantly, there is little about the picture aside from its title to specifically support such identifications.

The pair of 100s came, she states, "because at that point I wanted to contrast straight line with a curved one—as in much of the composition. A single straight vertical line followed by the two circles becomes '100.' I made the 100 and liked it and, because I wanted a play of symmetry, added another reflective 100," she says. The artist observes that the so-called "hand of God" that came next was originally a red oval shape and that its four vertical, upper "finger" elements were added later. About the yellow shape at the upper left corner—which she calls the "golden sun" —she comments, "You could say it's a star or planet, but it really isn't.

"*Eden,*" she prefers to say, "is about arabesque and linear division, and about symmetry and nonsymmetry." Certainly, the range and scale of the multiple passages are widely varied, from the long sweeping brown lines to very small, bunched curves. These latter elements, she notes, are drawn from childhood memory of cartoons, where similar markings indicate a figure in motion, although here they act "as a necessary part of the abstract drawing."

Notes:
1. E. C. Goossen, "Two Younger Painters," *Monterey Peninsular Herald*, 25 February 1957.
2. E[lizabeth] P[ollet], "In the Galleries," *Arts Magazine* 31 (March 1957): 54.
3. E. C. Goossen, "Helen Frankenthaler," *Art International* 5 (20 October 1961): 79.
4. B. H. Friedman, "Towards the Total Color Image," *Artnews* 65 (Summer 1966): 67.
5. Carl Belz, "Helen Frankenthaler's *Eden*," *Artnews* 80 (May 1981): 157.
6. John Elderfield, "Specific Incidents," *Art in America* 70 (February 1982): 106.

(Continued on page 94)

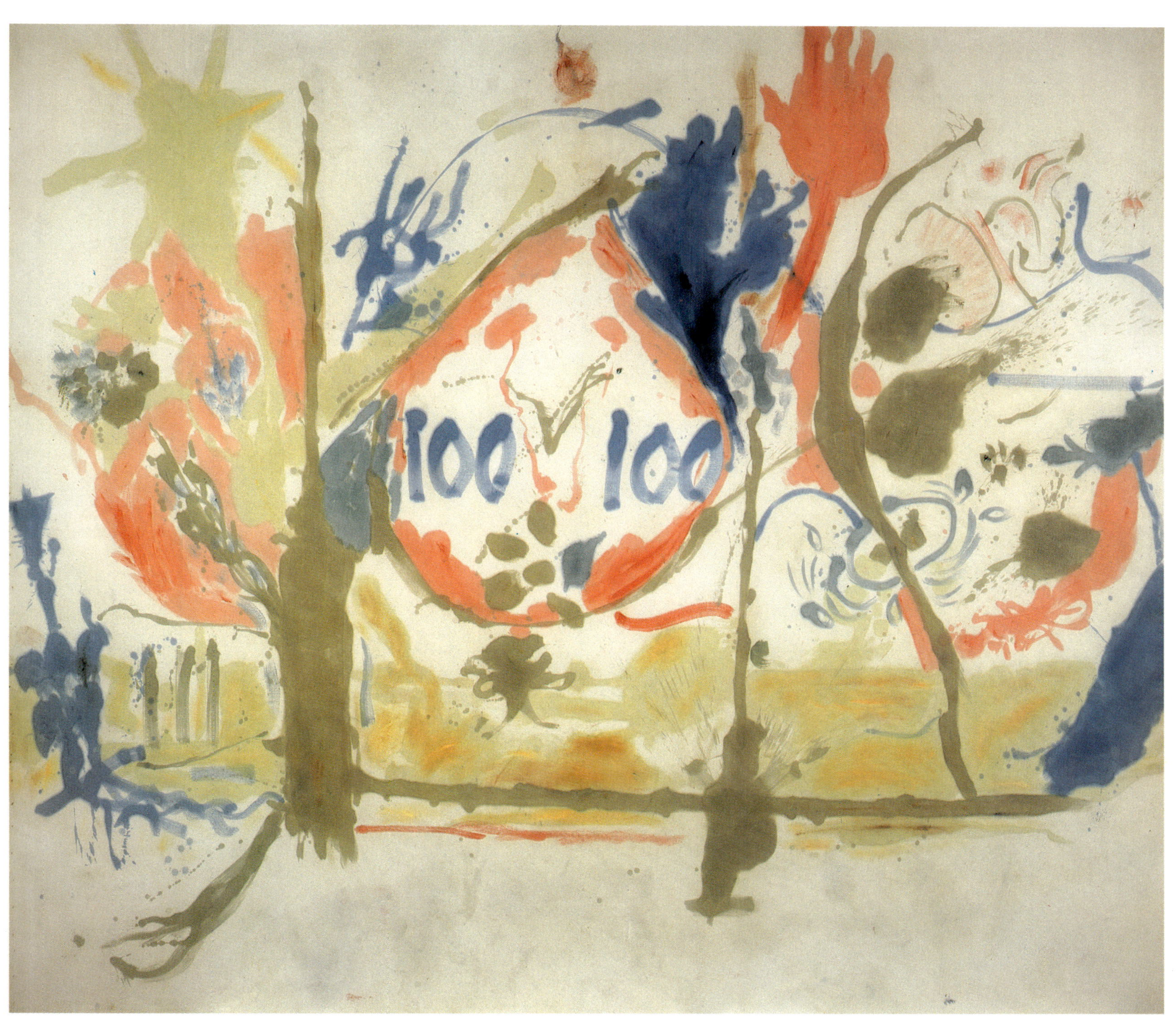

100 100

3. *Round Trip.* 1957

Oil on canvas

5′10¼″ x 5′10¼″ (178.4 x 178.4 cm.)

Inscribed, l.r.: Frankenthaler/57

Albright-Knox Art Gallery, Buffalo, New York. Gift of James I.
Merrill to the Room of Contemporary Art, 1958

"In *Round Trip,*" observed Elaine Gottlieb in 1958, "an intricate involvement of large, inexact forms presents enormous central tulips, two towers lower left, tracks to the right, accents of green, blue, and strange spreading blots that seem like things remembered but never quite recalled."[1] Writing of this work and other 1957 pictures twelve years later, Barbara Rose called them "pictures of an intense originality and an apparently joyous abandon."[2]

Like the earlier *Eden* (cat. no. 2), *Round Trip* has certain elements that suggest a symmetrical composition, such as the two red shapes in the upper center or the two darker forms at the lower corners. "It is symmetrical and not symmetrical," says Frankenthaler, "an aesthetic play on the idea that repeated motifs are never truly identical." Within this structure, however, are numerous other passages—often smaller—that break up the mirrored layout. These include not only the trails of yellow at the bottom and the upper right, but also smaller lines in black and green, as well as many X-like forms scattered throughout the lower region. "It may contain 'joyous abandon,'" the artist comments, "but it is also full of incident."

The title, *Round Trip,* refers to the picture's overall unity. "One should not look for imagery," Frankenthaler remarks. "What *Round Trip* should imply is that the picture starts and returns to itself, comes full circle. In that sense, it is satisfied in its order."

Notes:

1. E[laine] G[ottlieb], "In the Galleries," *Arts Magazine* 32 (January 1958): 55.

2. Barbara Rose, *Frankenthaler,* (New York: Harry N. Abrams, Inc., 1972), 86.

Provenance:

(Tibor de Nagy Gallery, New York)

Exhibition History:

New York: Tibor de Nagy Gallery, 1958

Buffalo, New York: Albright-Knox Art Gallery (cat. no. 51, ill.), 1958–59

New York: Whitney Museum of American Art (traveling exhibition, cat. no. 12, ill. p. 24), 1969

Buffalo, New York: Albright-Knox Art Gallery (checklist), 1972

Albany, New York: Executive Mansion (cat.), 1974

Selected Critical References:

Gottlieb, *Arts Magazine* (January 1958), comm. p. 55

Overy, *The Financial Times,* 20 May 1969, ill.

Alloway, *Artnews* (November 1971), comm. p. 89

Contemporary Art 1947–72, 1972, color ill. p. 71

Price, 1972, color ill. p. 289

Rose, 1972, comm. p. 86, ill. pl. 28

Sandler, 1978, ill. p. 63

Elderfield, 1989, comm. p. 109, color ill. p. 111

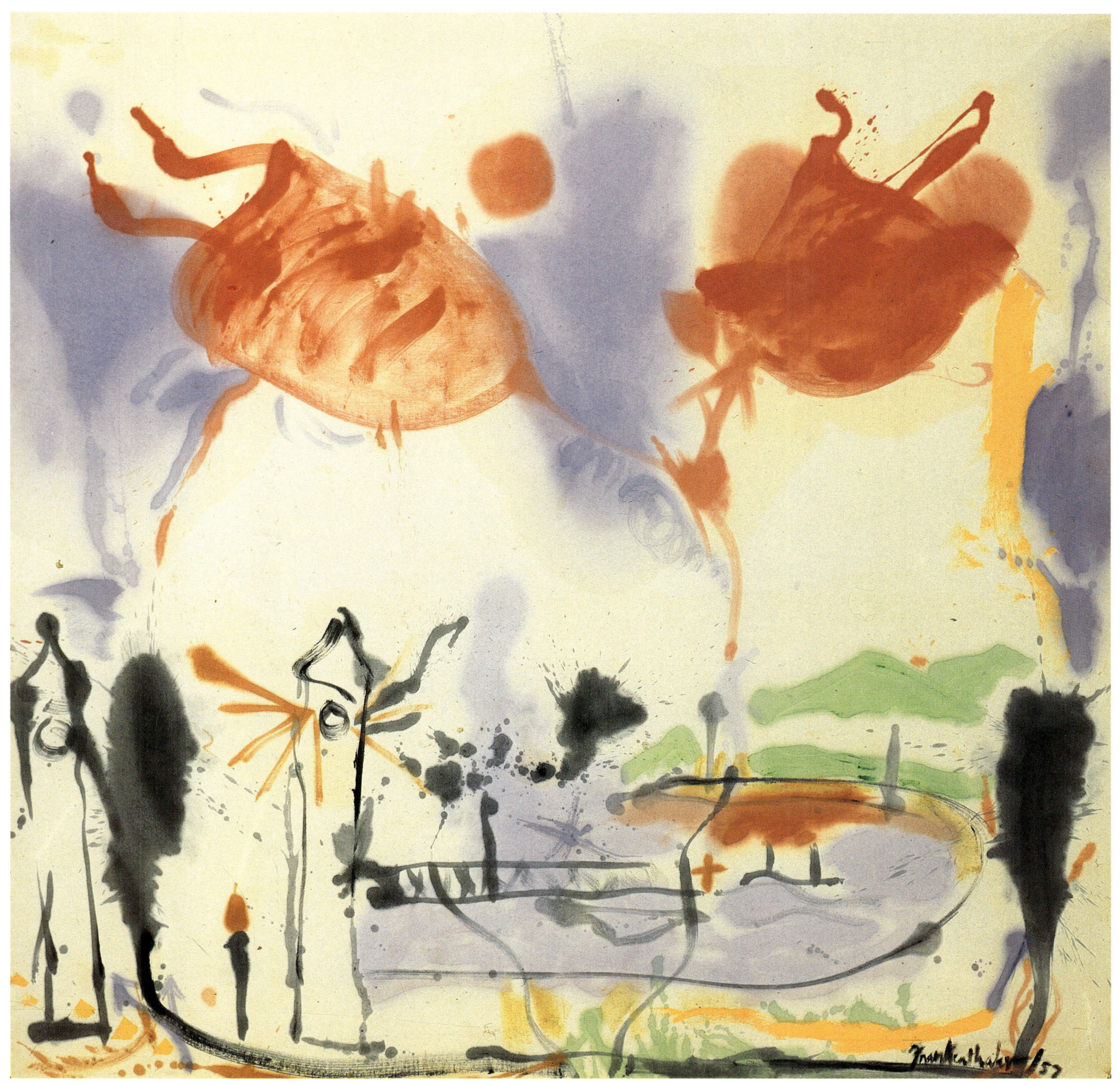

4. *Winter Hunt.* 1958
Oil on canvas
7'7" x 3'10½" (231.1 x 118.1 cm.)
Inscribed, l.r.: Frankenthaler '58
Los Angeles County Museum of Art. Gift of David Geffen

In this exhibition, *Winter Hunt* is joined by two related paintings, *Nude* and *Las Mayas* (cat. nos. 5, 6). These works share a general format: they are tall, vertical compositions, closely related in size, and they employ generous amounts of unpainted, raw canvas. Furthermore, each contains decipherable imagery, conveying themes that are less abstract than other earlier or later works.

In the present picture, the image is the angled fox at the left-hand side of the composition, most clearly identified by its two tri-angular ears and round, bulging eye. This animal was first remarked upon in the literature by Robert Taylor in 1981: "like the fox in 'Winter Hunt'"[1]; then by John Elderfield in 1982: "However specific in its imagery her work becomes at times—and it is occasionally very specific (witness the fox in *Winter Hunt*) . . . ."[2]

Curving around and piercing into the fox are numerous swirls and sweeps of a drawing more intense than in other works, suggestive of the "hunt" of the picture's title, while the empty white field at the top may have suggested the "winter" reference in the naming of the picture. "I was very aware of leaving that exact space at the top untouched as a necessary part of the drawing," comments the artist. Harris Rosenstein, in a 1969 review, described the picture as "a snapping electric snarl of black and brown."[3] Frank O'Hara, writing in 1960, referred to the "tragic"[4] tone of the painting. Their impressions have been more recently echoed in the artist's description of *Winter Hunt* as being "perhaps at first impulsive, with an element of whim. But as the picture developed it gained impact, intensity. There is a ferocity in it." With such character and mood, it stands apart from the other themes in her work in this exhibition.

Notes:
1. Robert Taylor, "Frankenthaler Show Splendid and Revealing," *Boston Globe,* 10 May 1981, p. A33.
2. John Elderfield, "Specific Incidents," *Art in America* 70 (February 1982): 105.

3. Harris Rosenstein, "The Colorful Gesture," *Artnews* 68 (March 1969): 31.
4. O'Hara, Frank. *Helen Frankenthaler Paintings,* (New York: The Jewish Museum, 1960), 7. [Reprinted in O'Hara, Frank. *Art Chronicles: 1954–1966,* (New York: George Braziller, 1975), 127.]

Provenance:
(Galleria dell'Ariete, Milan)
Mr. Guglielmo A. Cavellini, Brescia, Italy
(André Emmerich Gallery, New York)
Mr. David Geffen, California

Exhibition History:
New York: André Emmerich Gallery, 1959
São Paulo: Museu de Arte Moderna, 1959
Paris: Galerie Lawrence (cat. color frontispiece), 1961
Milan: Galleria dell'Ariete (cat.), 1962
New York: Whitney Museum of American Art (traveling exhibition, cat. no. 15, comm. p. 10, ill. p. 28), 1969
Reno, Nevada: Sierra Nevada Museum of Art (cat.), 1979
Waltham, Massachusetts: Rose Art Museum, Brandeis University (cat. no. 37, color ill. p. 46), 1981
Fairfield, Connecticut: Whitney Museum of American Art in Fairfield County (cat.), 1983
New York: André Emmerich Gallery, 1984–85

Selected Critical References:
It Is (Winter–Spring 1959), ill. p. 68
Goossen, *Art International* (20 October 1961), ill. p. 78
Berkson, *Arts Magazine* (May–June 1965), comm. p. 50
Rosenstein, *Artnews* (March 1969), comm. p. 31
K., D., *Spandauer Volksblatt,* 12 October 1969, comm.
Alloway, *Artnews* (November 1971), comm. p. 89
Rose, 1972, ill. pl. 57
O'Hara, 1975, comm. p. 127, ill. p. 126
Katzen, *Art Journal* (Summer 1980), ill. p. 258
Taylor, *Boston Globe,* 10 May 1981, ill. p. A33
Elderfield, *Art in America* (February 1982), comm. pp. 105–6
Raynor, *The New York Times,* 2 October 1983, comm. p. 24
The Robert O. Anderson Building, 1986, color ill. p. 87
Elderfield, 1989, comm. p. 126, color ill. p. 128

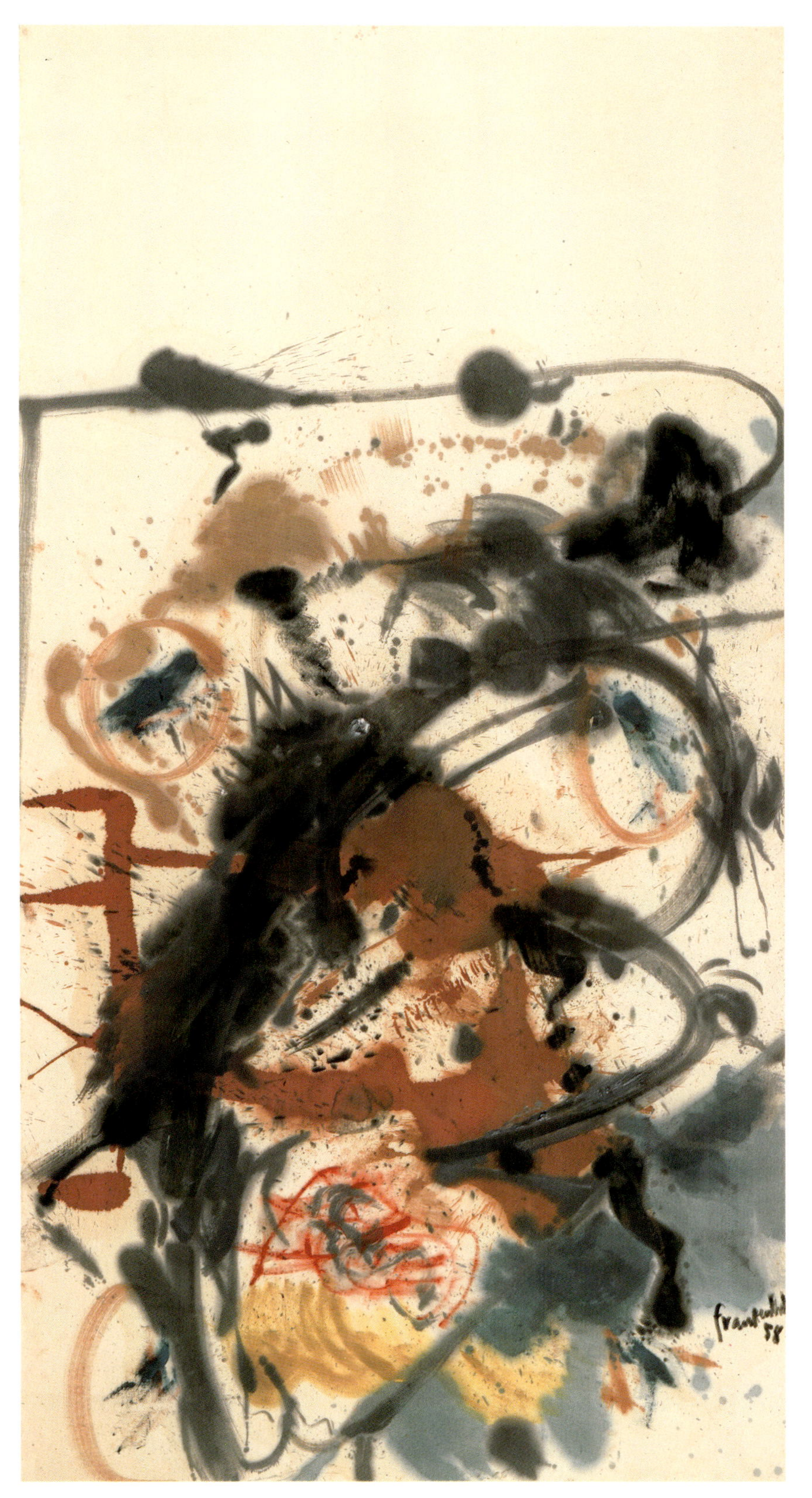

5. *Nude.* 1958
Oil on canvas
8′5½″ x 3′9½″ (257.8 x 115.6 cm.)
Inscribed, l.r.: Frankenthaler '58
Private Collection

"It's called *Nude,*" says Frankenthaler of this picture, "because there is a nude there. If one had to project an image and read into this picture, the square at the top with its dividing line with two dots could be perceived as a head of sorts and beneath it breastlike shapes with dots as nipples. The silhouette of the main shape below has a somewhat curvaceous attitude. The picture's basic order and success have nothing whatsoever to do with a nude." Painted in 1958, *Nude* is the second of the three vertical paintings included in the present exhibition (see cat. nos. 4, 6).

Another tall panel, *Nude* was begun in a much more linear fashion than the final composition would indicate. "I worked on it for quite a while, both on the floor and up on the wall," the artist recalls. "It started out as a ropey outline, to which I made later additions. Part of what I had in mind was a play on symmetry." Some of the original character can still be seen in the linear reddish passages at the right and in certain of the blue lines as well.

By filling in the denser red at the upper areas, Frankenthaler gives greater definition to the shape and pushes the white canvas forward as the white surface of an abstracted figure. This effects a quality not unlike that found in Rubens and may account for the reference to Rubens in Barbara Rose's discussion of this painting.[1]

The abstracted imagery in *Nude* was recognized in its literature, as seen, for example, in John Ashbery's description of it as "scrappily figurative,"[2] while other authors cited its more formal qualities. Most salient of these discussions is Dore Ashton's on the head of the figure: "In *Nude* of 1958 . . . Frankenthaler introduces an idea which gradually assumed great importance in her work. The idea is symbolized by the presence of a squared form. The square, still open, still relatively ambiguous, serves as an abstract pictorial device. It is a way of relating to the rectangular limits of the canvas and a reference to another kind of space — circumscribed, equilibrated."[3]

The artist also emphasizes this square head and connects it to its "echo" in the square placed at the lower edge, which she calls an "animal-like figure." Frankenthaler is equally insistent on other aspects of *Nude*'s pictorial makeup, especially its great variety of linear markings, from the "loopy" passages to the line around the chest to the strict horizontal crossing the lower section, stopping just tangent to the left blue. She comments: "I used dots as lines. They may have started with a few accidental drops from the brush. I seized the accident and put it to work by continuing the dots to make the equivalent of a line that I needed there." This latter device, hinted at in the upper horizon of *Winter Hunt,* will take on "thematic" importance in *Las Mayas,* completed after *Nude.*

Notes:
1. Barbara Rose, *Frankenthaler* (New York: Harry N. Abrams, Inc., 1972), 86.
2. John Ashbery, "Paris Notes," *Art International* 5 (20 November 1961): 50.
3. Dore Ashton, "Helen Frankenthaler," *Studio International* 170 (August 1965): 54–55.

Exhibition History:
Kassel, West Germany: *Documenta II* (cat. no. 3, ill. p. 165), 1959
New York: André Emmerich Gallery, 1959
New York: The Jewish Museum (cat. no. 16, ill. p. 11), 1960
Paris: Galerie Lawrence, 1961
Milan: Galleria dell'Ariete (cat. no. 5), 1962
New York: Whitney Museum of American Art (traveling exhibition, cat. no. 11, comm. p. 10, ill. p. 27), 1969
Bordeaux, France: Centre d'Arts Plastiques Contemporains de Bordeaux (cat. ill. p. 17), 1981
Berlin, West Germany: Berlinische Galerie (cat. no. 16–15, ill. p. 440), 1988

Selected Critical References:
Tillim, *Arts Magazine* (May 1959), ill. p. 56
Seelye, *Artnews* (March 1960), comm. p. 57
Ashbery, *New York Herald Tribune,* 18 October 1961, comm. p. 50
———, *Art International* (20 November 1961), comm. p. 50
Ashton, *Studio International* (August 1965), comm. pp. 54–55
Rose, *Artforum* (September 1965), ill. p. 56
Rosenstein, *Artnews* (March 1969), comm. and ill. p. 31
Rose, 1972, comm. pp. 80–81, 86; colorpl. 20
Elderfield, 1989, comm. pp. 126, 137, 141, 144, 172, 397; color ill. p. 129

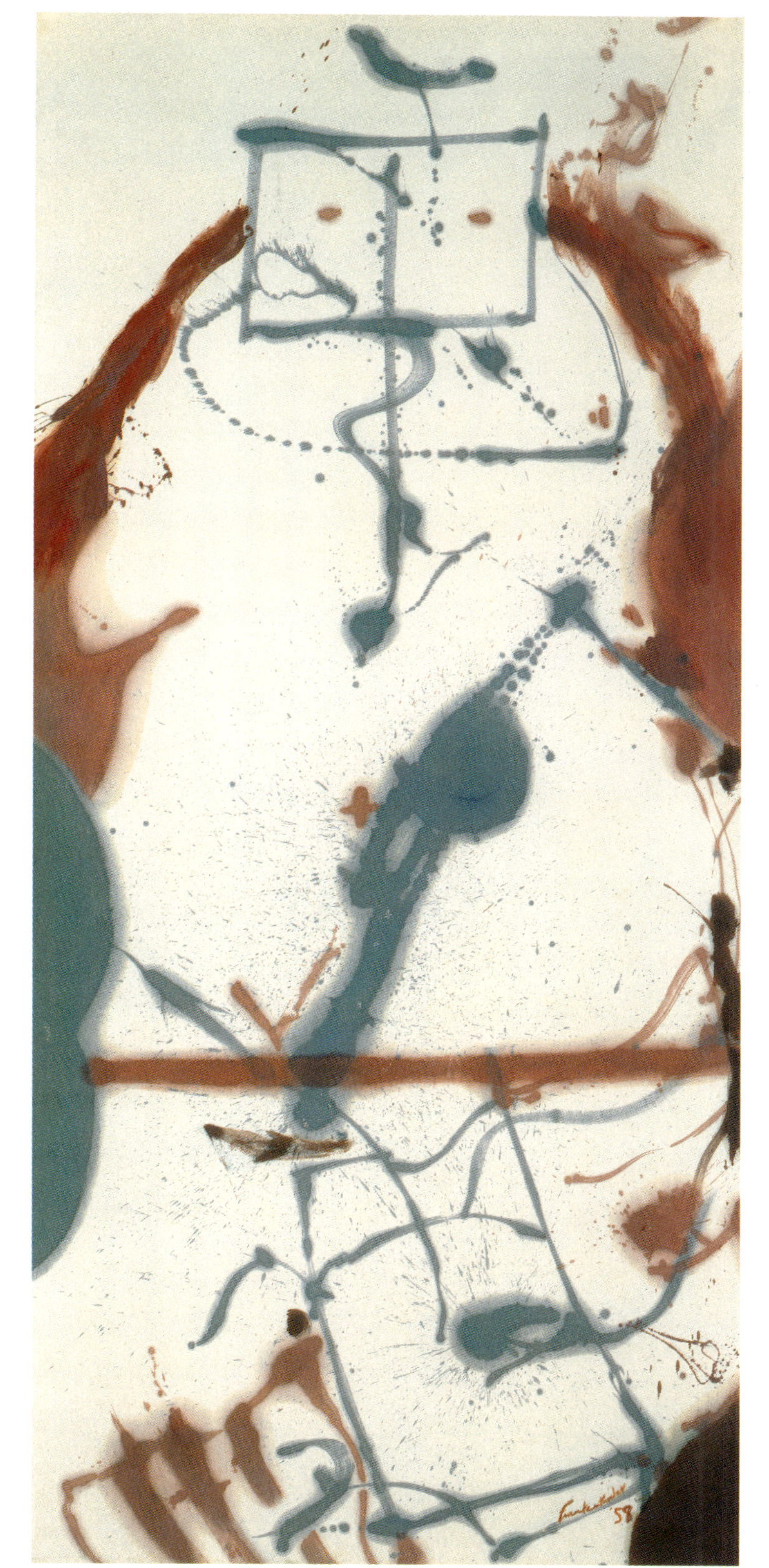

6. *Las Mayas.* 1958
Oil on canvas
8'4" x 3'7¾" (254 x 109.9 cm.)
Inscribed, l.r.: HF 58
Collection Norman and Irma Braman

Walking through an exhibition at the Walker Art Center in Minneapolis with H. Harvard Arnason in 1961, the British art historian Sir Herbert Read was confronted with the picture *Las Mayas.* As later reported, Read remarked: "This is unquestionably a lovely painting. The saturated blotter effect of the thin paint on the unprimed canvas is very compelling. Yet I am somewhat uneasy about it. The accidental element seems to be carried too far."[1]

How ironic is Read's comment on *Las Mayas*'s accidental element. With its Spanish title, it is often taken as just "an allusion to Goya."[2] In fact, whole sections of the painting's structure are based directly on Goya's *Mayas on a Balcony* (fig. 2) in the collection of The Metropolitan Museum of Art in New York. This relationship may not at first be apparent, for Frankenthaler inverted the composition in her final orientation of *Las Mayas.* Turning her picture upside down (she worked on it in both orientations; see fig. 1), we can identify several image transpositions: the triangular, wrapped head with eyes at the upper right, the figure with rounded hat to the left, and a hint of the *Mayas* in the center. Most dramatically, the abstract line of the earlier *Nude* (cat. no. 5) here becomes the upper railing of the balcony grillwork, and the empty white center zones—areas of unpainted canvas that *Las Mayas* shares with *Winter Hunt* (cat. no. 4) and *Nude*—reflect the lighter color areas in the Goya.

To be sure, the Frankenthaler is a much more vertical and elongated composition than that found in the Metropolitan picture, and within the scheme of her "Goya" are other, unrelated passages. As she has commented: "It was intended as an incidental but useful takeoff—not a parody. The ideas, the format, and the colors in the Goya fueled my own ideas. *Las Mayas* was also painted as an homage to Goya."

Such homage pictures—similar "incidental takeoffs"—occur periodically throughout Frankenthaler's career, including three other works (cat. nos. 24, 33, 34) in the present exhibition.

Notes:
1. Sir Herbert Read and H. Harvard Arnason, "Dialogue on Modern U.S. Painting," *Artnews* 59 (May 1960): 36.
2. B. H. Friedman, "Towards the Total Color Image," *Artnews* 65 (Summer 1966): 67.

Provenance:
(Galleria dell'Ariete, Milan)
Mr. Luciano Pistoi, Turin
(André Emmerich Gallery, New York)

Exhibition History:
Kassel, West Germany: *Documenta II* (cat. no. 2, ill. p. 164), 1959
New York: André Emmerich Gallery, 1959
Minneapolis, Minnesota: Walker Art Center (cat. no. 19, ill. p. 22), 1960
New York: The Jewish Museum (cat. no. 15, ill. p. 11), 1960
Los Angeles: Everett Ellin Gallery, 1961
Paris: Galerie Lawrence, 1961
Milan: Galleria dell'Ariete (cat. no. 4), 1962
Paris: Salles de la Fondation de Paris Nationale des Arts Plastiques et Graphiques (traveling exhibition, cat. ill.), 1977

Selected Critical References:
Butler, *Art International* (February–March 1960), ill. p. 55
Read and Arnason, *Artnews* (May 1960), comm. p. 36, ill. p. 34
Ashbery, *Art International* (20 November 1961), ill. p. 50
Friedman, *Artnews* (Summer 1966), comm. p. 67
Rose, 1972, ill. pl. 60
Touraine, *Art Press International* (March 1977), ill. p. 22
Rubinstein, 1982, ill. p. 326
Elderfield, 1989, comm. pp. 126, 137; color ill. p. 129

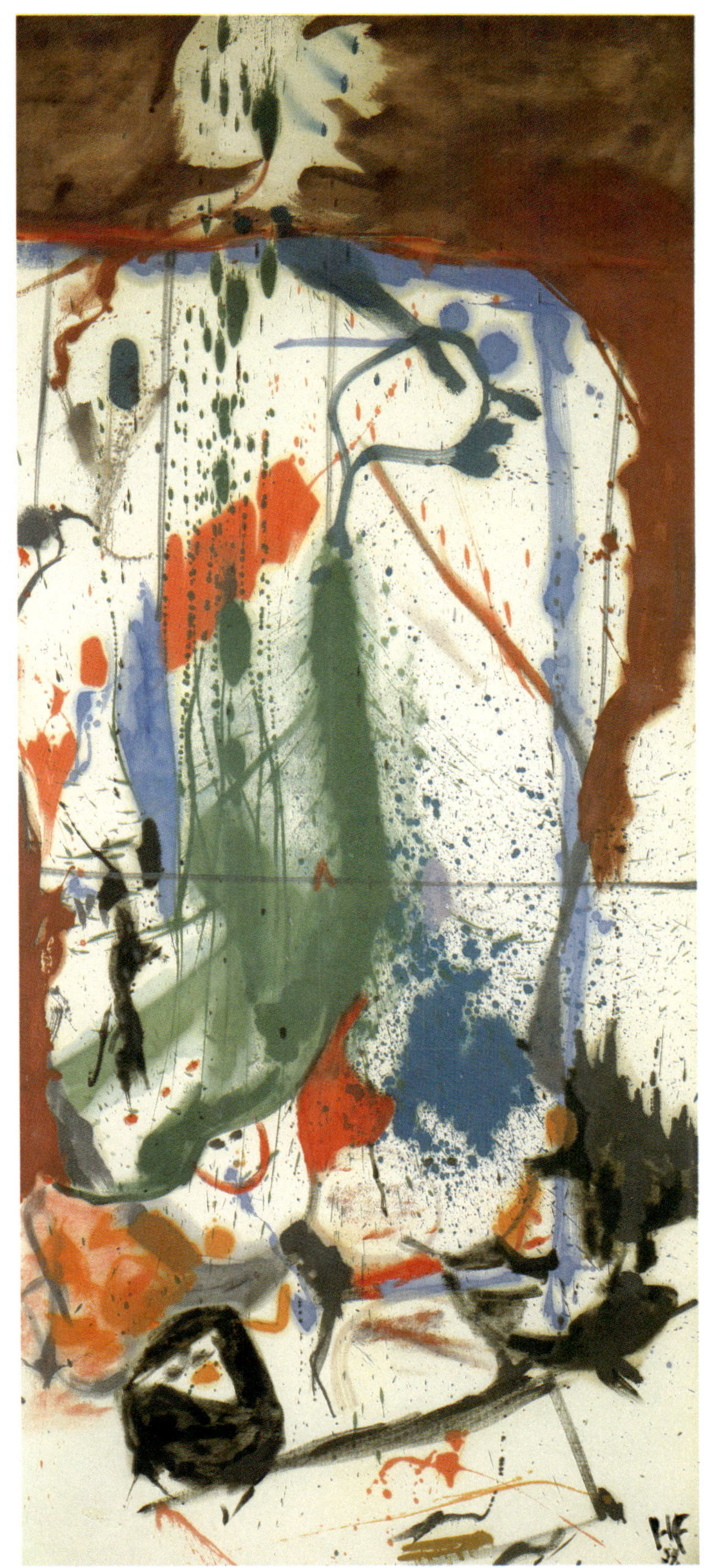

7. *Mother Goose Melody.* 1959
Oil on canvas
6'10" x 8'8" (208.2 x 264.1 cm.)
Inscribed, l.r.: Frankenthaler '59
Virginia Museum of Fine Arts. Gift of Sydney and Frances
Lewis

Beginning with *Mountains and Sea* (cat. no. 1), many of the 1950s works in this exhibition tend toward a kind of compositional symmetry, at least in terms of the distribution of pictorial weight. *Mother Goose Melody* represents a dramatically different kind of organization. "How do you make one side dense and weighty and the other side open and ropey and still have it work together?" says Frankenthaler of this picture. Here, the left side of the canvas is filled with a trio of elongated blackish shapes while the right section is left open, crossed with looping curves of red and gray and smaller semicircular elements of black and yellow. At the upper left, the squared drawing—here with an enclosed circle—makes another appearance (see *Nude*, cat. no. 5), while across the bottom, tying the sides together, is an irregular broad yellow band.

Highly successful as a picture, this marked asymmetry may have something to do with the special nature of this work. In many ways *Mother Goose Melody* seems to be the most lighthearted work in Frankenthaler's oeuvre. Early critics had some sense of these aspects, regarding its more personal nature either in a negative fashion—Robert Coates commented in 1960 that "there are times, too, when she verges on the coyly sentimental, as in *Mother Goose Melody*"[1]—or in a more positive way, as in Frank O'Hara's description of the same year: "On the sentimental side, the superb *Mother Goose Melody* . . . [does] not fail to refer to emotional enthusiasms which are real and likeable. . . ."[2] In a similar manner William Berkson referred to the way in which Frankenthaler's drawing established "the rocking-horse gaiety of *Mother Goose Melody*."[3] More precise readings of the picture have rarely been made. In 1966 B. H. Friedman wrote of the allusion "to the artist and her two sisters in *Mother Goose Melody*,"[4] an analysis made more specifically by Barbara Rose's subsequent comment that "in *Mother Goose Melody*, for example, the three central figural shapes might refer to Frankenthaler and her two sisters."[5] In 1981 Robert Taylor wrote (more accurately): "Frankenthaler's allusions to fig-

urative art are never tied to the literal, though shapes are evident; they don't seem superimposed upon an abstract design, but from out of it . . . [as does] the goose in *Mother Goose Melody*."[6]

Recently the artist has commented more specifically about painting *Mother Goose Melody*: "It was done in a garage in Falmouth, Massachusetts. When I made it, I first started on the left with the dark shapes. Each is the same but different. It was probably then I thought of 'three sister-shapes.' But they could just as well have been four green octagonals that day. Then I wanted something circular at the right. The lines made a sort of stork figure—the whole thing had a nursery-rhyme feeling."

If the three Frankenthaler sisters, Helen, Gloria, and Marjorie, are suggested in the abstract shapes, the stork is only slightly less so, identifiable in its black and red triangular beak, round head and eye, and in the general curving red line in the white area. "Some people read these long lines at the right [vertical, in gray] as the legs of the stork," she further noted, "but they were already there as necessary lines.

"I next put in the yellow passage at the bottom, going from side to side. Then I added the square and round shapes at the upper left—what some people see as the 'clock on the nursery-room wall.' I just put a square there. My first concern was drawing; I never consciously put down a clock. Then I added the blue next to the three dark shapes, blue that 'hugs in' on each side. The picture is about left side versus right side, but then it's woven together."

Notes:
1. Robert Coates, *The New Yorker* 36 (9 April 1960): 159.
2. Frank O'Hara, *Helen Frankenthaler Paintings* (New York: The Jewish Museum, 1960), 7.
3. William Berkson, "Poet of the Surface," *Arts Magazine* 39 (May–June 1965): 50.
4. B. H. Friedman, "Towards the Total Color Image," *Artnews* 65 (Summer 1966): 67.
5. Barbara Rose, *Frankenthaler* (New York: Harry N. Abrams, Inc., 1972), 22.
6. Robert Taylor, "Frankenthaler Show Splendid and Revealing," *Boston Globe*, 10 May 1981, p. A33.

(Continued on page 94)

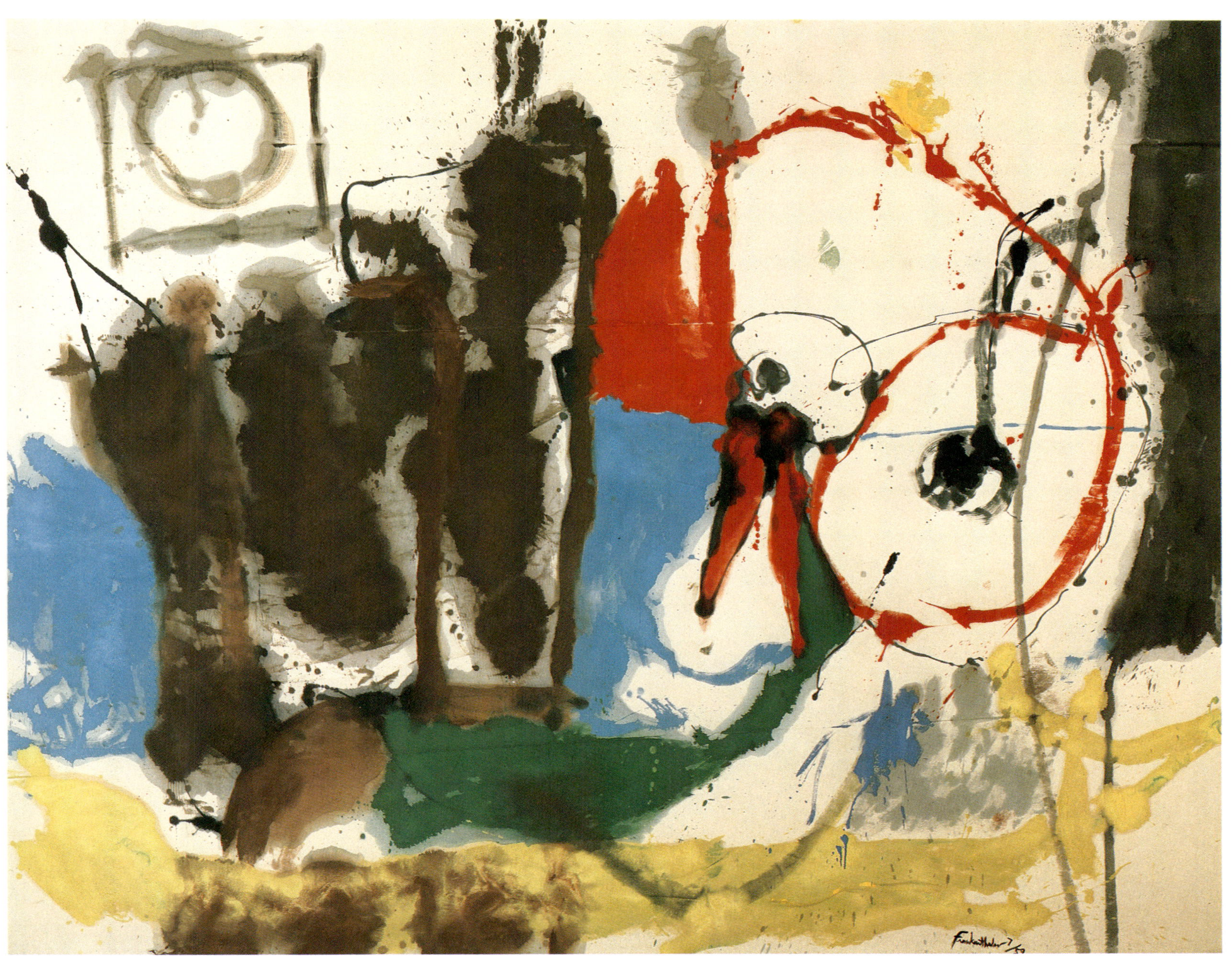

8. *Swan Lake I.* 1961
Oil on canvas
7'5⅛" x 7'9¾" (226.4 x 238.1 cm.)
Inscribed, l.r.: Frankenthaler
Private Collection

"When I was young there was a magazine I loved called *Child Life*," says Frankenthaler. "Each edition had a game in the puzzle section in which there were hidden yet definable images within the obvious images. For example, if you saw a landscape with trees, you could with care decipher a rabbit hidden in the leaves of a tree or find a duck camouflaged in a pond. I looked forward to this challenge and was good at the game. Looking back, the 'swans' in *Swan Lake I* remind me of that childhood experience. However, the former was a game, *Swan Lake I* involved making a picture." Not unlike seeing or finding the rabbit in the negative spaces of a tree, the swans in *Swan Lake I* were found rather than planned: "I started with blue, and a rather arbitrary beginning," recalls the artist. "At some point I recognized the birdlike shape— I was ready for it—and I developed it from there."

The "swans" in this large painting are white, unpainted canvas, their shapes defined by the blue paint of the surrounding areas. This blue "lake" sits on passages of green and yellow and is bordered by a nearly closed brown rectangle. The suggestion of a square within a square and its implied symmetry is further defined by dark brown passages to each exterior side of the lighter brown rectangle. The picture has a tripart rhythm, alternating positive and negative, balance and imbalance, and closing and opening. Where the painting differs from earlier work is in having a more densely defined center, with open white canvas around all of its edges. This more focalized quality—"I like the looking-in of it," says Frankenthaler — would lead to the more symmetrical work of the mid-1960s.

Swan Lake I also marked a rare time in her work in which Frankenthaler developed a series of pictures around a particular image or theme, including *Swan Lake II*.[1] Painted on a canvas of nearly identical size, *Swan Lake II* is especially close to *Swan Lake I*. The artist recalls that the birds in the second picture were outlined in charcoal before any paint was applied, and they took their shapes from the initial composition. "I wanted a shape that happened to be a swanlike shape," she notes. *Swan Lake II* is more subdued in its palette, using only various shades of blue, gray, and brown.

Unfortunately, *Swan Lake I* became known also as *Swan Lake II*, causing some confusion in subsequent literature. For example, when one realizes it was the variant and not *Swan Lake I* that was shown in Paris at the Galerie Lawrence in 1961, one understands John Ashbery's description of it there as "a large and beautiful blue canvas."[2]

Swan Lake I also suffered another kind of misfortune; it was damaged in a fire in 1976. The painting has been painstakingly restored with the ongoing advice of the artist, and, because of their generosity and their understanding of its importance, its owners have agreed to its public exhibition.

Notes:
1. *Swan Lake II* was finished after *Yellow Caterpillar.*
2. John Ashbery, "Paris Notes," *Art International* 5 (20 November 1961): 50.

Provenance:
The artist

Exhibition History:
New York: Whitney Museum of American Art (traveling exhibition, cat. no. 19, ill. p. 32), 1969

Selected Critical References:
Goossen, *Art International* (20 October 1961), ill. p. 79
Ashbery, *Art International* (20 November 1961), comm. p. 50
Rosenstein, *Artnews* (March 1969), comm. p. 31
Rose, *Artforum* (April 1969), cover ill.
———, 1972, comm. pp. 42, 90 [referred to as *Swan Lake II*]; colorpl. 12
Carmean, *Art International* (April–May 1978), comm. pp. 30–31 [referred to as *Swan Lake II*]; ill. p. 31
Elderfield, 1989, comm. pp. 145, 154, 398; color ill. p. 148

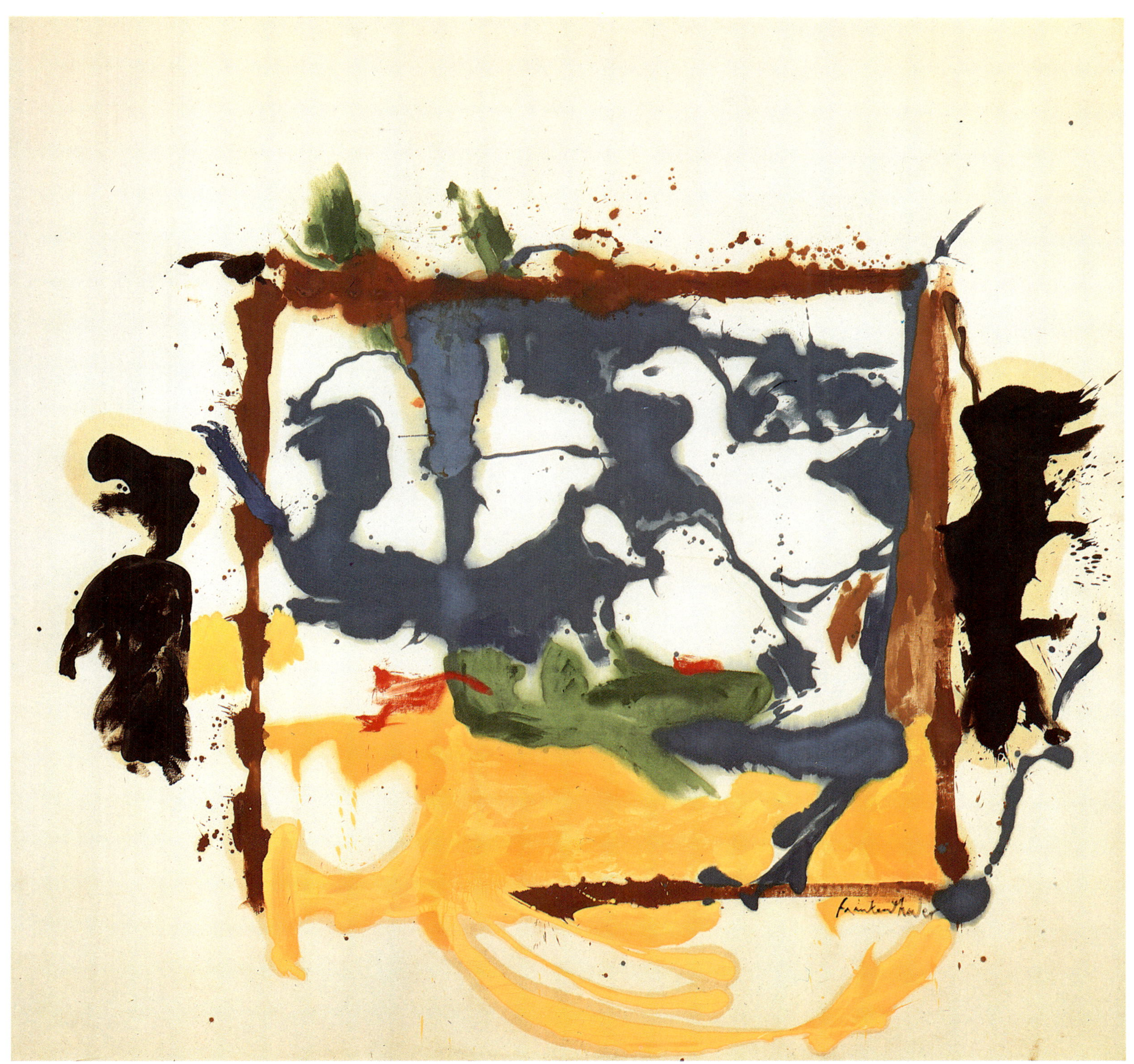

9. *Yellow Caterpillar.* 1961
Oil on canvas
7'9¾" x 10' (238.1 x 304.8 cm.)
Inscribed, c.r.: Frankenthaler
The Eli and Edythe L. Broad Collection

Yellow Caterpillar follows *Swan Lake I* and shares with it a more centralized massing of forms and a surrounding of empty white canvas. *Yellow Caterpillar* precedes *Swan Lake II,* as we can see in a studio photograph showing the completed *Yellow Caterpillar* on the studio wall and *Swan Lake II* still on the studio floor. The palettes are also similar, rich blues and intense yellow set off by a deep brown. *Yellow Caterpillar* further recalls the earlier work in that it "also plays the game of positive and negative shapes," says Frankenthaler, "although here they work differently." While the negative spaces in the earlier work might conjure up swans, in *Yellow Caterpillar* they are totally abstract.

The largest shape in *Yellow Caterpillar* is the long yellow passage at the top for which the work is named. This horizontal is echoed by the blue passages that start and stop, creating a second, broken horizontal slightly below center. The two brown shapes that interrupt this second line form enclosing shapes, with the one on the left again suggestive of the framing rectangle of *Swan Lake I.*

"I had the paint in buckets," Frankenthaler comments, "and I poured it as well as brushed it in certain areas. The shapes were determined in counterpoint with each other." Other, more detailing elements were added to the large forms, such as the thinner, semirectangular brown shape at the upper right center. Its feathering edge of darker brown over the lighter area introduces what the artist calls "flat chiaroscuro—on the cusp of shading yet keeping its place in space." The halo of oil that bled out from the paint into the surrounding canvas is not seen by her as shading but rather as "something that often comes unwittingly yet can serve as a bridge between the shape and the negative canvas."

Provenance:
The artist
Mr. Henry Geldzahler, New York
(André Emmerich Gallery, New York)

Exhibition History:
Paris: Galerie Lawrence (cat. ill. n.p.), 1961
New York: The Metropolitan Museum of Art (cat. no. 82, color ill.
    p. 75), 1969–70

Selected Critical References:
Goossen, *Art International* (20 October 1961), ill. p. 79
Ashbery, *Art International* (20 November 1961), comm. p. 50
Rose, 1972, ill. pl. 104
Clothier, *Artnews* (January 1988), color ill. p. 145
Elderfield, 1989, comm. p. 154, color ill. p. 151

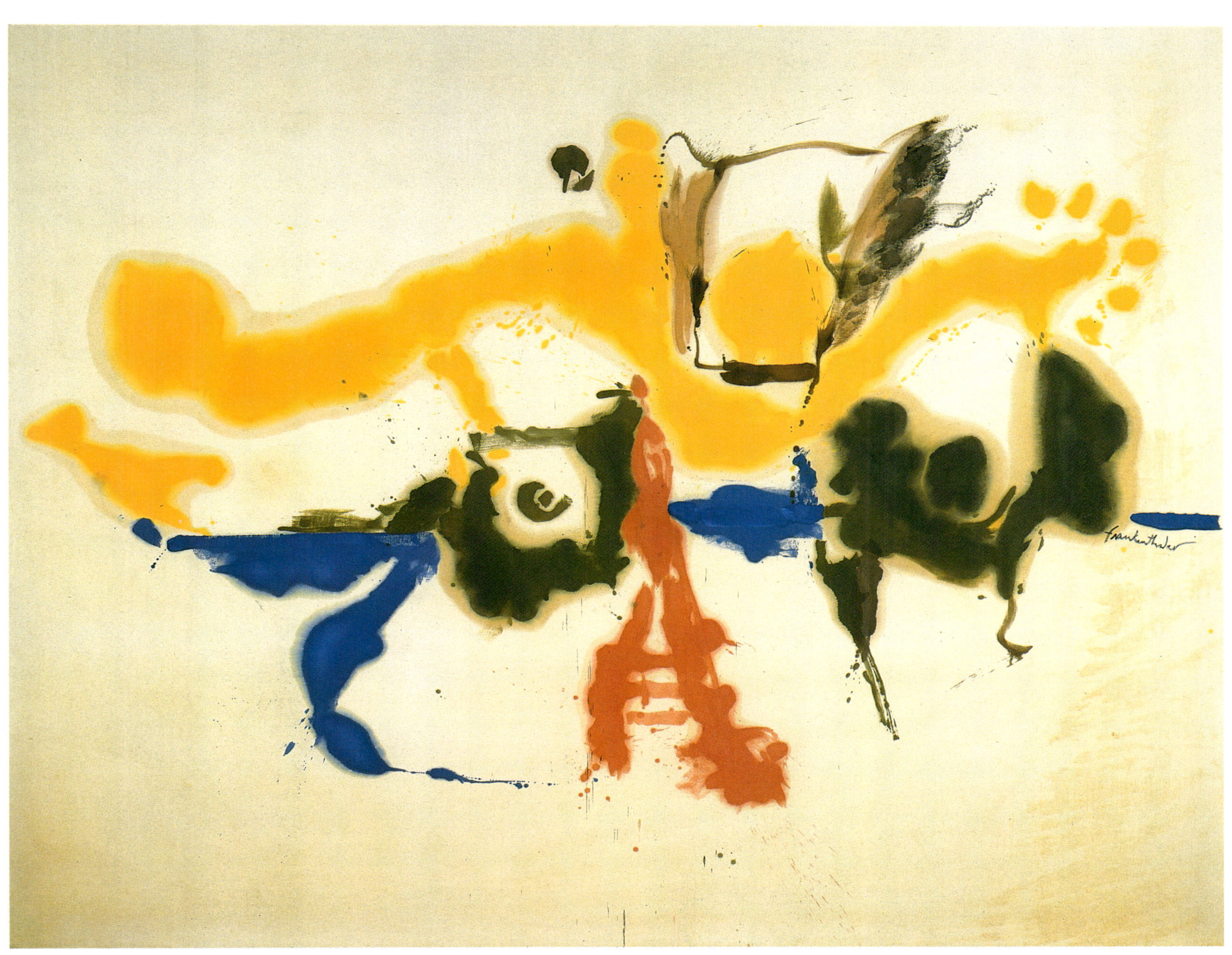

10. *Arden.* 1961
Oil on canvas
7'3½" x 10'¼" (222.3 x 305.4 cm.)
No inscription
Whitney Museum of American Art, New York. Gift of the artist. 69.170

"In 1961 there is an increasing amount of raw canvas space in the background for an image in such paintings as *Arden,*" wrote Harris Rosenstein, "which by their forms that could only be acceptably laid down by her stain technique, and in their biting color and commanding placement, seem to bring to a culmination the 'hard' qualities of Frankenthaler's work."[1] *Arden,* along with *Yellow Caterpillar* and *Seascape with Dunes* (cat. nos. 9, 11) are three works in the present exhibition that represent a new direction in Frankenthaler's work in the early 1960s. With long (ten to eleven feet), horizontal formats, these works overall are more controlled and restrained than her earlier paintings; their compositions exhibit—by placement of color shapes and drawing—a greater serenity.

Certainly the title of this work suggests repose. Lawrence Alloway observed in 1971 that her *Arcadia* "and *Arden,* the forest in *As You Like It,* are open references to the sites of pastorals, as is *Eden* [see our cat. no. 2]."[2] Without citing *Arden* directly, Barbara Rose had made a similar connection in 1972: "When looking at some of Frankenthaler's landscapes, particularly those of the fifties and early sixties, with such suggestive titles as *Eden* and *Arcadia,* one may be struck by associations with . . . the innocence of the paradise lost or garden of love theme."[3]

Frankenthaler agrees that "the title might be a garden reference. However," she continues, "the title was suggested to me by a studio visitor. When I needed a title, I had nothing in mind. *Arden* does make reference to an ideal or spiritual place, and—with the pink surrounded by the greens—you can conceive of it as an enclosed place. But the picture is abstract."

Arden represents a development out of certain ideas seen in the Swan Lake pictures (see cat. no. 8). Here, the positive shapes made of color and the negative shapes made from enclosed white canvas are used in a similar manner, with positive and negative interweaving through the composition. The green triangle at the lower left, for example, is echoed by the white (painted) triangle in the center and the triangle hinted at in the pinks above that area.

Running throughout the whole are the green color shapes, which form a line that serves to further interconnect the other, more disparate elements of the composition. "This line was originally blobs of green color—placed locally. After that, I joined them together," says the artist. Much the same was true initially of the pinks, which, as she notes, "are different pinks – they do not repeat pigments." Part of one of the pinks was also used to establish the three small verticals in the center of the white triangle, a trio meant to echo the longer green ones at the left: a lighter touch that, she says, "may also have been a note of whim as well as a necessary bridge."

Notes:
1. Harris Rosenstein, "The Colorful Gesture," *Artnews* 68 (March 1969): 31.
2. Lawrence Alloway, "Frankenthaler as Pastoral," *Artnews* 70 (November 1971): 89.
3. Barbara Rose, *Frankenthaler* (New York: Harry N. Abrams, Inc., 1972), 50.

Exhibition History:
New York: Whitney Museum of American Art (traveling exhibition, cat. no. 17, ill. p. 35), 1969
New York: Whitney Museum of American Art (checklist), 1974
Tokyo, Japan: The Seibu Museum of Art (cat. no. 4, colorpl. 4), 1976
Jacksonville, Florida: Jacksonville Art Museum (traveling exhibition, cat. color ill. n.p.), 1977–78
Bordeaux, France: Centre d'Arts Plastiques Contemporains de Bordeaux (cat. ill. p. 20), 1981

Selected Critical References:
Rosenstein, *Artnews* (March 1969), comm. pp. 31, 68
Alloway, *Artnews* (November 1971), comm. p. 89
Rose, 1972, comm. p. 50, colorpl. 89
Nemser, *Feminist Art Journal* (April 1972), ill. p. 23
Munro, 1979, comm. p. 208, ill. p. 209
Elderfield, 1989, comm. p. 154, color ill. p. 152

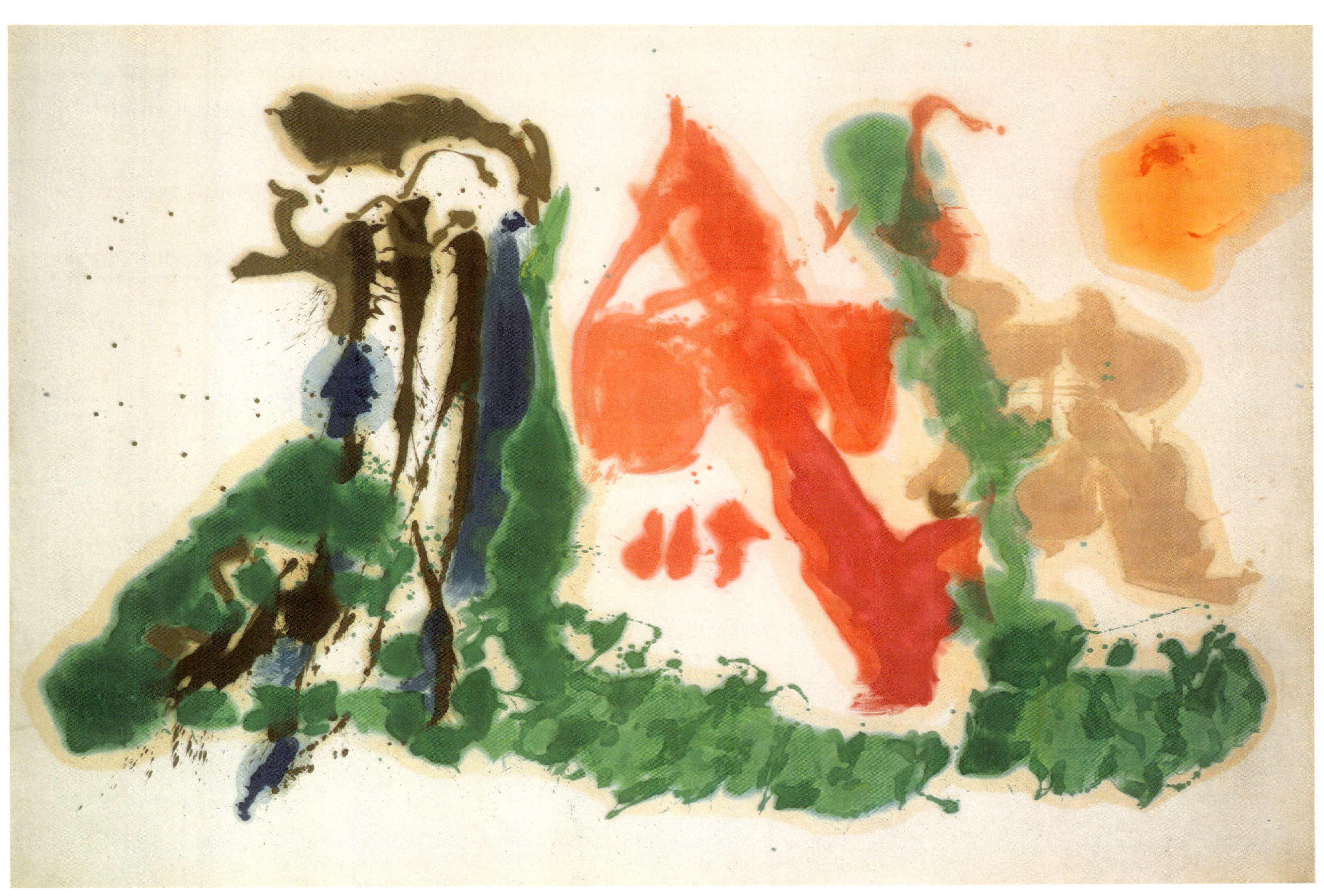

11. *Seascape with Dunes.* 1962
Oil on canvas
5'10" x 11'8" (177.8 x 355.6 cm.)
Inscribed, c.r.: Frankenthaler
Grey Art Gallery and Study Center, New York University Art
Collection. Gift of the artist, 1963

Frankenthaler says of the title of this work, "The picture conjures up horizons and could have a resemblance or reference to dunes." This abstract reference in the title, and the fact that *Seascape with Dunes* was painted on Cape Cod in Massachusetts, led to more specific readings of the work. *Time* magazine, for example, described the picture's palette in terms of "the oceanic blues, yellow sands, the faded greens of marsh grass, and the savage reds of black plums," and said of its composition: "Militant playfulness seems to predominate in *Seascape with Dunes.* Its thorny blobs march across the canvas in a shape like a sea horse at bay."[1]

Other critics were less descriptive but nevertheless retained oceanic or water metaphors in their more formal analyses of the picture.[2] In the literature, only Hilton Kramer avoided metaphors, choosing instead to write of this work (and two other examples) that "Miss Frankenthaler is indeed a more traditional composer."[3]

The artist says of *Seascape with Dunes:* "The title is misleading. It is actually a play of reds and of rhythms and of the ambiguities of symmetry. It might have a playful quality, but it is seriously playful, thought out." And, indeed, red dominates, with three shapes aligned vertically in the center of the canvas, two more at the left and right tops, and one small passage at the left margin. All around them are smaller shapes and lines of color of widely varying character and scale (the changes in sizes of elements in *Seascape with Dunes* are remarkable). Interwoven throughout this mixture are the "horizons," one of green and brown between the top two center reds, the other a long brown passage (again a frequently used element in her work) that moves from the left margin across the center, going between the lower red shapes. Indeed, this lower "horizon" almost serves as a seesaw-like board, poised among the center lines of red, holding the weight of the other areas in balance.

Notes:
1. "Heiress to a Tradition," *Time* 93, no. 13 (28 September 1969): 69.
2. See, for example, Christopher Andreae's description of the color areas as "islands" with their turpentine seepages as indicating "various depths of the ocean round a landmass" in *Christian Science Monitor,* 19 March 1969, p. 12.
3. Hilton Kramer, "Abstraction and the Landscape Paradigm," *The New York Times,* 2 March 1969, sec. 2, p. 31.

Exhibition History:
Urbana, Illinois: Krannert Art Museum (cat. ill. p. 99), 1963
Venice: XXXIII Venice Biennale (traveling exhibition, cat. ill. p. 27), 1966
New York: Whitney Museum of American Art (traveling exhibition, cat. no. 23, ill. p. 36), 1969
Yonkers, New York: The Hudson River Museum (cat.), 1971
Houston: The Museum of Fine Arts (cat. no. 14, ill. p. 51), 1974
New York: Grey Art Gallery and Study Center, New York University (cat. color ill. p. 43), 1975
Jacksonville, Florida: Jacksonville Art Museum (traveling exhibition, cat. ill. n.p.), 1977–78

Selected Critical References:
Geldzahler, *Artforum* (June 1966), ill. p. 34
Lowe, *Museum News* (November 1966), ill. p. 16
Hudson, *The Washington Post,* 1 January 1967, ill. p. G8
Kramer, *The New York Times,* 2 March 1969, comm. sec. 2, p. 31
Andreae, *Christian Science Monitor,* 19 March 1969, ill. p. 12
Time, 28 March 1969, comm. p. 69
Brett, *The Times,* 26 May 1969, comm. p. 5
Rose, 1972, comm. p. 90, colorpl. 110
Elderfield, 1989, comm. p. 154, ill. p. 155

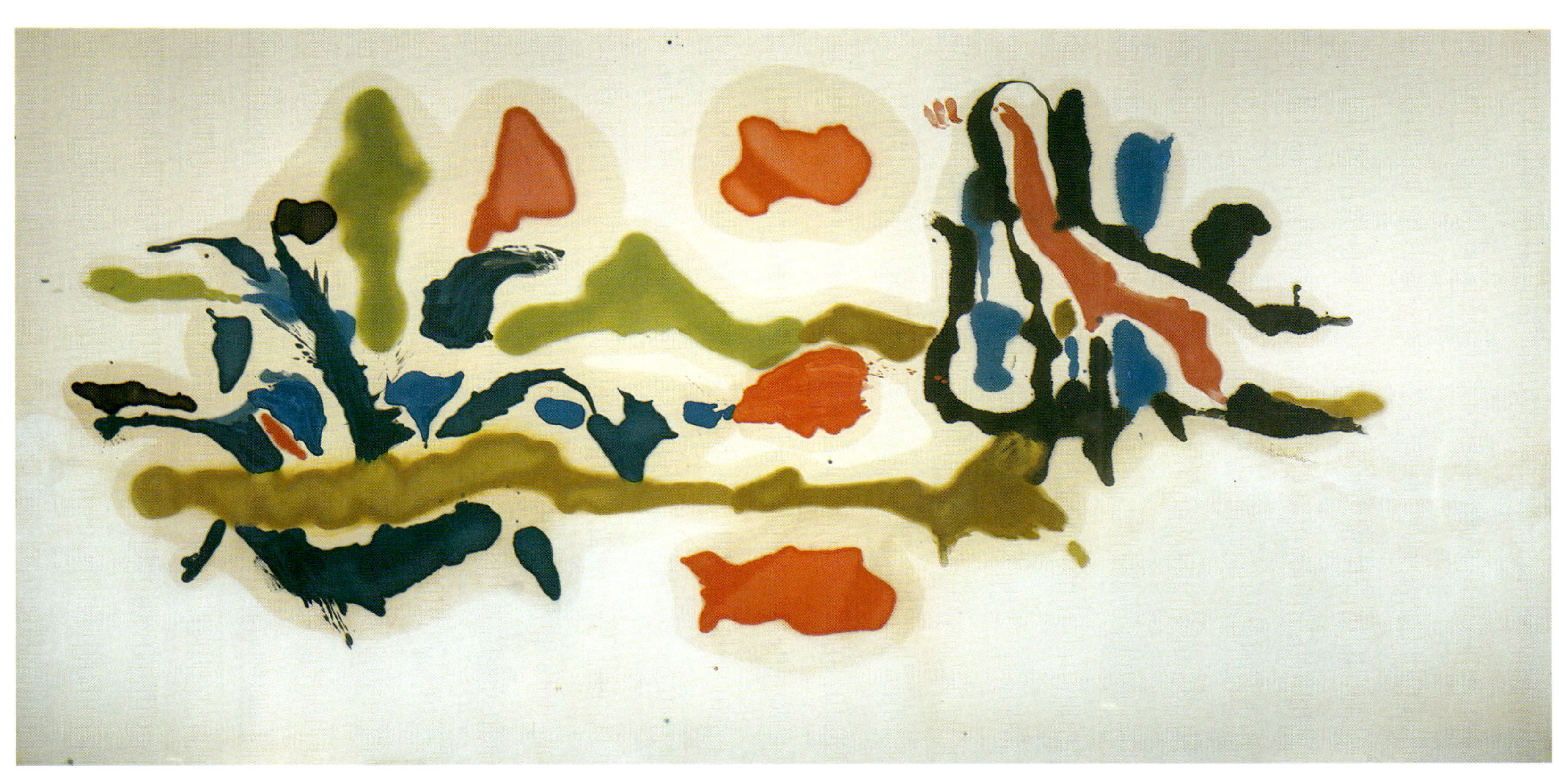

12. *The Bay.* 1963
Acrylic on canvas
6'8¾" x 6'9¾" (205.1 x 207.6 cm.)
Inscribed, l.r.: Frankenthaler
The Detroit Institute of Arts, Michigan. Gift of Dr. and Mrs.
Hilbert H. DeLawter

Although seemingly linked by its seaside title, *The Bay,* of 1963, with its rippling blue shape looming over a field of green and gray, differs dramatically from the earlier *Seascape with Dunes* (cat. no. 11) and its intricate, point-to-point composition of widely varied elements. But the differences are more than just compositional. *The Bay* established a new direction in Frankenthaler's art, introducing ideas that would dominate her work until the end of the decade.

Curiously, this work is one of the few to have been titled by Frankenthaler before being completed, in this case after only the dominant blue area had been painted. "In seeing the silhouettes of blue and raw canvas, I thought of the bay — of weather, but in terms of abstract shapes," she recalls. Painted in a bayside studio, *The Bay* "was the first of the Provincetown pictures. It was literally 'bay bound.'" To be sure, the artist insists the painting does not depict Provincetown Bay, which her studio overlooked, and it "is not intended to represent a particular body of water." Like other "themes" in her art — especially those of place — it comes from that experience, however, and she said of *The Bay:* "Anything that happens affecting your sensibility has an effect on what you make. My work is not a matter of direct translations, but something is bound to creep into your head or heart."

The facture of *The Bay* underscores Frankenthaler's comments on its poetic associations. As she notes: "The blues were painted first in various horizontal gestures. It looks like one blue, but there are many." Indeed, close observation reveals that the horizontal strata are still present and are clearly made of blues of *different* pigments, most likely nine distinct blues in all. It is this layering — through color variation — that gives the shapes of blue their "billowy" or "weather-like" effect. "I painted the blues and left it to dry," she recalls. "When I came back, I was surprised. I then added the green and it felt done. I came back, put in the gray — a sort of gray banner — then the red sienna 'dot.' Then I looked it at and said to myself, stop, get out of here." Again, this question of "Is it finished?" plays a crucial role in her work.

Provenance:
(André Emmerich Gallery, New York)

Exhibition History:
London: Kasmin Limited (cat.), 1964
Detroit, Michigan: Detroit Institute of Arts (cat. no. 20), 1965
Venice: XXXIII Venice Biennale (traveling exhibition, cat. color ill. p. 10), 1966
Grand Rapids, Michigan: Grand Rapids Art Museum (cat. no. 70), 1967
New York: Whitney Museum of American Art (traveling exhibition, cat. no. 24, comm. p. 13, ill. p. 41), 1969
Grand Rapids, Michigan: Grand Rapids Art Museum (cat. no. 102, ill. n.p.), 1977

Selected Critical References:
Braun, *Detroit Free Press,* 6 May 1965, ill.
Geldzahler, *Artforum* (June 1966), color ill. p. 37
Lynton, *Art International* (September 15, 1966), comm. p. 80
Lowe, *Museum News* (November 1966), ill. p. 15
Gold, *The Sun,* 8 October 1967, comm. p. D20
———, *The Sun,* 23 March 1969, comm. p. D22
Battcock, *Art and Artists* (May 1969), ill. p. 55
Grinke, *The Spectator,* 16 May 1969, comm.
Hunter, 1970, ill. p. 33
Alloway, *Artnews* (November 1971), comm. p. 89
Rose, 1972, comm. p. 96, colorpl. 1
Elderfield, 1989, comm. pp. 166, 398; color ill. p. 169

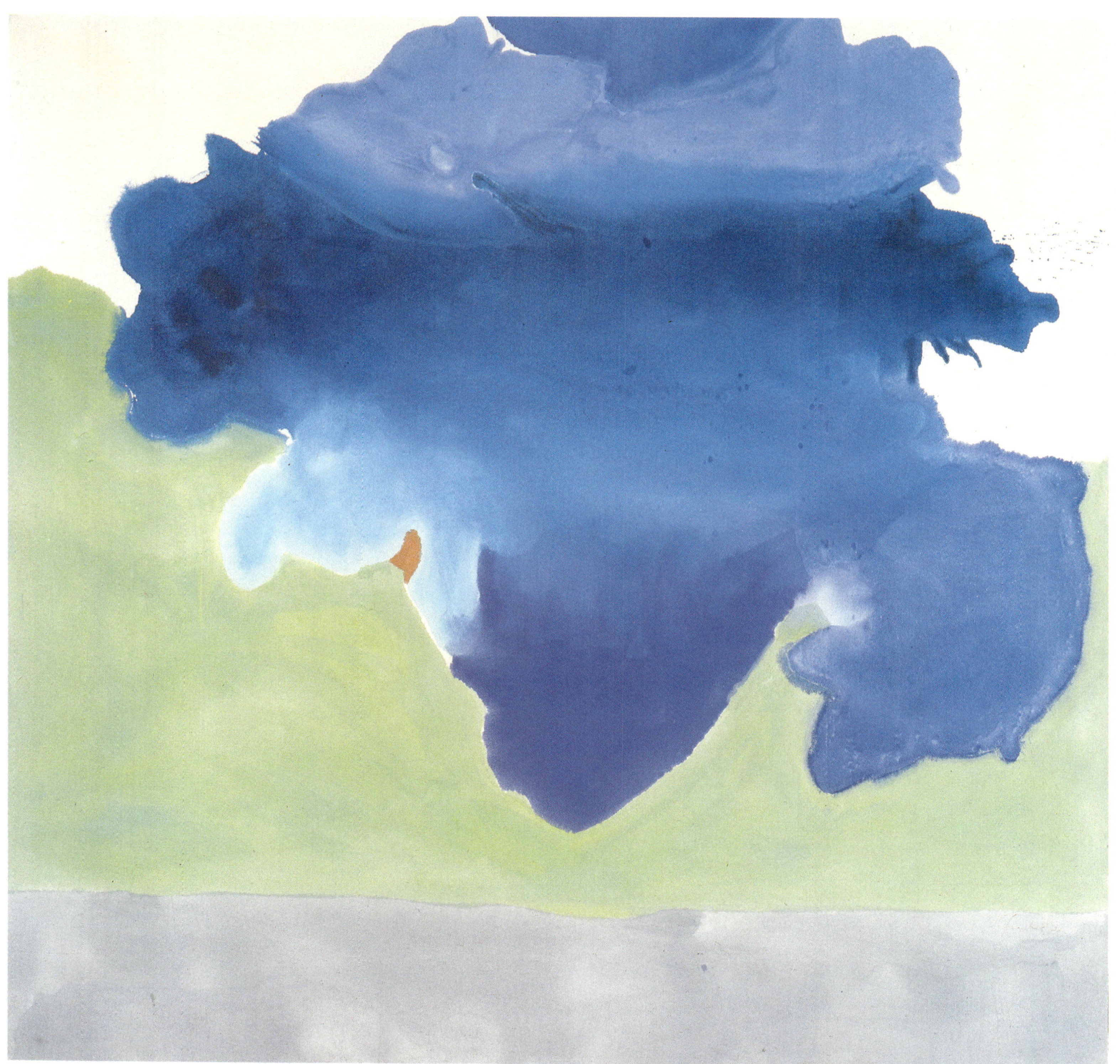

13. *Small's Paradise.* 1964
Acrylic on canvas
8'4" x 7'9⅝" (254 x 237.7 cm.)
Inscribed, verso: Frankenthaler "Small's Paradise" (1964)
    100 x 93¾"
National Museum of American Art, Smithsonian Institution,
    Washington, D.C. Gift of George L. Erion

"It is a play on interiors, shapes within shapes," Frankenthaler recently remarked of the composition of *Small's Paradise.* Previously she had referred to this work and the related *Buddha's Court* (cat. no. 14) as "interiors. They are things inside of things."[1]

How interesting that the idea of "interior," of enclosure rather than landscape, would come to the fore in her work during the mid-1960s. To be sure, there were earlier interiors (including *Mother Goose Melody,* cat. no. 7), but Frankenthaler's art to this point had been predominantly one of landscape associations. Even so, the notions of exterior or interior continue an underlying theme of *place.*

Enclosure after enclosure governed the making of the picture. "I started with the red shape in the middle," she recalls, "and then added the precise pink square around it." This squarish shape, enclosing an irregular form, continues another dominant Frankenthaler motif (see *Nude, Mother Goose Melody, Swan Lake I,* and *Yellow Caterpillar,* cat. nos. 5, 7, 8, 9), but does so here in the form of a field of encasing color rather than as an open, linear outline.

The inverted **U** shape of light green surrounding the pink was added next, along with the blue band below. This long, crossing horizontal is another frequently used element in the artist's work. She recalls: "The picture existed for quite a while without the other, outer green. At the bottom, I let it remain open, with raw canvas."

When asked earlier about titling her paintings, Frankenthaler had said: "I usually name them for an image that seems to come out of the pictures. . . . I don't like sentimental titles. The picture *Small's Paradise* had a Persian shape in it; also, I had been to that nightclub recently."[2] The nightclub reference is to a Harlem establishment of the same name that featured jazz music;[3] while the "Persian shape" likely indicates forms in certain Persian manuscript illustrations (sometimes of Paradise), where an irregular shape is often found enclosed by other shapes. Interestingly in this regard, many such illustrations have irregularly formed areas extending past the square formats of the center areas, something akin to the composition of *Small's Paradise.*

Frankenthaler recently added another kind of abstract association, related to the "small" in the title, saying that the tightly defined edges in *Buddha's Court* and *Small's Paradise* were like "those I recognized much later in Persian court miniatures and Japanese painting — combining detail and precision within vast settings."

Notes:
1. E.A. Carmean, Jr., "On Five Paintings by Helen Frankenthaler," *Art International* 22 (April–May 1978): 30.
2. Henry Geldzahler, "An Interview with Helen Frankenthaler," *Artforum* 4 (October 1965): 38.
3. William Kloss, "Helen Frankenthaler: *Small's Paradise,*" *Treasures from the National Museum of American Art* (Washington, D.C.: Smithsonian Institution Press, 1985), 164.

Provenance:
(André Emmerich Gallery, New York)

Exhibition History:
London: Kasmin Limited (cat.), 1964
New York: Whitney Museum of American Art (traveling exhibition, cat. no. 32, comm. p. 13, ill. p. 45 [first state]), 1969
Jacksonville, Florida: Jacksonville Art Museum, 1977–78
Mexico City: Museo del Palacio de Bellas Artes (cat. no. 79, color ill. p. 199), 1980
Munich: Haus der Kunst (cat. no. 22, ill. p. 40), 1981–82
Washington, D.C.: National Museum of American Art (traveling exhibition, cat. no. 75, comm. and color ill. p. 164), 1986–87

Selected Critical References:
Bowen, *The Arts Review* (May–June 1964), comm. p. 25
Geldzahler, *Artforum* (October 1965), comm. p. 38
Friedman, *Artnews* (Summer 1966), comm. p. 68
Rosenstein, *Artnews* (March 1969), comm. p. 60
Rose, *Artforum* (April 1969), comm. p. 33, ill. p. 31
Alloway, *Artnews* (March 1971), comm. p. 89
Rose, 1972, comm. p. 96, colorpl. 14
Carmean, *Art International* (April–May 1978), comm. p. 30
Elderfield, 1989, comm. pp. 172, 180; color ill. p. 179

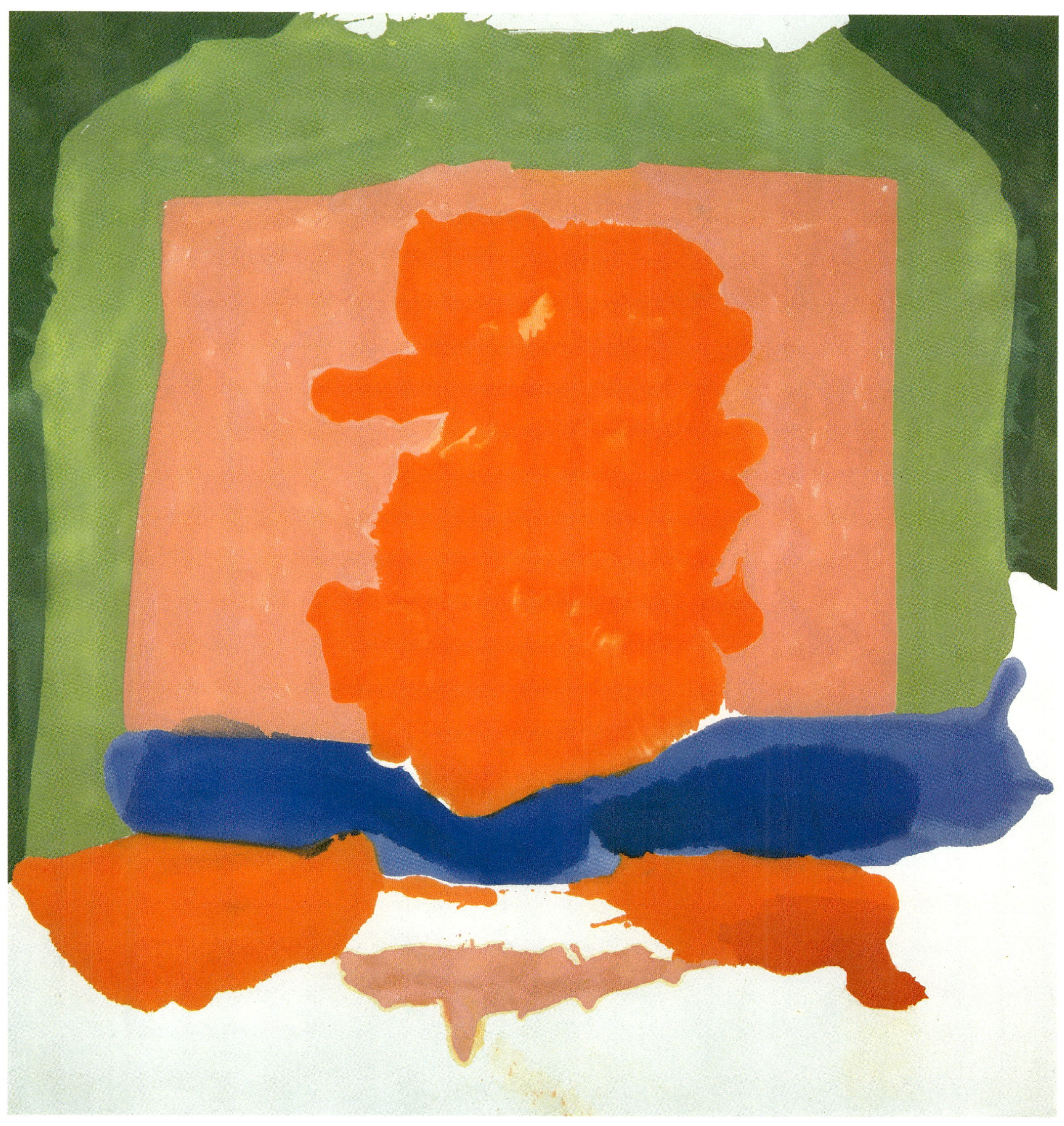

14. *Buddha's Court.* 1964
Acrylic on canvas
8'2" x 7'10" (248.9 x 238.8 cm.)
Inscribed, l.r.: Frankenthaler
Collection Mr. and Mrs. Robert K. Hoffman

Of the five related paintings from the mid-1960s in the present exhibition, both *The Bay* and *Small's Paradise* preceded *Buddha's Court,* which in turn was completed before *Interior Landscape* and, finally, *Tangerine* (cat. nos. 12, 13, 15, 16).[1] Of the quintet, *Buddha's Court* displays the densest composition, its surface entirely covered, without leaving any unpainted canvas. It is also the most enclosed composition — more interior than the others. Here the central image is encased in a brown field, surrounded by an orange border, which in turn is enclosed by a darker, brown-black band. We find here square within square within square, the furthest extension of a major Frankenthaler motif.

This "squareness" accords with the almost symmetrical layout of the central elements, giving the picture its extremely heretic composition. This near rigidity, combined with glowing color, supports the often mystical reading of the painting as, indeed, "Buddha in his court."

Like the "bay" of *The Bay*, the "mystical court" of this work wasn't always there. "For a long time there was no border," Frankenthaler recalls. "Adding it—the somber color—made it a magisterial 'place.'"

Critical reaction to the painting historically has echoed her comment. In 1965 Lawrence Campbell observed: "Her work was never clearer nor more mysterious. *Buddha's Court* . . . seemed to set the mind at rest before acting on the body."[2] And in the same year, William Berkson went further, saying of the upper ovals, "Like double images of the uplifted hands of a Buddha, they enforce a regal and friendly calm."[3] The following year B. H. Friedman said of the painting: "The blues have a quiet, almost religious *presence.* . . . In addition to these associations, there is a suggestion, too, in the upper blue forms, of the palms-out gesture of the Buddha."[4]

"But these are simply associations,"[5] Friedman concluded. And Frankenthaler would agree.

Notes:
1. E. C. Goossen, *Helen Frankenthaler* (New York: Whitney Museum of American Art, 1969), 13.
2. L[awrence] C[ampbell], "Helen Frankenthaler," *Artnews* 64 (May 1965): 10.
3. William Berkson, "Poet of the Surface," *Arts Magazine* 39 (May–June 1965): 46.
4. B. H. Friedman, "Towards the Total Color Image," *Artnews* 65 (Summer 1966): 68.
5. Ibid.

Provenance:
(André Emmerich Gallery, New York)
Mrs. Donald Straus, New York
(André Emmerich Gallery, New York)

Exhibition History:
New York: André Emmerich Gallery, 1965
New York: Whitney Museum of American Art (traveling exhibition, cat. no. 29, comm. p. 13, color ill. p. 47), 1969
Houston: The Museum of Fine Arts (cat. no. 16), 1974
New York: André Emmerich Gallery, 1975
New York: School of Visual Arts, 1976
Dallas: University Gallery, Southern Methodist University (checklist no. 6), 1977

Selected Critical References:
Kozloff, *The Nation* (5 April 1965), comm. p. 375
Campbell, *Artnews* (May 1965), comm. p. 10
Berkson, *Arts Magazine* (May–June 1965), comm. and ill. p. 46
Friedman, *Artnews* (Summer 1966), comm. p. 68, ill. p. 32
Burton, *Artnews* (November 1966), comm. p. 12
Rosenstein, *Artnews* (March 1969), comm. p. 68
Rosenberg, *The New Yorker* (29 March 1969), comm. p. 120
K., D., *Spandauer Volksblatt,* 12 October 1969, comm.
Alloway, *Artnews* (November 1971), comm. p. 89
Rose, 1972, comm. p. 96, colorpl. 34
Art Press International (March 1977), ill. p. 38
Carmean, *Art International* (April–May 1978), comm. p. 30
Rubinstein, 1982, comm. p. 329
Elderfield, 1989, comm. pp. 172, 180; color ill. p. 181

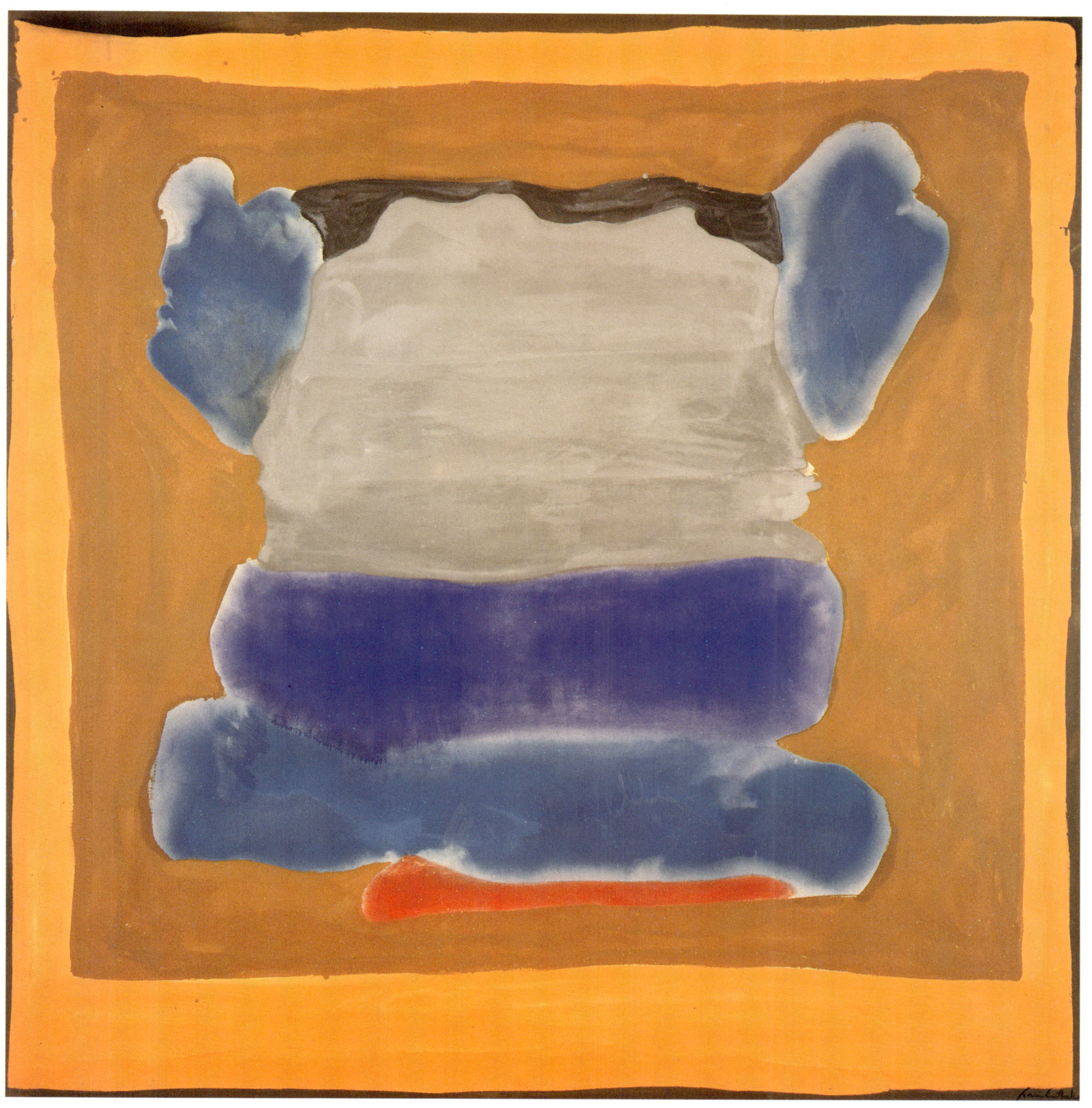

15. *Interior Landscape.* 1964
Acrylic on canvas
8′8⅞″ x 7′8⅝″ (266.4 x 234.6 cm.)
Inscribed, l.r.: Frankenthaler
San Francisco Museum of Modern Art. Gift of the Women's
Board

All five works from the mid-1960s in the present exhibition form a tightly related stylistic group. From *The Bay* to *Tangerine,* each painting plays off of a somewhat symmetrical format, the composition focused on a dominant central shape, which is enclosed, or at least partially surrounded, by color. All five works are painted on large, nearly square canvases. Within the range of Frankenthaler's more freely created oeuvre, these pictures of the mid-1960s are the closest she has come to painting in a "series" manner.

The present work, *Interior Landscape,* is even closer to the concept of series — or of work with an interrelated format — in that its general composition can be seen as a variant of one established earlier in *Small's Paradise*.[1]

Interior Landscape resembles *Small's Paradise* in its centered, irregular shape surrounded by a rectangular field of color. This "regular" field is further enclosed by an irregular band, which is itself bound by another color extending to the edge of the canvas. Below, a long horizontal crosses the surface — stopping short in the later painting. Below, in each, are two more independent shapes, connected by a second horizontal. In *Interior Landscape* this passage is quite geometric in character, echoing the upper blue rectangle that extends downward in this work toward the lower edge.

"It's called *Interior Landscape,*" says Frankenthaler, "because that's what it is — an interior landscape — an abstract picture." The central image, and those below, were generated most spontaneously. "The spikey outline of the yellow came from the original splash of paint, and I just left that spikey edge, which is unusual for me." The irregular edge of the yellow was further emphasized because, as Frankenthaler notes, "The gray-green border was painted with a small detailing brush in order to adhere to and not overlap the exact yellow edge."

Note:
1. See also E. C. Goossen's discussion of these works in *Helen Frankenthaler* (New York: Whitney Museum of American Art, 1969): 13.

Provenance:
(André Emmerich Gallery, New York)

Exhibition History:
London: Kasmin Limited, 1964
Cleveland: Cleveland Museum of Art (cat. no. 160, ill. n.p.), 1966
Detroit: Detroit Institute of Arts (cat. no. 26, ill. n.p.), 1967
San Francisco: San Francisco Museum of Art (cat. no. 25, ill. p. 25), 1968
New York: Whitney Museum of American Art (traveling exhibition, cat. no. 30, ill. p. 44), 1969
Des Moines, Iowa: Des Moines Art Center (cat. no. 12, color ill. n.p.), 1973
San Francisco: Bank of America World Headquarters Building, 1974
San Francisco: San Francisco Museum of Modern Art (brochure no. 12), 1977
San Francisco: San Francisco Museum of Modern Art, 1984

Selected Critical References:
Bowen, *The Arts Review* (May–June 1964), comm. p. 25
Reichardt, *Aujourd'hui* (October 1964), comm. p. 56, ill. p. 57
Baro, *Art International* (September 1967), comm. and color ill. p. 37
Arnason, 1968, comm. p. 623, colorpl. 251
Rosenstein, *Artnews* (March 1969), comm. p. 68, ill. p. 31
Time (28 March 1969), comm. p. 69, ill. p. 67
Rosenberg, *The New Yorker* (29 March 1969), comm. p. 120
Rose, *Artforum* (April 1969), comm. p. 33
L., W., *Telegraf,* 4 October 1969, comm.
Catalog of the Permanent Collection, 1970, comm. p. 41, colorpl. 51
Hunter and Jacobus, 1972, ill. p. 251
Rose, 1972, comm. p. 96, colorpl. 141
Baldwin, *Des Moines Sunday Register,* 4 March 1973, color ill. p. 15
Preble, 1976, colorpl. 41, ill. p. 226
Arnason, 1977, colorpl. 272
Rubinstein, 1982, comm. p. 329
Arnason, 1986, colorpl. 233

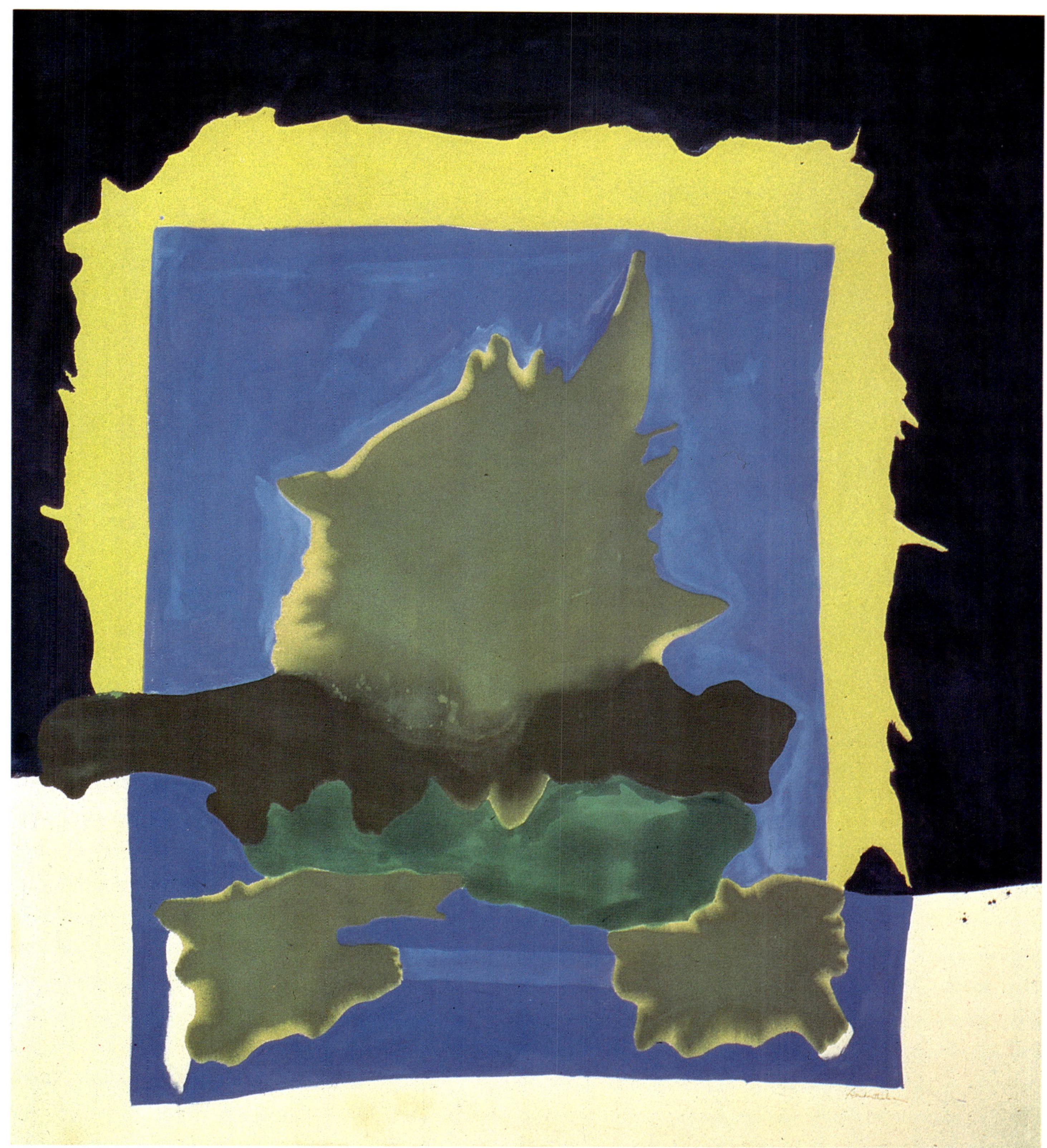

16. *Tangerine.* 1964
Acrylic on canvas
6'4" x 5'6" (193 x 167.6 cm.)
Inscribed, l.r.: Frankenthaler
Private Collection, courtesy of André Emmerich Gallery,
New York

Bad art history and bad criticism sometimes come from knowing an abstract picture's title and "reading" into the forms a corresponding image. What's more, such wrong associations get passed on — even codified — in further writing about the same work. Thus, in the literature certain forms in *Mother Goose Melody* (cat. no. 7) have gone from looking *like* a goose to *being* a goose.

We find a somewhat analogous case in *Tangerine,* the last picture from the mid-1960s included in this exhibition. Such "reading in" (see below) is especially ironic for this painting, which the artist describes as "probably my most abstract of this group." Knowing the previous four works in this "series" (see cat. nos. 12, 13, 14, 15), we can glean some idea of why. Composed of shapes in four different oranges (again from four different pigments), the center is dominated by the large, two-color irregular shape above, with two smaller, more horizontal orange shapes below: the latter shapes, joined by a green horizontal at bottom, are enclosed by a rectangle of unprimed canvas, distinct from the enclosing higher square of the earlier pictures. Green encloses the whole, except for the darker red crossing completely at the bottom. The exterior composition is direct and cool—in contrast to the glow of the interior oranges.

"It is called *Tangerine,*" Frankenthaler says, "because of the color — which is tangerine." And critics have avoided suggesting the picture, having no rounded shapes, is in any way a "still life" composition. However, other "readings in" have been suggested by careless interpretation of the picture's literature. For example, in his 1969 study of this work and the others in the "series," E. C. Goossen observed that within their format of enclosed irregular shapes and enclosing regular ones, the irregular shapes become more dominant overall, as in *Tangerine.* This path of increased compositional dominance he described thus: "In the progress from *Interior Landscape* to *Tangerine* . . . one feels he is witnessing the genie escaping from the bottle."[1] By 1982 this metaphor describing a stylistic *path* had been transformed, and we read of

"*Tangerine,* where the horizontal bands of color expand and flow upward like a 'genie escaping from the bottle.'"[2] Thus, for this critic, abstract forms mistakenly assume a descriptive quality.

Notes:
1. E. C. Goossen, *Helen Frankenthaler* (New York: Whitney Museum of American Art, 1969), 13.
2. Charlotte S. Rubinstein, *American Women Artists* (Boston: Avon Publishers, 1982), 330.

Provenance:
(André Emmerich Gallery, New York)

Exhibition History:
New York: Whitney Museum of American Art (cat. no. 35), 1965–66
New York: Whitney Museum of American Art (traveling exhibition, cat. no. 33, comm. p. 13, ill. p. 46), 1969
Houston: The Museum of Fine Arts (cat. no. 15, colorpl. 4), 1974
Bordeaux, France: Centre d'Arts Plastiques Contemporains de Bordeaux (cat. color ill. p. 27), 1981

Selected Critical References:
Campbell, *Artnews* (May 1965), ill. p. 10
Denvier, *Art International* (September 1969), ill. p. 66
Rose, 1972, colorpl. 143
Carmean, *The Art Gallery* (January 1974), color ill. p. 58
———, *Art International* (April–May 1978), comm. p. 30, ill. p. 32
Deschamps, 1981, colorpl. XXIV
Huth, *Connaissance des Arts* (October 1981), color ill. p. 83
Rubinstein, 1982, comm. p. 330, ill. p. 331
Berman, *Architectural Digest* (September 1983), color ill. p. 159
Hall, *House & Garden* (December 1983), color ill. p. 29
Elderfield, 1989, comm. pp. 172, 180; color ill. p. 182

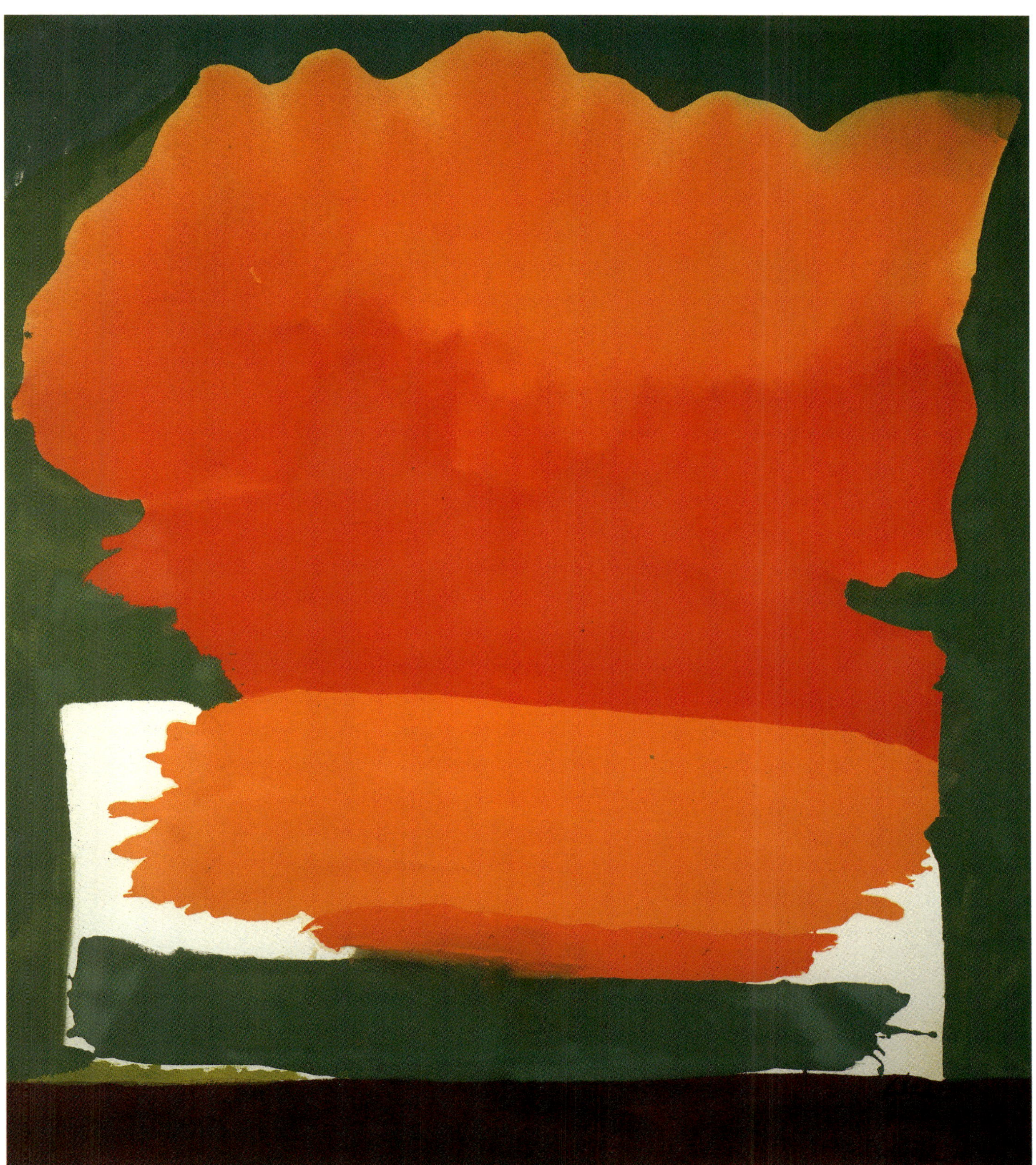

17. *Mauve District.* 1966
Acrylic on canvas
8'7" x 7'11" (261.6 x 241.3 cm.)
Inscribed, l.l.: Frankenthaler
Collection, The Museum of Modern Art, New York.
   Mrs. Donald B. Straus Fund, 1967

By 1967, only two years away from the symmetrical, "square" paintings of the mid-1960s (cat. nos. 13, 14, 15, 16), Frankenthaler had embarked on a radically different course, one fully exemplified in the painting *Mauve District.*

Comprised of only four colors — mauve, yellow, green, and black — *Mauve District* has been related to a contemporaneous group of paintings by the artist known as "color space" pictures.[1] *Mauve District* differs from these others — which use disparate shapes of colors — in the dominance of the huge field of mauve, a powerful visual anchor that relates the painting, indirectly, to the mid-1960s compositions.

About the mauve the artist notes: "The left-hand-border part of it was luck. My main concerns were edges — toward framing a *light.* It's very abstract — it's about color. In painting the other areas, I was concerned with colors that touched and joined — yellow and mauve, and colors held apart." Between the mauve and the other colors passes an open area of unpainted canvas, predicting the channels, or "cables/crevices," of the early 1970s pictures, while the solid mauve is a filling-in of a squarish shape, and the "hanging downward" character of this mauve field looks toward the "banner" paintings of the next years.

Compositionally, *Mauve District* is a very restrained picture, something relatively new at this point in Frankenthaler's art. This quality — in combination with its subtle coloration — prompted an interesting critical reception to the painting. Scott Burton, writing in 1966, called it "semi-geometric,"[2] while Michael Benedikt, in the same year, referred to its "wayward compositional logic."[3] The following year Jane Livingston would describe *Mauve District*'s composition as having a "mottled quality,"[4] while Hilton Kramer would stress its "conservative force."[5] In 1969 E. C. Goossen would contrast within the work "the mauve district as real as a curtain and as ambivalent as the light at sunset" with "the precision of the edges of the forms," calling the latter evidence of a "calculating intelligence,"[6] an opinion echoed in Jerry Bowles's

observation that *Mauve District* showed "an obvious interest in resolving design in a linear, reasoned, and nonaccidental manner."[7]

Notes:
1. Michael Benedikt, "New York Letter," *Art International* 10 (December 1966): 64. This group includes, for example, *Four Color Space,* 1966.
2. S[cott] B[urton], "Helen Frankenthaler," *Artnews* 65 (November 1966): 12.
3. Benedikt, "Letter," 64.
4. Jane Livingston, "Los Angeles Reviews," *Artforum* 5 (May 1967): 62.
5. Hilton Kramer, "Sixties in Retrospect," *The New York Times,* 2 July 1967, sec. 2, p. D19.
6. E. C. Goossen, *Helen Frankenthaler* (New York: Whitney Museum of American Art, 1969), 16.
7. Jerry Bowles, "Helen Frankenthaler," *Arts Magazine* 43 (March 1969): 22.

Provenance:
(André Emmerich Gallery, New York)

Exhibition History:
New York: André Emmerich Gallery, 1966
Los Angeles: Nicholas Wilder Gallery, 1967
New York: Whitney Museum of American Art (traveling exhibition, cat. no. 36, comm. p. 14, ill. p. 49), 1969
Northampton, Massachusetts: Smith College Museum of Art (cat. no. 20, ill. n.p.), 1974
New York: *American Art from The Museum of Modern Art* (traveling exhibition organized by The Museum of Modern Art, 1979–80

Selected Critical References:
Burton, *Artnews* (November 1966), comm. p. 12
Benedikt, *Art International* (December 1966), comm. p. 64
Livingston, *Artforum* (May 1967), comm. and ill. p. 62
Kramer, *The New York Times,* 2 July 1967, ill. sec. 2, p. D19
Rubin, *The Museum of Modern Art Members Newsletter* (October 1968), ill. n.p.
Bowles, *Arts Magazine* (March 1969), comm. p. 22
Alloway, *Artnews* (March 1971), comm. p. 89
Rose, 1972, ill. pl. 164
Elderfield, 1989, comm. pp. 202, 203; color ill. p. 195

18. *The Human Edge.* 1967
Acrylic on canvas
10'4" x 7'9¼" (315 x 237 cm.)
Inscribed, verso, stretcher: "The Human Edge" Summer 1967
Everson Museum of Art, Syracuse, New York. Museum Purchase to Honor Max W. Sullivan, Director, on the Occasion of the Opening of the New Building, 1968

Looking at *The Human Edge,* Frankenthaler recalls that "the top color shapes were done first, the four panels." Initially, we might find this comment puzzling, seeing only three panels — gray, orange, and pink. But in fact the gray shape is divided into two, with a denser tone at the left. Other, more subtle color variations are also evident—the orange and the pink are denser at the top, with an even paler orange horizontal band crossing at the bottom of the larger orange shape. The grays and the orange align with the edges of the canvas, while the pink shape tilts at an angle, seeming to go behind the orange one.

Across the bottom of the picture runs a horizontal "stroke" of deep blue, again with subtle tonal variations, and a horizontal, near–black band, which turns upward and runs along the left exterior of the picture. The blue and black are tangent in the middle, with small areas of white canvas between them at the margins. "I was very conscious of those shapes," says the artist, "of how they were the same, and different."

Seeing the rectangular color panels hanging down from the top edge over the horizon of blue (painted before the black), one could associate the picture with flags in a sky over a dark ocean. Certainly critical reception to *The Human Edge* has supported such a reading. Ralph Pomeroy, in 1968, called it "a strange band of horizontals overhung with banners of grays, orange, and raspberry,"[1] while Scott Burton in the same year referred to the "vertical, suspended . . . 'flags' [that] flutter slightly."[2]

The black horizontal and its extension up the left side work against this association. "As I looked at the picture, I asked myself, is it finished?" recalls Frankenthaler. "Sometimes an action demands another action. In its earlier state the 'banners' were so linear, so precise, without reference. The [black] framing softens the rigid 'banner' concept. At first I thought, keep it rigid and hard edged, then, no, I want a human edge, not a hard edge like some of those others."

This latter reference is to the so-called "Hard-Edge" color painters, with whom Frankenthaler was often compared by critics. Thus the title *The Human Edge* is stated in contrast to "Hard-Edge" and refers both to the irregularity of the black shape on the left "edge" of the work as well as to the irregular profile of the black shape itself.

Notes:
1. Ralph Pomeroy, "The Fall of France," *Art and Artists* 3 (June 1968): 36.
2. S[cott] B[urton], "Helen Frankenthaler," *Artnews* 67 (May 1968): 13.

Provenance:
(André Emmerich Gallery, New York)

Exhibition History:
New York: André Emmerich Gallery, 1968
New York: Whitney Museum of American Art (traveling exhibition, cat. no. 41, color ill. p. 55, exhibited only at Whitney), 1969

Selected Critical References:
Willard, *New York Post Magazine,* 20 April 1968, comm. p. 14
Burton, *Artnews* (May 1968), comm. p. 13, ill. p. 14
Mellow, *Art International* (15 May 1968), comm. and ill. p. 68
Pomeroy, *Art and Artists* (June 1968), comm. p. 36
Time (28 March 1969), color ill. p. 67
Rose, *Artforum* (April 1969), comm. p. 33, ill. p. 30
————, 1972, comm. p. 100, ill. pl. 171
————, *Partisan Review* (1973), comm. p. 89
Wess, *Everson Museum of Art Bulletin* (January 1985), comm. and ill. n.p.
Elderfield, 1989, comm. pp. 202, 337; color ill. p. 138

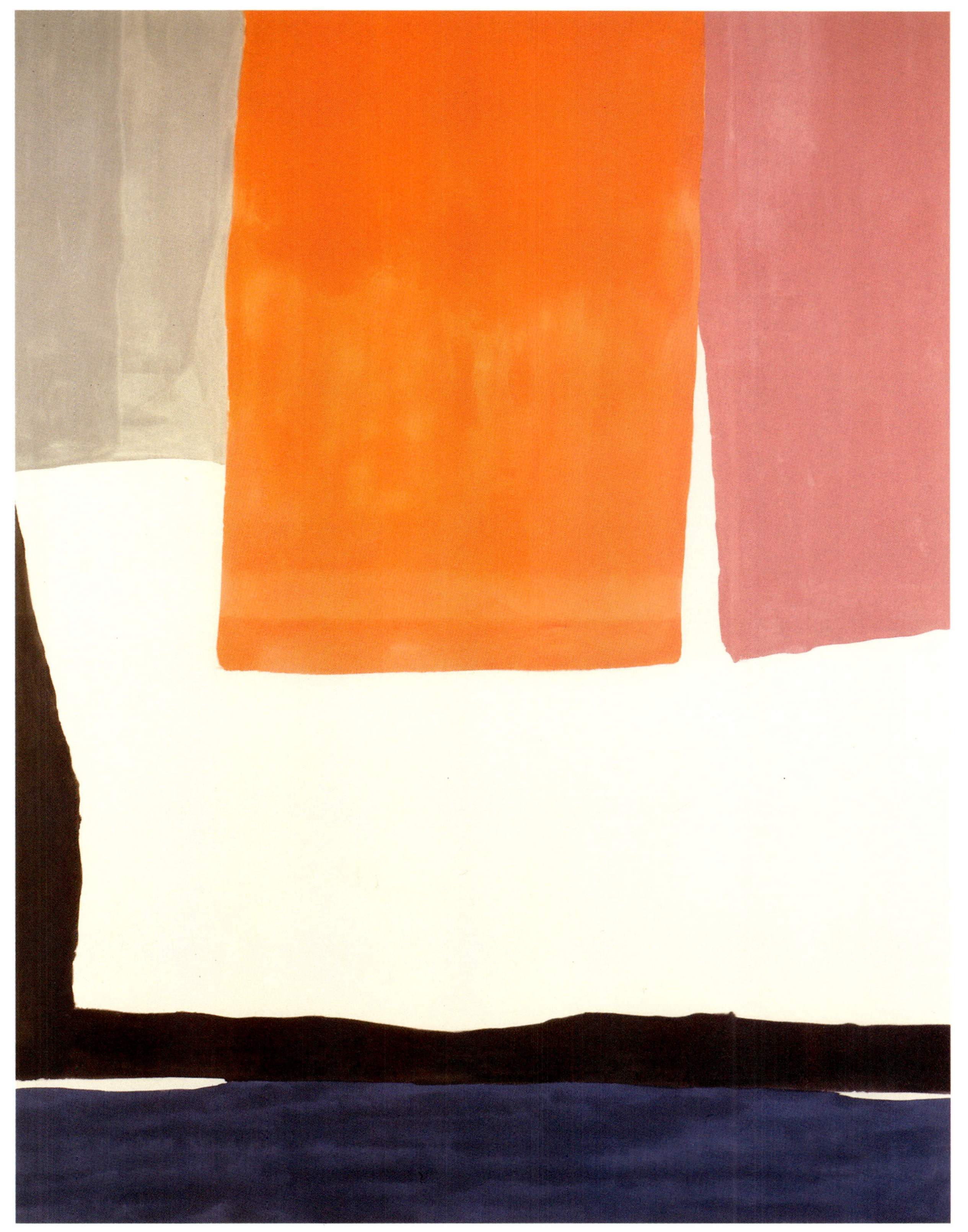

19. *Flood.* 1967
Acrylic on canvas
10'4" x 11'8" (315 x 355.6 cm.)
No inscription
Whitney Museum of American Art, New York. Purchase with
funds from the Friends of the Whitney Museum of American Art

Whenever the painting *Flood* has been exhibited, it has usually received almost rapturous reviews, as when critic James R. Mellow called it "a grand and spacious abstraction . . . [an] ambitious and successful Turneresque performance."[1] Other authors have used phrases such as "magnificent, grandiloquent beauty"[2] and "sumptuous gorgeousness,"[3] although another writer, who panned the picture, referred to it as the "aptly-named *Flood.*"[4]

Flood is one of the most atmospheric and dramatic works in Frankenthaler's oeuvre up to this point in her career. Here massive shapes of color flow horizontally across the surface, their pathway seemingly determined by the huge, dark-pink shape at the top. Going beyond the often-found references to "place" and nature in her work, *Flood* seems to present the forces of nature— and a sense of unleashed power that will subsequently return in another grand painting, entitled *Nature Abhors a Vacuum* (cat. no. 25).

Flood is also dramatically different from other, more precisely composed works of around the same time, such as *Mauve District* and *The Human Edge* (cat. nos. 17, 18). "It is a strange picture in that regard," says the artist. "It was the last painting of that summer. I started at the top with the pink and then added the layers and filled in the green. It was still wet, and I was dissatisfied with it, so I went to a kind of brushiness. The whole painting, for me, was constructed in an unusual way."

The last area painted was the blue horizontal across the bottom. "When I got to the bottom left," Frankenthaler recalls, "I left that gap of white as a space—as I left the air spaces in *Nature Abhors a Vacuum.*"

About the "aptly-named" title of *Flood* the artist notes: "It was painted in my 'tree-house' studio, a studio on the second floor, in stands of pine. It was not painted by the Bay. The studio floor was small, and I wanted to work on a canvas as large as possible. Once the canvas was laid down I had only about a foot of margin to stand on between the canvas edges and the wall. I recall that there was a lot of liquid paint on the floor. The studio was flooded with color."

Notes:
1. James R. Mellow, "New York Letter," *Art International* 13 (20 May 1969): 56.
2. Harris Rosenstein, "The Colorful Gesture," *Artnews* 68 (March 1969): 68.
3. Barbara Rose, "Painting Within the Tradition: The Career of Helen Frankenthaler," *Artforum* 7 (April 1969): 33.
4. John Canaday, "Art: The Whitney Museum Annual," *The New York Times,* 13 December 1967, p. 54.

Provenance:
(André Emmerich Gallery, New York)

Exhibition History:
New York: Whitney Museum of American Art (cat. no. 40), 1967–68
New York: Whitney Museum of American Art (traveling exhibition, cat. no. 40, color ill. p. 54), 1969
New York: Whitney Museum of American Art (checklist), 1974
New York: Whitney Museum of American Art Downtown at Federal Reserve Plaza (checklist no. 6, color ill. n.p.), 1988

Selected Critical References:
Canaday, *The New York Times,* 13 December 1967, comm. p. 54
Rosenstein, *Artnews* (March 1969), comm. p. 68, color ill. p. 30
Rosenberg, *The New Yorker* (29 March 1969), comm. p. 120
Rose, *Artforum* (April 1969), comm. p. 33, ill. p. 32
Mellow, *Art International* (20 May 1969), comm. p. 56
Lucie-Smith and White, 1970, color ill. p. 38
Alloway, *Artnews* (March 1971), comm. p. 89
Hunter and Jacobus, 1972, colorpl. 723
Rose, 1972, comm. pp. 76, 100; colorpl. 25
Guest, *Arts Magazine* (April 1975), comm. p. 59
Rubinstein, 1982, comm. p. 329
Sandler, 1988, ill. p. 27
Yarrow, *The New York Times,* 16 April 1988, ill. p. 12
Elderfield, 1989, comm. pp. 202–3, 228, 235, 296, 334; color ill. p. 199

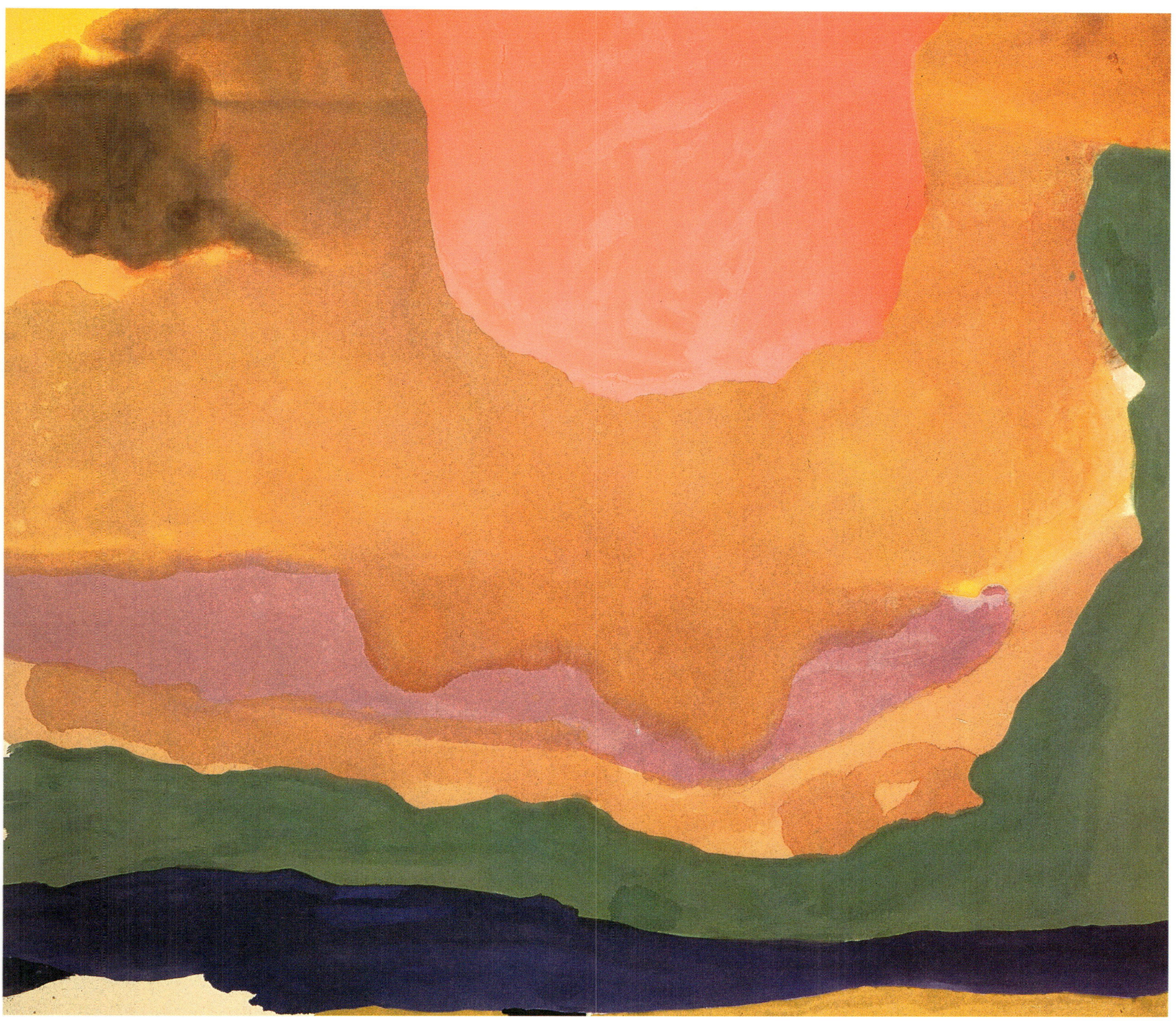

20. *Summer Banner.* 1968
Acrylic on canvas
6'¼" x 7'9⅝" (183.5 x 237.8 cm.)
Collection Mr. and Mrs. Fayez Sarofim

Summer Banner is one of the most reductive of Frankenthaler's paintings. Comprised only of a long blue horizontal, shapes of red and orange, and the white canvas, the picture is a study in restraint and nuance. Although the colors are each subtly modeled, their shapes and exterior edges carry the compositional impact. The red form, cropped at the left edge, seems cut from a larger shape, a feeling reinforced by the way in which the white canvas cuts into the red above the blue line. The right-side orange, by contrast, seems more solid, like a banner suspended from the upper edge. But even here this firmness is challenged by the bowing edge at the right, where the white canvas moves into the shape. The long blue horizontal flows across the bottom, nearly touching the orange at the right and implying a connection with the red but, again, outside of the confines of the canvas.

Interestingly, the restraint of *Summer Banner*'s composition was seen by critics as indicative of a new quality both in the artist and in her work. Jerry Bowles called it a "more carefully *planned* approach to design. It is the work of one who can no longer be classified an action painter,"[1] while Barbara Rose suggested that the picture "proves the victory of character over virtuosity, a battle any natural painter has to win over his own talent."[2] Other writers were less enthusiastic about Frankenthaler's work of the late 1960s, although some gave this picture their approval, as in Harris Rosenstein's comment that "her work in this area is not without a suggestion of a problem. When with a precise adjustment of color and placement of forms, as in *Summer Banner,* for example, it does come off, there is ample evidence that the effort is worthwhile."[3]

Curiously, despite the "hanging" color forms and the ocean-like blue horizontal, the critical literature does not refer to the picture as a seascape of sorts. The title itself is a later addition: when the picture was finished it was initially hung with the blue across the upper edge (see photograph, p. 4).

Notes:
1. Jerry Bowles, "Helen Frankenthaler at the Whitney," *Arts Magazine* 43 (March 1969): 22.
2. Barbara Rose, "Painting Within the Tradition: The Career of Helen Frankenthaler," *Artforum* 7 (April 1969): 32.
3. Harris Rosenstein, "The Colorful Gesture," *Artnews* 68 (March 1969): 68.

Provenance:
(André Emmerich Gallery, New York)

Exhibition History:
New York: Whitney Museum of American Art (traveling exhibition, cat. no. 45, color ill. p. 57), 1969
Houston: Congregation Beth Israel (cat. no. 26), 1982

Selected Critical References:
Bowles, *Arts Magazine* (March 1969), comm. p. 22
Rosenstein, *Artnews* (March 1969), comm. p. 68, color ill. p. 29
Rose, *Artforum* (April 1969), comm. p. 32
Battcock, *Art and Artists* (May 1969), ill. p. 54 [mistitled *Buddha's Court*]
Alloway, *Artnews* (November 1971), comm. p. 89
Rose, 1972, colorpl. 180
Carmean, *Art International* (April–May 1978), comm. p. 30
Fuchs, Kenneth, *Out of Dark: After Three Paintings by Helen Frankenthaler* [musical score]. New York: Juilliard Festival of Contemporary Music, 24 January 1985
Elderfield, 1989, comm. p. 202, color ill. p. 201

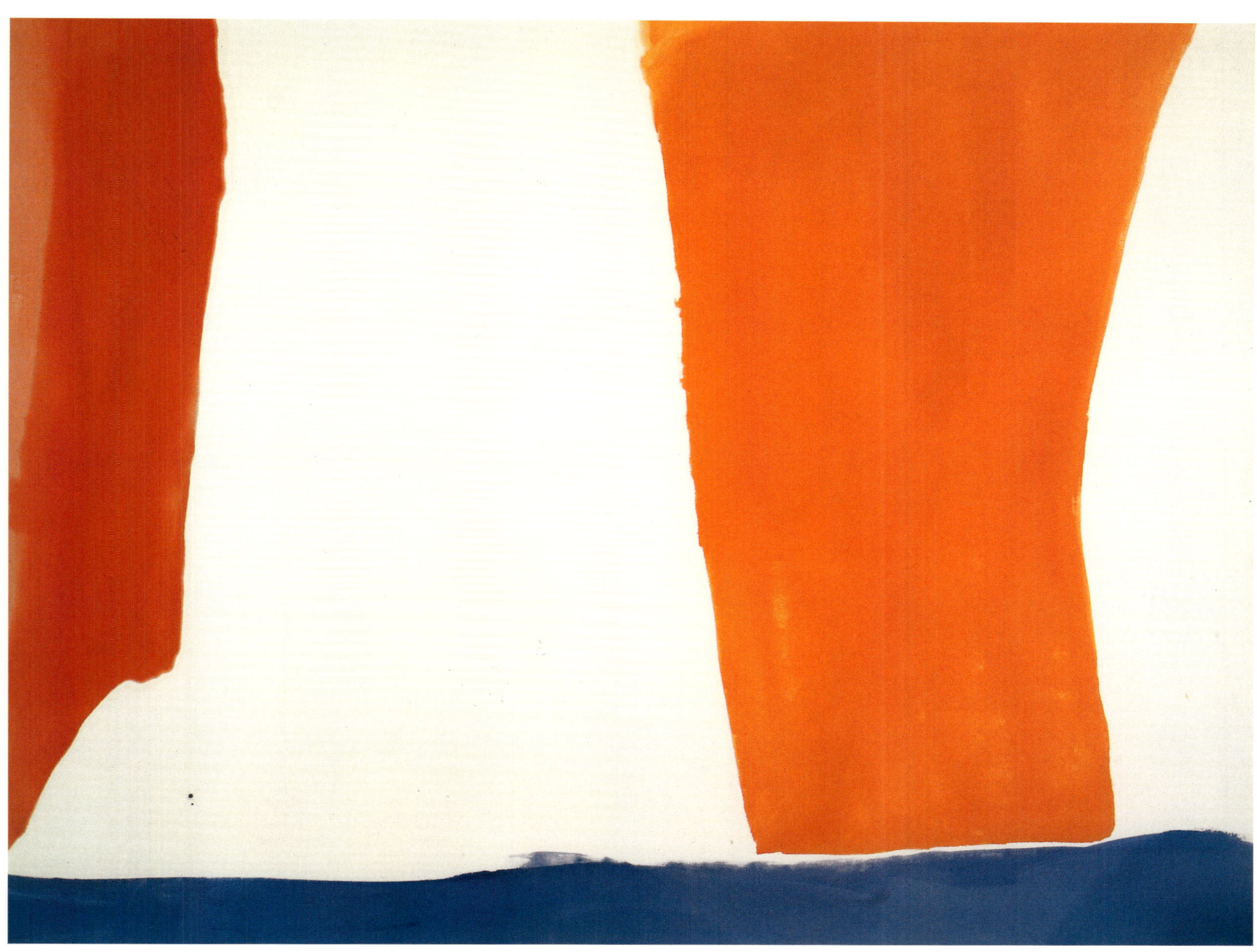

21. *Sesame.* 1970
Acrylic on canvas
8′10″ x 6′10½″ (269.2 x 209.6 cm.)
Inscribed, verso, stretcher: Sesame 1970 106″ x 82½″ Franken-
thaler 1970
Private Collection

"I was going to Morocco," says Frankenthaler of the lines in
Sesame, "and as an artist you think of the visits Matisse and Dela-
croix had made there. In art and decoration, I knew iconography
was forbidden by religion. Linear or arabesque motifs were used
to replace and rival imagery—on walls, reliefs, tiles, gates, railings
—an ordered mélange of patterns."

Sesame is a landmark picture in Frankenthaler's work, one
where the independent line reasserts itself in a manner rarely
seen since those that control so much of *Mountains and Sea*
(cat. no. 1). Indeed, in addition to acknowledging the Moroccan
influence, the artist notes that "in making *Sesame,* I went back
to *Mountains and Sea,* as I have from time to time in making
other works."

Sesame is, she states, "a closing in; it's almost an allover picture.
I put in the colors first. Once the painting was dry and placed
against the wall, I put in the lines with a felt-tip pen. I later went
over the lines in paint using a fine brush."

The picture went through a process of many additions and was
"worked on both on the floor and the wall," she notes. "Many
decisions were made while it was up on the wall." These proce-
dures also lent a certain Orientalizing quality, for as Frankenthaler
observes: "There is the aspect of the Oriental rug, which can rest
above, below, or head-on. Pictures of this period have a kind of
bird's-eye flying-carpet view—as if you were looking downward.
However, all paintings must be judged on the wall."

Sesame marked the start of new formal considerations that
would inform much of Frankenthaler's painting over the next few
years. She points to the four different compositional "placements"
of the painting: its overall flatness, the play of the left side versus
the right side, the interior of the white crossing passage—what
she refers to as a "cable or crevice"—and the drawn lines, about
whose space making she observes, "I was very conscious of
threading line through the 'cable/crevice.'"

The title *Sesame* carries a double reference: one is to the ocher
color of sesame seeds—not unlike the way in which *Tangerine*
refers to the orange of the fruit—while the other is to the magical
command first given by Ali Baba, "Open, sesame," used here, as
Frankenthaler states, "because the picture is open."

Exhibition History:
New York: André Emmerich Gallery, 1971
Toronto: David Mirvish Gallery, 1971
Houston: The Museum of Fine Arts (cat. no. 18, ill. p. 52), 1974
Washington, D.C.: Corcoran Gallery of Art (traveling exhibition,
   cat. no. 5, ill. n.p.), 1975

Selected Critical References:
Heywood, *The Montreal Star,* 20 February 1971, ill.
Raphael, *Vie Des Arts* (Autumn 1971), ill. p. 66
Alloway, *Artnews* (November 1971), comm. p. 89
Nemser, *Arts Magazine* (November 1971), comm. p. 51, ill. p. 53
Metzger, *The Herald,* 28 June 1975, comm.
Holmes, *Houston Chronicle,* 21 October 1975, comm. p. 12
Goodman, 1980, comm. p. 6
Elderfield, 1989, comm. pp. 214, 218, 226; color ill. p. 215

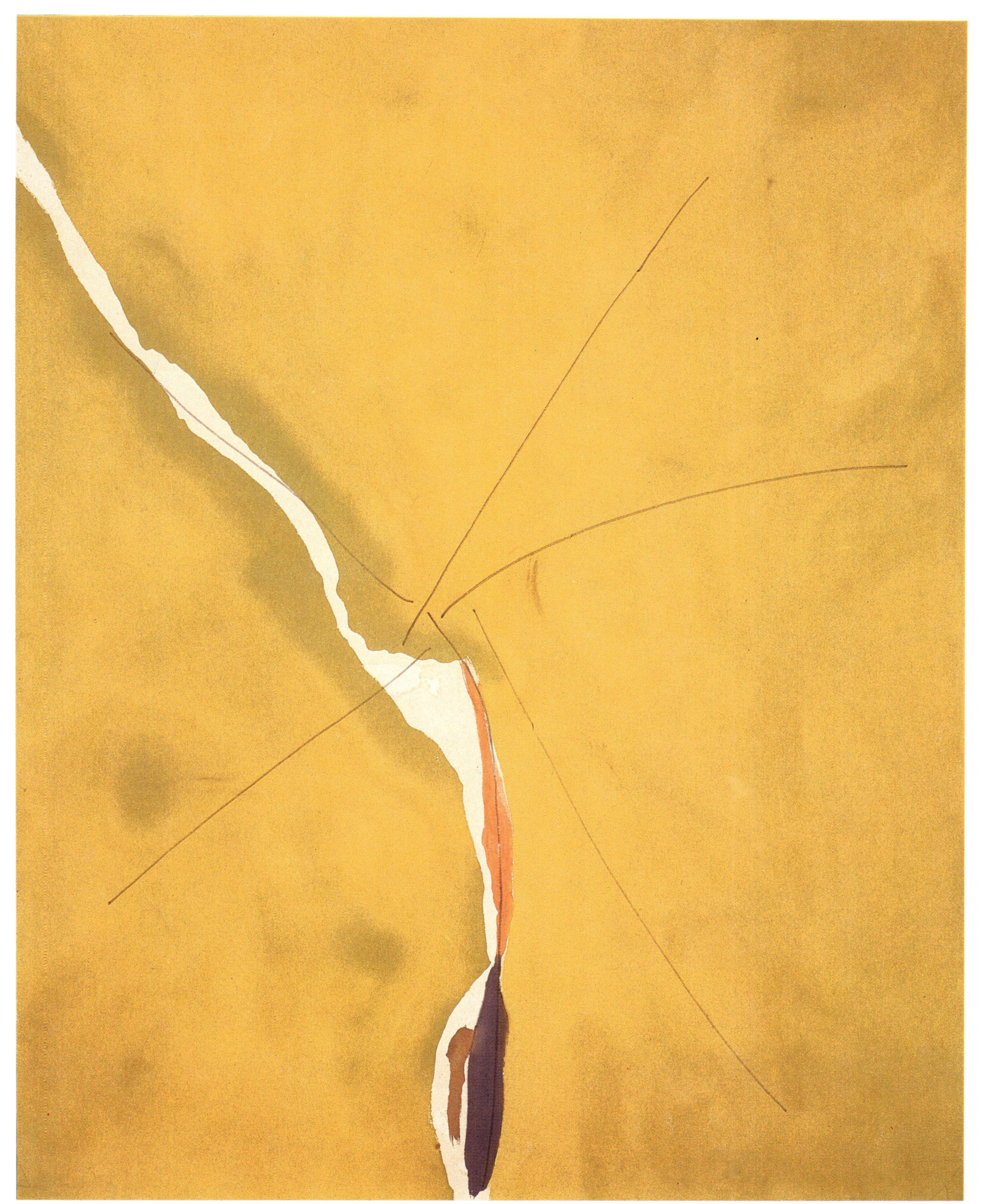

22. *Chairman of the Board.* 1971
Acrylic on canvas
6'10" x 16'2" (208.3 x 492.8 cm.)
Nina and Gordon Bunshaft Collection

In her long (and prestigious) career, only rarely has Frankenthaler experienced a bad reception for a group of new works or had one picture in particular maligned. One of the exceptions to this rule is *Chairman of the Board*, in the present exhibition. Seen first at the André Emmerich Gallery in New York in 1971, this large canvas was the focus of several negative reviews. Carter Ratcliff, for example, inferred from its "too many bravura, and at the same time, hesitant, black lines scrawled about . . . a reluctance to commit herself,"[1] while, going in the opposite direction, Kermit S. Champa declared that "the painting finally feels too constricted. Its oppositions seem overwrought and presented with too much definitiveness."[2] As to its found formal qualities, Hilton Kramer, in reviewing the exhibition as a whole, said of Frankenthaler's new pictorial vocabulary, "mostly it does not work,"[3] and a few years later, Barbara Guest would fuse *Chairman of the Board*'s color and large scale into a description of "solid gold Cadillacs."[4]

This reception stands in sharp counterpoint to the artist's exuberance and confidence in making *Chairman of the Board*. She remembers: "It was about a 'grand sweep.' I had the basic idea in my head — I knew how the lines would dance in. I felt sure of myself." The picture follows a semisymmetrical layout, with a white "crevice/cable" separating vast areas of orange, this negative shape descending from the upper left to the lower center, then rising to the upper right. In the center of the crevice is a cluster of small color shapes, with a separate pink shape at the upper right, also within the white passage. Running across the surface, from the center, are nine lines of greatly varying length.

"The composition opens up and out," the artist comments, "and I emphasized the clean cut of the 'crevice/cable.' The edges of the orange were very carefully done. The lines were made all at once, in one 'fell swoop,' lines that echo shapes and 'bridge the gap' literally—from the outside to the inside of the crevice. They are also necessary because they create another kind of space—the same as in *Sesame*."

Aside from a special commission painting done for Expo '67 in Montreal,[5] *Chairman of the Board* was the largest painting in Frankenthaler's oeuvre to that date, and this was a factor in establishing its title. She recalls: "Big sweep; big scale."

Notes:
1. Carter Ratcliff, "New York," *Art International* 16 (January 1972): 68.
2. Kermit S. Champa, "New Work of Helen Frankenthaler," *Artforum* 10 (January 1972): 59.
3. Hilton Kramer, "Frankenthaler Paintings Displayed at 2 Galleries," *The New York Times*, 10 November 1971, p. 27.
4. Barbara Guest, "Helen Frankenthaler: The Moment and the Distance," *Arts Magazine* 49 (April 1975): 59.
5. *Guiding Red*, 1967, measured 30 by 16 feet. The painting is no longer extant.

Provenance:
(André Emmerich Gallery, New York)

Exhibition History:
New York: André Emmerich Gallery (color ill. n.p.), 1971
Toronto: David Mirvish Gallery, 1971

Selected Critical References:
Wilson, *Toronto Daily Star*, 8 May 1971, ill.
Champa, *Artforum* (January 1972), comm. p. 59, ill. p. 56
Time (20 March 1972), color ill. p. 74
Masheck, *Artforum* (March 1973), comm. p. 87
Guest, *Arts Magazine* (April 1975), comm. p. 59
Elderfield, 1989, comm. pp. 226, 228, 244; color ill. p. 222

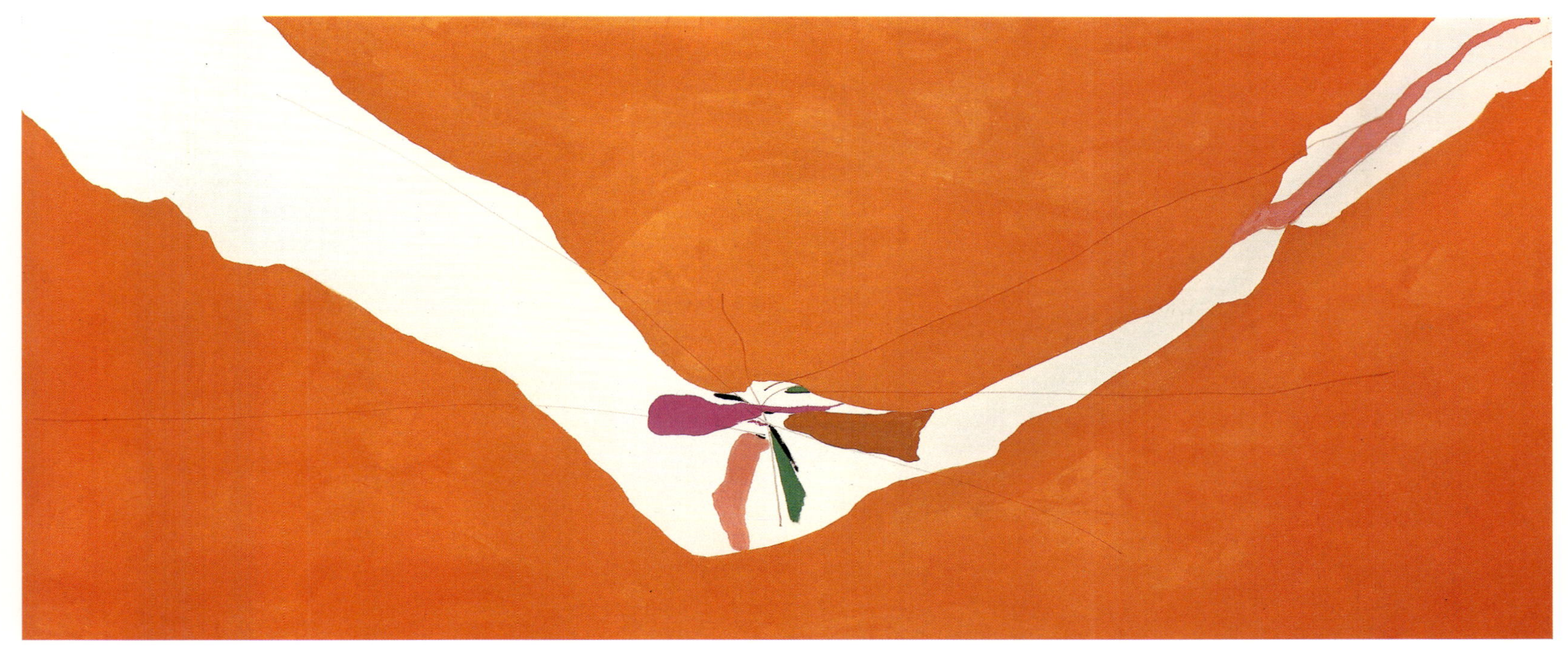

23. *Burnt Norton.* 1972
Acrylic on canvas
5'9½" x 7'11½" (176.5 x 242.6 cm.)
Inscribed, recto, l.r.: Frankenthaler
    verso, stretcher: Dec. 1972 69½" x 95½" "Burnt Norton"
Private Collection

In many ways *Burnt Norton* exemplifies "classic" aspects of Frankenthaler's work: rolling passages of color, a symmetrical/asymmetrical layout, and the use of a lower crossing horizontal passage. But the picture is also quite different from much of her art, in its coloration, layering, detailing, and mood. More somber than earlier paintings, it contrasts a deep rose with a rich, olive-brown color, the latter not easily arrived at. "Under that brown lies all kinds of activity," she notes, "whole passages; an obliterated, billowing blanket." The subtlety of these zones is relieved by the energy of the lower pale-blue line. "I worked on that line for weeks," she recalls. "I finally relieved it with the light passages under and to the left of the line."

The predominantly horizontal orientation of *Burnt Norton*'s composition has led critics to associate it with landscapes. However, aside from some authors' brief phrases, such as "mysterious" or "romantic," only Hilton Kramer described the import of the painting, writing, "She has reached for something harder—an imagery that is richer in implication than the literal surface that gives it visual life."[1]

"*Burnt Norton* is a deep, serious, cathartic picture," says the artist. "I get a sense of peace and order from it—there is something contemplative about it that reminds me of *Buddha's Court* [cat. no. 14]."

About the title and its reference to the T. S. Eliot poem of the same name she comments: "I was thinking about Eliot, making order out of chaos, of light and dark. Like Eliot's poem, the painting's simplicity is arrived at after a great deal of complexity. My work is never playful. This seemed at the time an especially serious and weighty picture to solve."

Note:
1. Hilton Kramer, "Helen Frankenthaler," *The New York Times*, 1 December 1973, p. 27.

Exhibition History:
New York: André Emmerich Gallery, 1973
Washington, D.C.: Corcoran Gallery of Art (traveling exhibition, cat. no. 14, ill. n.p.), 1975

Selected Critical References:
Kramer, *The New York Times*, 1 December 1973, comm. p. 27
Kim, *Arts Magazine* (November 1974), comm. p. 75, color ill. p. 77
Guest, *Arts Magazine* (April 1975), comm. p. 59
Hudson, *Art International* (15 June 1975), comm. p. 97
Holmes, *Houston Chronicle*, 21 October 1975, comm. and ill. sec. 1, p. 12
Elderfield, 1989, comm. p. 235, color ill. p. 231

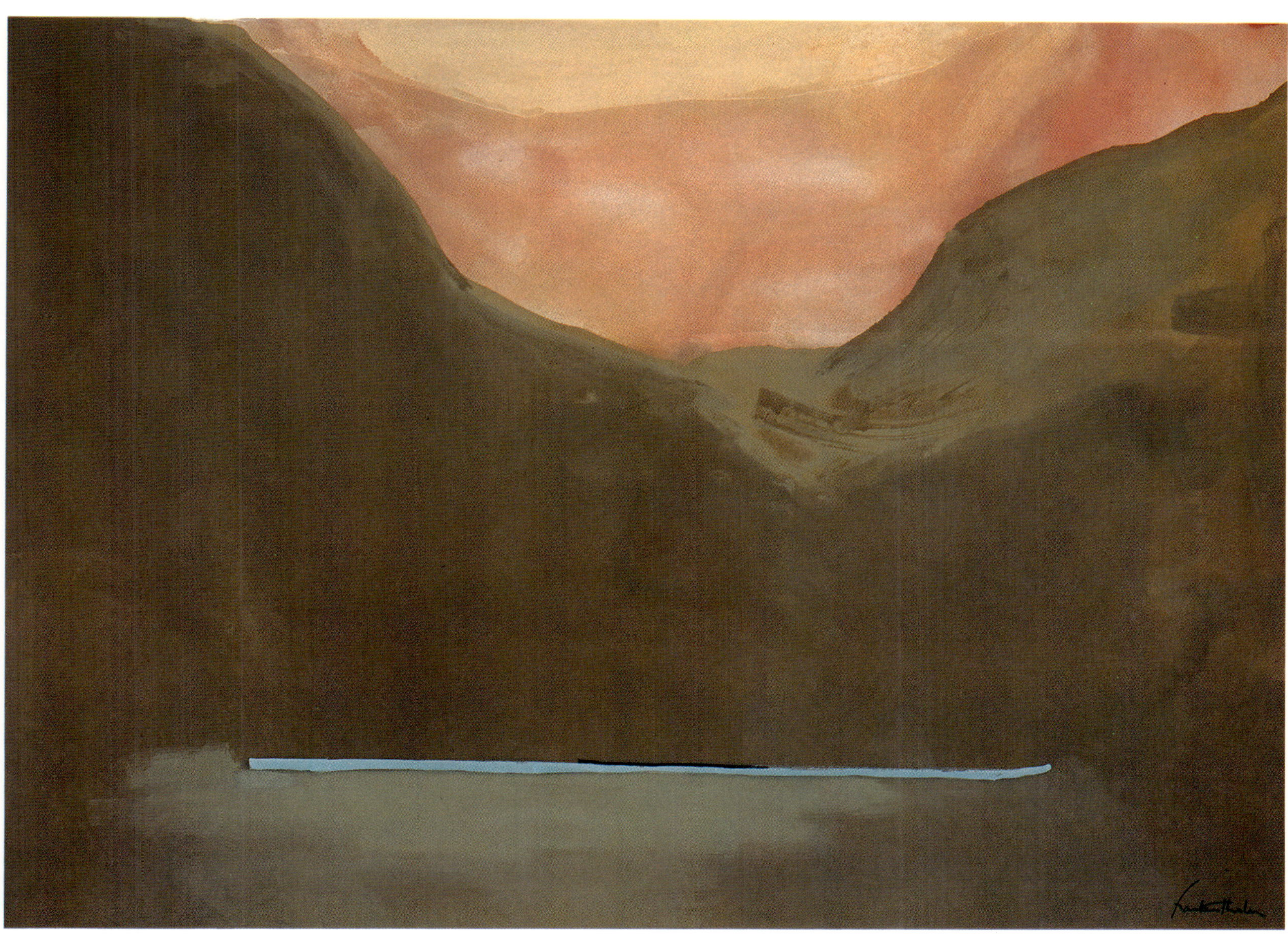

24. *Hint from Bassano.* 1973
Acrylic on canvas
7'1" x 18'11¼" (215.9 x 577.2 cm.)
Inscribed, l.r.: Frankenthaler 73
Collection Mr. and Mrs. David Mirvish, Toronto, Ontario

"I was in Princeton and visited Norton Simon's collection, on view at the time," Frankenthaler recalls. "It included a beautiful painting by Bassano. What made it so good? I liked it so much that I wanted to copy it." The picture she describes is *Flight Into Egypt* by Jacopo da Ponte, called Il Bassano, a relatively large (47 by 78 inches) canvas painted around 1540. It was included in the exhibition *Selections from the Norton Simon, Inc. Museum of Art,* shown at The Art Museum, Princeton University, in 1972.

Frankenthaler continues: "In my studio I mixed the colors, taking clues from Bassano. First of all, I wanted to get the stroke and the color of this master." *Hint from Bassano* is one of several works in Frankenthaler's career that are based on pictures by Old Master painters. In some, such as *Las Mayas* (cat. no. 6), the artist uses as point of departure the compositional structure of the earlier work, while others hew more closely to the "copied" image. *Hint from Bassano* is much more abstracted—a "hint"—and draws from the color and general touch of the sixteenth-century work. Frankenthaler cites having made other works that use similar color sources, among them several pictures by Titian and Rembrandt.

One can see what attracted Frankenthaler to *Flight Into Egypt:* in the right portion of the picture are the leading angel and Joseph,

covered in swirling lengths of multihued cloth — rich greens, blues, pinks, and orange that reappear in the present work. Indeed, the flowing movement of the garb and the darker shadows in the Bassano, when isolated, recall similar passages of color, shape, and movement in her contemporaneous work such as *Nature Abhors a Vacuum* (cat. no. 25). Frankenthaler captures these aspects abstractly in her variation, especially by using thin washes of color that allow the white of the canvas to parallel the Venetian touch of Bassano, whose "colors are vibrant and shot through with light."[1]

This sense of light and color, placed in a huge horizontal format, gives the painting what Frankenthaler calls "cinerama" quality: "I was involved at that time with a commission, and I had been asked to make scaled-down maquettes; instead, I decided to make several large canvases of which this is one."

Note:
1. David W. Steadman, *Selections from the Norton Simon, Inc. Museum of Art* (Princeton, New Jersey: The Art Museum, Princeton University, 1972), 18.

Provenance:
(David Mirvish Gallery, Toronto)

Exhibition History:
Toronto: David Mirvish Gallery, 1973
Washington, D.C.: Corcoran Gallery of Art (traveling exhibition, cat. no. 20, ill. n.p.), 1975
Fort Worth: The Fort Worth Art Museum (cat. no. 6, color ill. p. 29), 1985

Selected Critical References:
Russell, *The New York Times,* 2 May 1975, comm. p. 20
Hudson, *Art International* (15 June 1975), comm. p. 97
Holmes, *Houston Chronicle,* 21 October 1975, comm. sec. 1, p. 12
Elderfield, 1989, comm. p. 235, color ill. p. 237

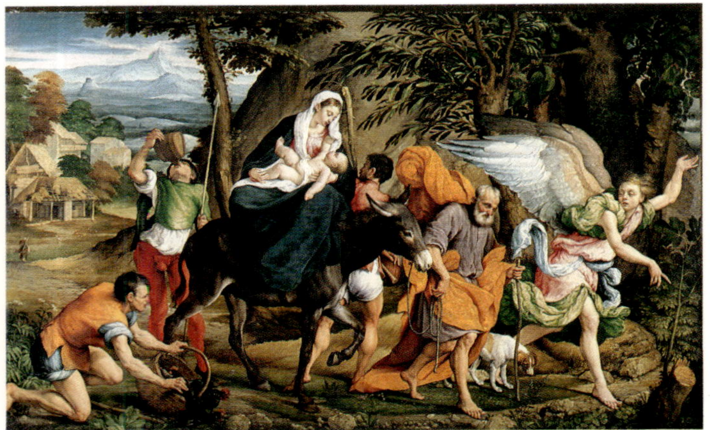

Fig. 4   Jacopo da Ponte, called Il Bassano
Flight into Egypt. c. 1540
Oil on canvas
47 x 78" (119 x 198 cm.)
Norton Simon Art Foundation

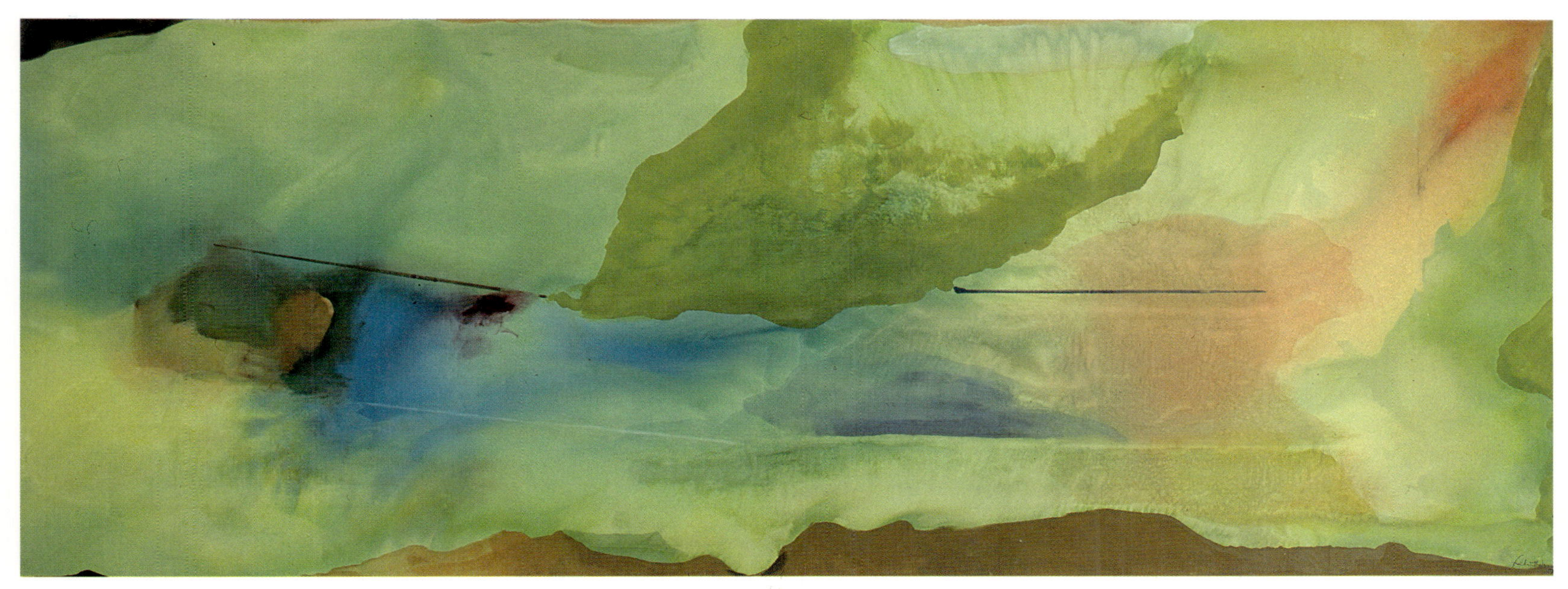

25. *Nature Abhors a Vacuum.* 1973
Acrylic on canvas
8'7½" x 9'4½" (262.9 x 285.8 cm.)
Inscribed, l.r.: Frankenthaler '73
Private Collection, courtesy of André Emmerich Gallery,
    New York

"But the real achievement of the show," John Russell wrote of a 1975 Frankenthaler exhibition, "lies in paintings of the scale of epic—among them . . . *Nature Abhors a Vacuum.*"[1] Other critics have responded with similar accolades, calling the picture "aggressive and powerful,"[2] "cosmic,"[3] "most beautifully realized,"[4] and "baroque."[5]

Nature Abhors a Vacuum is a grand painting, both in its physical size—it is over nine feet square – and in the visual power of its composition. Organized around huge sweeps of color moving horizontally across the surface, this picture calls to mind the earlier *Flood* (cat. no. 19), the strongest precedent in her oeuvre for a painting of this import.

Like *Flood,* the color passages in *Nature Abhors a Vacuum* are modeled, although in the later picture the ranges between opaque and near transparent are far more pronounced. Color shapes in *Nature Abhors a Vacuum* are also more individualized, with much more eccentric profiles. Where the two pictures most differ, formally, is in their use of white. In *Flood,* the entire surface is flooded with color, save for the tiny white "gap" at the lower left corner. By contrast, white areas—negative shapes of canvas, which Frankenthaler calls "air spaces"—are found throughout *Nature Abhors a Vacuum.* Furthermore, they are of three quite different characters.

The role of the so-called "negative spaces" of white canvas has played a major role in Frankenthaler's art throughout her career, seen most emphatically as the "swans" in *Swan Lake I* (cat. no. 8). A similar kind of opening can be found in *Nature Abhors a Vacuum,* at the upper left profile of the green, or in the small opening in the topmost yellow. A more authoritative use of negative space appeared in pictures of 1970–72, in the "cable/crevice" cutting through the color areas of works like *Sesame* and *Chairman of the Board* (cat. nos. 21, 22). A vestige of the crevice can also be found in *Nature Abhors a Vacuum* in the white passage from the left margin, through the center, upward to the right.

A third, "new" kind of negative space makes its appearance in

this work: this is found in the smaller, horizontal, nearly straight-edged passages that appear at the top, lower center, and bottom of the work. These introduce negative space as drawing—as line rather than shape—and will inform much of Frankenthaler's work during the next years. Made by placing strips of wood or tape on the canvas so as to block the flow of paint into that area, the negative lines are the first things established in the picture.

The title *Nature Abhors a Vacuum* is not the artist's but was suggested by a friend after seeing the picture. "It was appropriate," Frankenthaler notes, "because all spaces are color filled, something that Nature herself is capable of doing."

Notes:
1. John Russell, "Art: Helen Frankenthaler at Corcoran," *The New York Times,* 2 May 1975, p. 20.
2. Judith Von Baron, "Helen Frankenthaler," *Arts Magazine* 48 (December 1973): 72.
3. Diana Loercher, "Has Modern Art Run Out of Ways to Be Abstract?" *The Christian Science Monitor,* 6 December 1973, p. 30.
4. Barbara Guest, "Helen Frankenthaler: The Moment and the Distance," *Arts Magazine* 49 (April 1975): 59.
5. Ann Holmes, "Frankenthaler's Canvases Soar with Buoyancy," *Houston Chronicle,* 21 October 1975, sec. 1, p. 12.

Provenance:
(André Emmerich Gallery, New York)

Exhibition History:
New York: André Emmerich Gallery (cat. color cover), 1973
New York: National Institute of Arts and Letters, 1974
Northampton, Massachusetts: Smith College Museum of Art (cat. no. 22), 1974
Richmond: Virginia Museum of Fine Arts (cat. color ill. p. 33), 1974
Washington, D.C.: Corcoran Gallery of Art (traveling exhibition, cat. no. 23, color ill. n.p.), 1975
Fort Lauderdale: Museum of Art (comm. p. 65, colorpl. 30), 1986

Selected Critical References:
Von Baron, *Arts Magazine* (December 1973), comm. p. 72
Loercher, *The Christian Science Monitor,* 6 December 1973, comm. p. 30

(Continued on page 94)

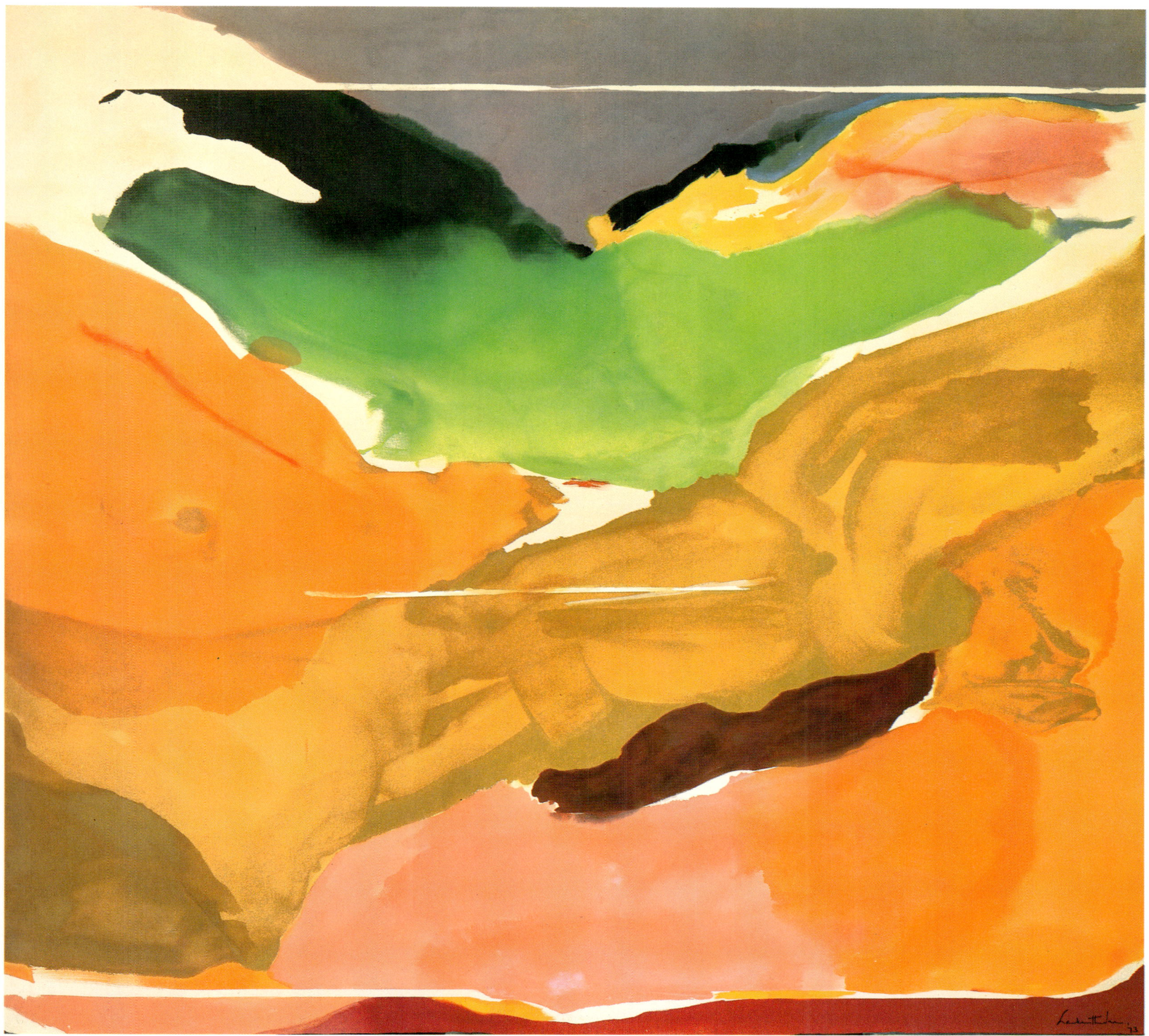

26. *Ocean Drive West #1.* 1974
Acrylic on canvas
7'10" x 12' (238.8 x 365.8 cm.)
Inscribed, recto, 1.1.: Frankenthaler '74
   verso, stretcher: 94" x 144" July 1974 "Ocean Drive West"
   (#1)
Private Collection

With its vast surface of subtly modeled blue, *Ocean Drive West #1*
is one of Frankenthaler's most serene pictures, its calm tempered
by light- and dark-blue shapes, interrupted only by the small areas
of other colors, areas John Russell called "tart and unpredictable
color accents [used] to jolt us clear of daydream."[1]

Its making was one of serenity, begun with lines of tape on the
canvas surface, a step akin to that used to initiate *Nature Abhors a
Vacuum.* Frankenthaler recounts: "I tinted the entire canvas with a
pale-blue wash, except for the two areas that I had taped, one at
the lower right, the other at bottom left. Then I laid down assorted
horizontal tapes on top of the wet tint. Once the canvas had dried,
I mixed a darker blue. I applied the second coat of darker blue
carefully, adjusting the drawing of every horizontal mark on the
surface. Before the darker blue field was dry, I said to myself, leave
that open, stick with the raw canvas. I looked at the painting for a
long time, then added the orange, the darker blue, and the black.
The whole surface moves around in space and has a magic mood."

Given its composition, its blue coloration, and its title, one
would associate *Ocean Drive West #1* with earlier, so-called "seaside pictures," including *Mountains and Sea, Seascape with Dunes,*
and *The Bay* (cat. nos. 1, 11, 12). Frankenthaler comments on the
elongated shapes: "Unrelated to *land* islands, they are islands
within this vast blue surface, made of horizontal *lines.*"

Ocean Drive West #1 was painted in summertime in a studio on
the Shippan Point coastline of Connecticut. "It was done there,"
she observes, "but one is always *someplace.* On Ocean Drive West
you are always staring at horizon lines—horizon lines that vary.
There are hazed-out parts of Long Island across the Sound, parts
of it can be visible, parts not." But what she gleans from this situ-
ation are abstraction and metaphor: "I wasn't looking at nature or
seascape but at the drawing within nature—just as the sun or
moon might be about circles or light and dark."

Note:
1. John Russell, "Art: Helen Frankenthaler at Corcoran," *The New
York Times,* 2 May 1975, p. 20.

Exhibition History:
Washington, D.C.: Corcoran Gallery of Art (traveling exhibition,
   cat. no. 27, color ill. n.p.), 1975

Selected Critical References:
Russell, *The New York Times,* 2 May 1975, p. 20
Holmes, *Houston Chronicle,* 21 October 1975, comm. sec. 1, p. 12
Elderfield, 1989, comm. pp. 254, 402; color ill. p. 262

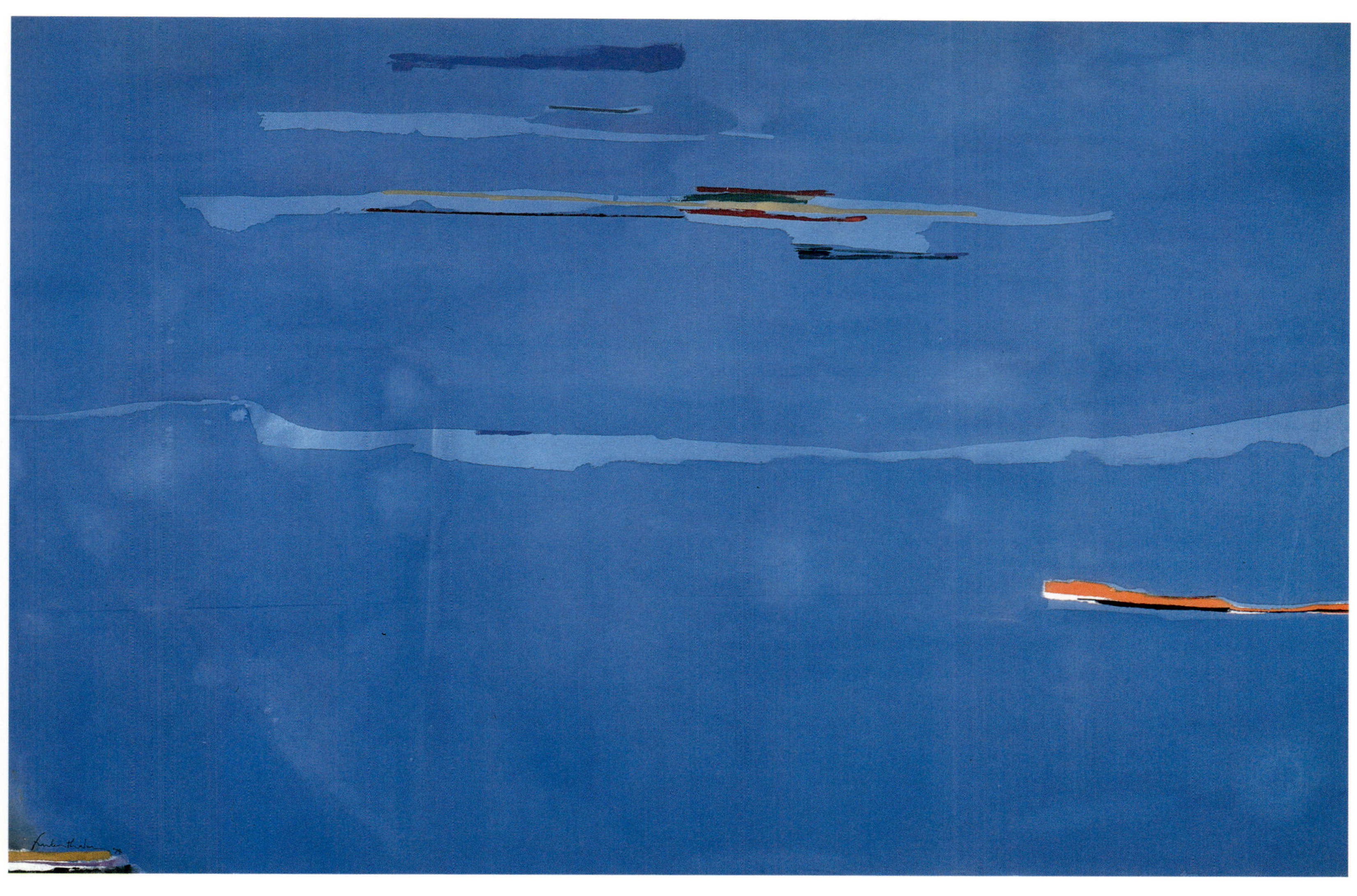

27. *Lush Spring.* 1975
Acrylic on canvas
7'9" x 9'10" (236.2 x 299.7 cm.)
Inscribed, verso: Frankenthaler
Phoenix Art Museum, Arizona. Museum Purchase with
   Matching Funds Provided by COMPAS and the National
   Endowment for the Arts

In a brief but insightful review of her 1975 exhibition at André
Emmerich Gallery, Hilton Kramer wrote: "The paintings of Helen
Frankenthaler occupy a distinctive place in the recent history of
American abstract painting. . . . We feel ourselves in the presence
of imaginary landscapes — landscapes distilled into a chromatic
essence." Turning to specific works in the show, Kramer continued, "What is best here is *Lush Spring,* an orchestration of vibrant,
watery greens in which the shifting lights and shadows of nature
are evoked without even being precisely described."[1] Harry Wood,
writing the next year, would second Kramer's account, saying
Lush Spring "is in no sense a seascape or even a landscape. It is
more universal than that, implying the surge of spring life."[2]

The artist agrees with this connection, remarking that "*Lush
Spring* is a verdant picture—filled with greens that might cause a
seasonal or climatic association." There is also the continuing
sense of place. She notes, "It was painted in the countryside at my
studio on Long Island Sound."

The greens of *Lush Spring* also mark another change in Frankenthaler's art, one hinted at in *Ocean Drive West #1* (cat. no. 26). In
that slightly earlier work, as in others, the artist had begun by
placing sticks and tape onto the raw canvas surface to create a
negative space; however, in *Ocean Drive West #1,* she chose to use
a rich blue for the positive surface rather than the many different
colors she had used in *Nature Abhors a Vacuum* (cat. no. 25), for
example. *Lush Spring* takes this direction further; here the entire
canvas initially was painted a uniform solid green, a color satura-
tion the artist calls a "tint." "*Lush Spring* was among the first works
where the surface was tinted," she recalls. "With a tinted surface
you have a ready-made plane that differs from raw canvas. This
picture is a play on greens; every green here does not contain the
green of another; they are each composed of different pigments."

With its richer yet subdued palette, its straightforward composition, and its sense of weight resting on the lower, dark-green

horizontal, *Lush Spring* is compositionally set apart from other
contemporary works by the artist. Sensing this, Ingeborg Hoesterey wrote in 1976 of *Lush Spring,* "It is astonishing how much
what is for my eyes the most important painting in the exhibition
reminds one of *Mountains and Sea.*"[3]

Notes:
1. Hilton Kramer, "Art: Lyric Vein in Frankenthaler Paintings," *The
New York Times,* 15 November 1975, p. 21.
2. Harry Wood, "Frankenthaler Has an Unobtrusive Presence,"
Phoenix Lecture, 11 March 1976, p. 38.
3. Ingeborg Hoesterey, "New York," *Art International* 20 (February–March 1976): 63.

Provenance:
(André Emmerich Gallery, New York)

Exhibition History:
New York: André Emmerich Gallery (cat. color ill. n.p.), 1975

Selected Critical References:
Kramer, *The New York Times,* 15 November 1975, comm. p. 21
Lorber, *Arts Magazine* (February 1976), comm. p. 12
Hoesterey, *Art International* (February–March 1976), ill. p. 63
Wood, *Phoenix Lecture,* 11 March 1976, comm. and ill. p. 38
The Art Gallery (August–September 1976), color ill. p. 44
Elderfield, 1989, comm. p. 255, color ill. p. 271

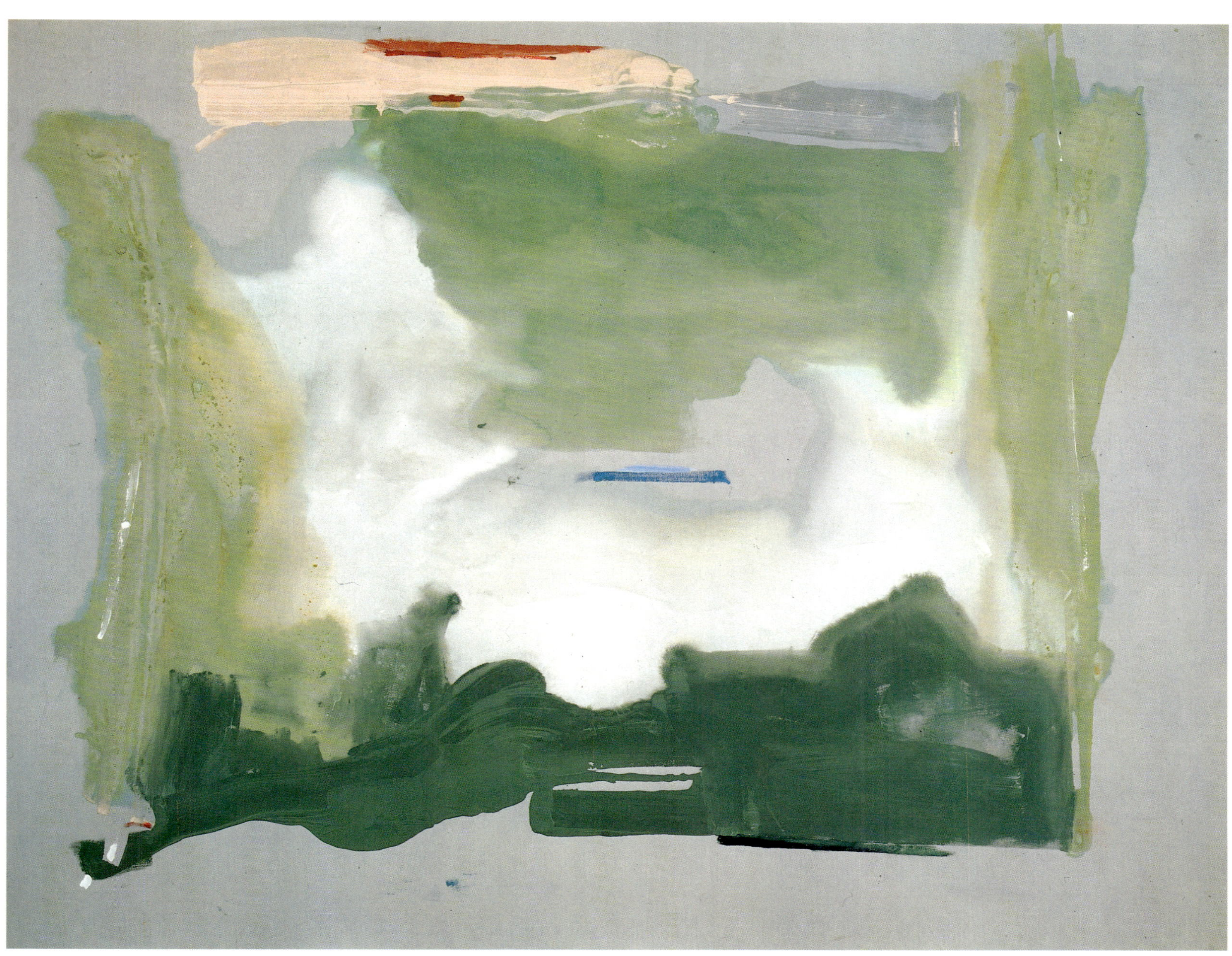

28. *Tulip Tint.* 1975
Acrylic on canvas
7'4" x 6'4" (223.5 x 193 cm.)
Inscribed, verso: Frankenthaler   1975   a/c   7'4" x 6'4"
Collection Mr. and Mrs. Ellwood M. Haynes

Tulip Tint extends an idea first explored in *Ocean Drive West #1* (cat. no. 26). In that earlier work, small elements of surface were scattered across a vast surface like islands in an ocean, as the title implies. In *Tulip Tint*, these surface interruptions have grown much larger and extend nearly the height of the entire canvas. With this greater authority, they present a shaping/drawing new to Frankenthaler's work.

Tulip Tint has a thin but richly modeled surface, not unlike those seen in the billowing shapes in pictures of the mid-1960s. But in those pictures, the softer central forms were surrounded by strange, more sharply drawn shapes placed between the central zone and the picture's physical exterior. By contrast, in *Tulip Tint*, the shaping/drawing, made of unpainted, canvas-reserved areas, now runs through the atmospheric tinted surface.

Tulip Tint began with an unpainted canvas, to which Frankenthaler attached long pieces of tape. "I used tape as drawing," she recalls. "I created variations, such as the curve at the right where I bent the tape, allowing for some seepage under it for softness of the edges. I knew how and where the tape and the tint might require softening." Beginning to cover the remaining surface with washes of varying colors of tint, the artist removed some of the tapes while the canvas was wet, allowing the paint to seep into the previously masked areas. In other portions of the work, some of the remaining tapes were moved and adjusted in response to the developing work. As with the initial tapes, when these were removed they left white canvas areas. These reserved passages were subsequently articulated with colors along their edges, as at the lower left, or with painted touches within the white, such as the tan, green, and pink passages at the upper right.

"It's a very abstract picture," says Frankenthaler, "and its title comes from having tulip-like colors and using a tint. The picture is very much the essence of a side of what I am about."

Provenance:
(André Emmerich Gallery, New York)
Mr. and Mrs. William K. Street, Tacoma, Washington
(Charles Cowles Gallery, New York)

Exhibition History:
New York: André Emmerich Gallery (cat. color n.p.), 1975

Selected Critical Reference:
Elderfield, 1989, comm. p. 255, color ill. p. 272

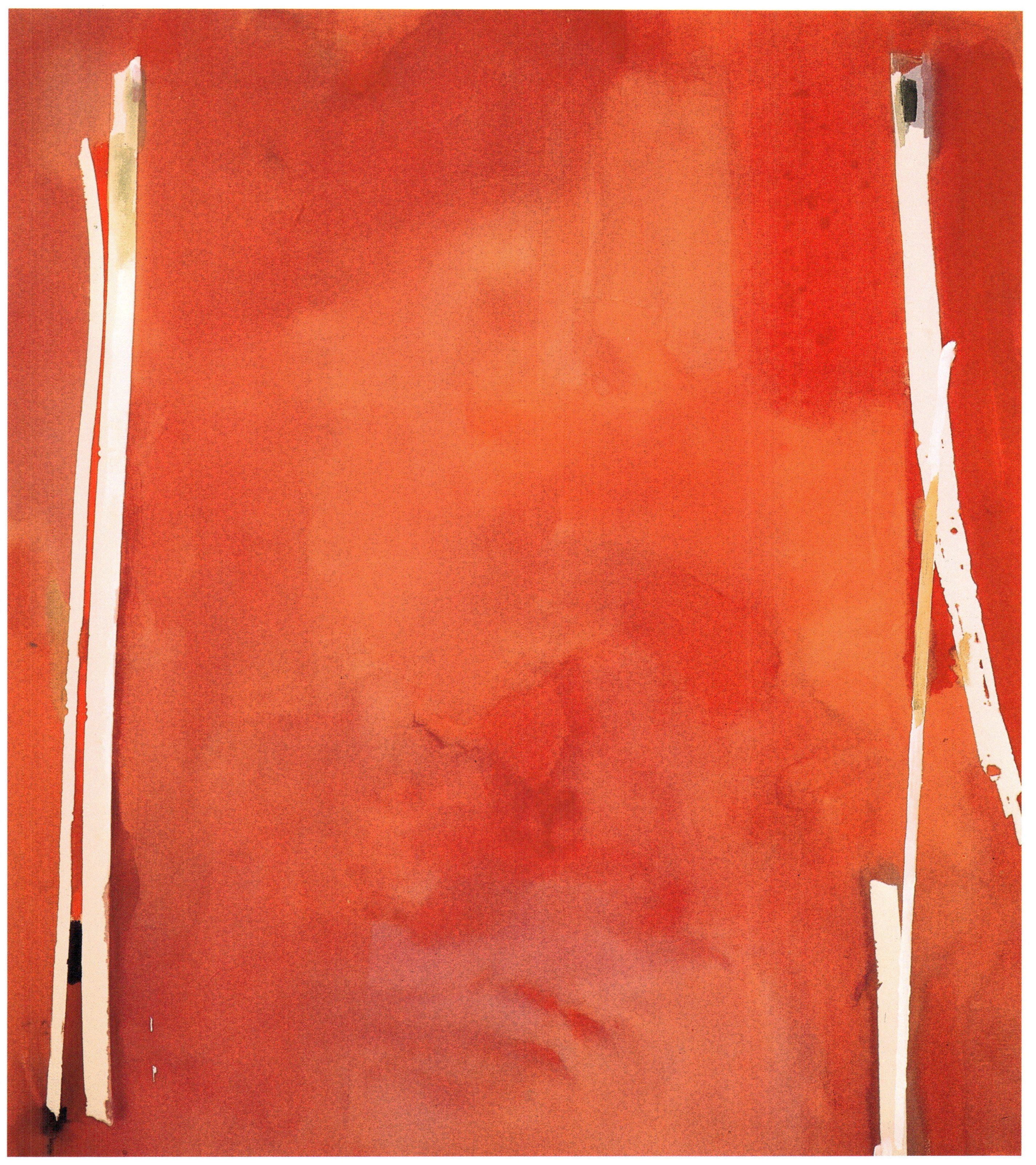

29. *Natural Answer.* 1976
Acrylic on canvas
8 x 11' (243.8 x 335.3 cm.)
Inscribed, recto, 1.1.: Frankenthaler
   verso, r.c.: Frankenthaler "Natural Answer" 1976 a/c
   96 x 132"
Art Gallery of Ontario.
   Gift of Mr. and Mrs. Morris Emer, 1985

In 1976 Frankenthaler visited Arizona to give a lecture at the Phoenix Art Museum. During her talk she described her titles as abstract "handles of identity and recognition," adding that, "Touring Phoenix today, I came up with lots of good titles, but I don't have the pictures [for them] yet."[1] She returned to New York with more than a list of possible names: the palette of Arizona was also present "in terra cotta colors."[2] "However," she notes, "even before I made the trip, the palette of certain paintings had anticipated those colors. Then, pictures made upon my return summed up what I had experienced."

Two works in this exhibition record the impressions on her work of that trip: *Into the West* (cat. no. 30) and *Natural Answer.* These works mark another shift in her oeuvre, toward a more complex, illusionistic composition with greater atmospheric qualities. To be sure, other non–terra cotta works from this period— such as *M,* also in this exhibition (cat. no. 31), move in this direction as well.

With its glowing surface, *Natural Answer* is a compendium of subtle color changes and multiple small tonal accents, especially touches of white. It was, the artist recalls, a very different picture to paint: "I worked long and hard on it—going to and from it I must have walked miles. As I do with many works, I had to add crucial touches in terms of space, color, light, weight. Actions demand reactions."

With its long format, implied darker brown horizon line, and glowing upper areas, as well as its title, it is not surprising that *Natural Answer* has been linked to the landscape tradition. E. C. Goossen compared it to two American nineteenth-century works —"It is almost a dead ringer for Washington Allston's *Moonlit Landscape*" and recalls "[Frederic Edwin] Church's *Cotopaxi*"—and to the works of Turner.[3] "You could *project* some sort of sunset image, but I don't know if it's there," the artist herself says of the painting. "However, the painting is resolved the way nature is resolved: a natural answer."

Notes:
1. Harry Wood, "Frankenthaler Has an Unobtrusive Presence," *Phoenix Lecture,* 11 March 1976, p. 39.
2. Ibid.
3. E. C. Goossen, "Helen Frankenthaler: Notes on Some Recent Paintings," *Bennington Review* (April 1978): 46.

Provenance:
(André Emmerich Gallery, New York)
Mr. Robert Weiss
(M. Knoedler & Co., New York)
Mr. and Mrs. Morris Emer, Toronto

Exhibition History:
New York: André Emmerich Gallery (cat. color cover), 1977
Bennington, Vermont: Suzanne Lemberg Usdan Gallery, Bennington College (cat. comm. n.p., color ill. n.p.), 1978

Selected Critical References:
Frackman, *Arts Magazine* (February 1978), comm. p. 30
Goossen, *Bennington Review* (April 1978), comm. p. 46, color ill. p. 54
Clement, *The Fayette Observer,* 4 November 1983, comm.
Mays, *Globe and Mail,* 27 July 1985, comm.
Baele, *Ottawa Citizen,* 2 August 1985, comm.
Elderfield, 1989, comm. p. 287, color ill. p. 277

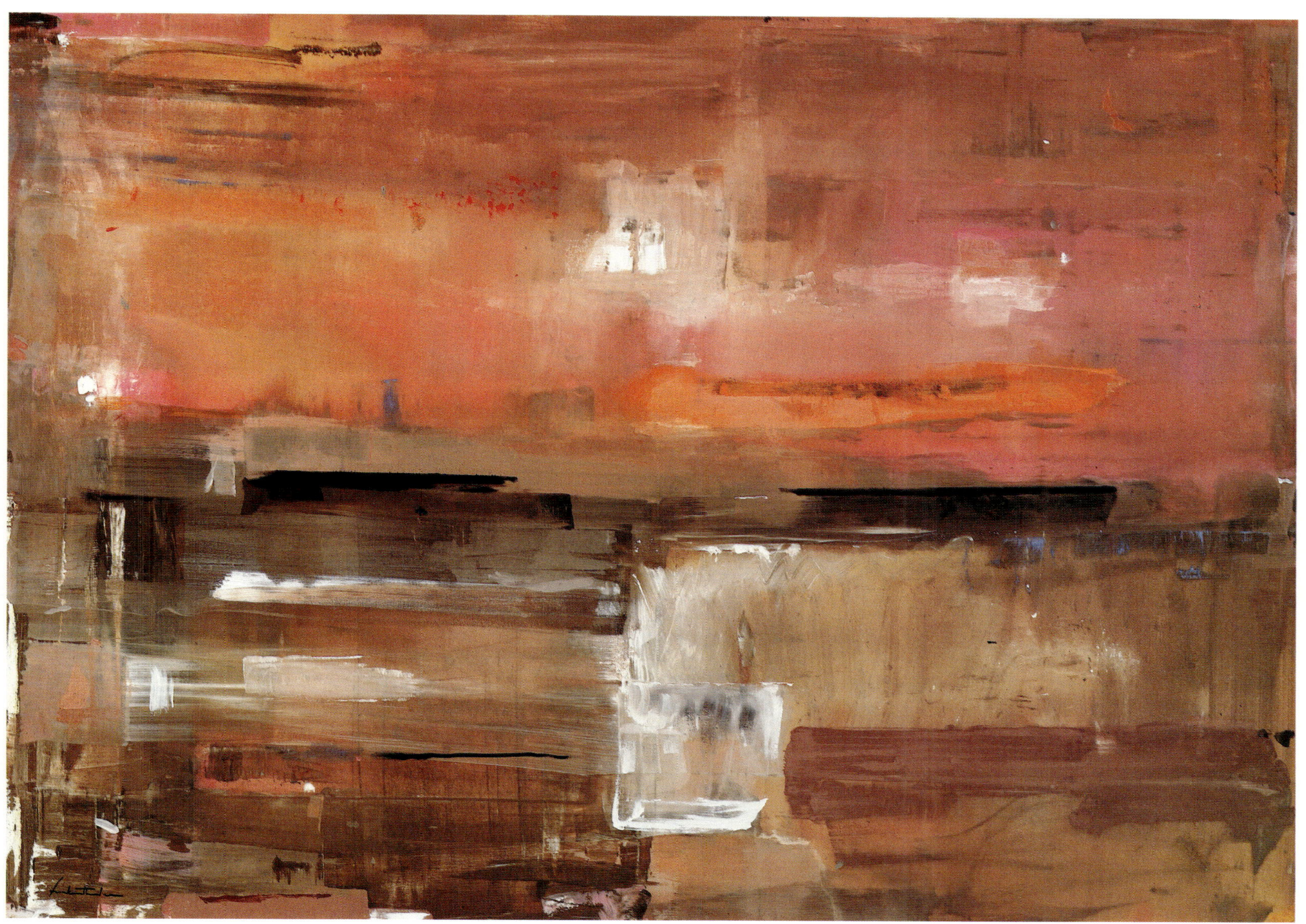

30. *Into the West.* 1977
Acrylic on canvas
8 x 11' (243.8 x 335.3 cm.)
Inscribed, recto, l.r.: Frankenthaler
verso, u.l.: Into the West 1977 acrylic on canvas 86" x 132"
(8' x 11') Frankenthaler '77
Private Collection

Along with *Natural Answer* (cat. no. 29), *Into the West* is one of Frankenthaler's late 1976–early 1977 pictures that were partially informed by the colors she saw on her first trip to Arizona in 1976. And, like *Natural Answer,* the present picture has been compared with works by earlier landscape painters. E. C. Goossen, for example, linked it to the Hudson River School,[1] while Michael McKinnon, in his 1982 analysis of *Into the West,* proposed that its "dark rectangle drifting out of a blackened smudge on the right is certainly redolent of Turner's mid-winter sunsets on the Thames Estuary and of Monet's drifting barges in *Impression, Sunrise.*"[2] Charlotte S. Rubinstein, on the other hand, proposed that parts of its surface "sometimes suggest clefts in rocks."[3]

Like *Natural Answer, Into the West* was also a difficult picture; "perhaps," says the artist, "even more so. As it was drying, I was working into it deeply, as never before to this extent, rubbing and correcting, adding one more thing and wondering, how much more could it take?" But unlike *Natural Answer,* which is a complex additive composition, *Into the West* emerged out of a series of subtractions. Where an earlier work like *Lush Spring* had been initiated with a solid color into the canvas (see cat. no. 27), the surface of *Into the West* was "painted, not tinted. At one point it was covered with paint — applied using sponge heads with strong sweeps of motion, changing direction constantly. The difficult part was to leave or add the chosen areas or strokes. Every millimeter of that huge surface had to have 'perfect' color placement yet look as if it all occurred in a flash." She further notes: "I remember almost pounding color into the picture; a different attitude from the one I had in *Natural Answer.* Comparing the two, the paint in *Natural Answer* rests more on the surface." Building on top of the resulting atmospheric surfaces are the small touches of color, in brown, white, and green. Frankenthaler has often employed these elements in her work (see *Arden* or *Seascape with Dunes,* cat. nos. 10, 11), but in *Into the West* and *Natural Answer,* they are more physically detached from the overall composition, introducing a kind of marking that would play a key role in her later pictures.

Notes:
1. E. C. Goossen, "Helen Frankenthaler: Notes on Some Recent Paintings," *Bennington Review* (April 1978): 46.
2. Michael McKinnon, comp., *The History of Western Art,* sec. 31: *Art of the '70s* (London: Visual Publications International, 1982), notes on the filmstrip.
3. Charlotte S. Rubinstein, *American Women Artists* (Boston: Avon Publishers, 1982), 330.

Exhibition History:
New York: André Emmerich Gallery (cat. color ill. n.p.), 1977
Bennington, Vermont: Suzanne Lemberg Usdan Gallery, Bennington College (cat. comm. n.p., color ill. n.p.), 1978

Selected Critical References:
Goossen, *Bennington Review* (April 1978), comm. p. 46
Carmean, *Art International* (April–May 1978), comm. p. 30
Munro, 1979, comm. pp. 210, 223
Rubinstein, 1982, comm. p. 330
Broder, 1984, color ill. p. 296
Elderfield, 1989, comm. pp. 287, 288; color ill. p. 283

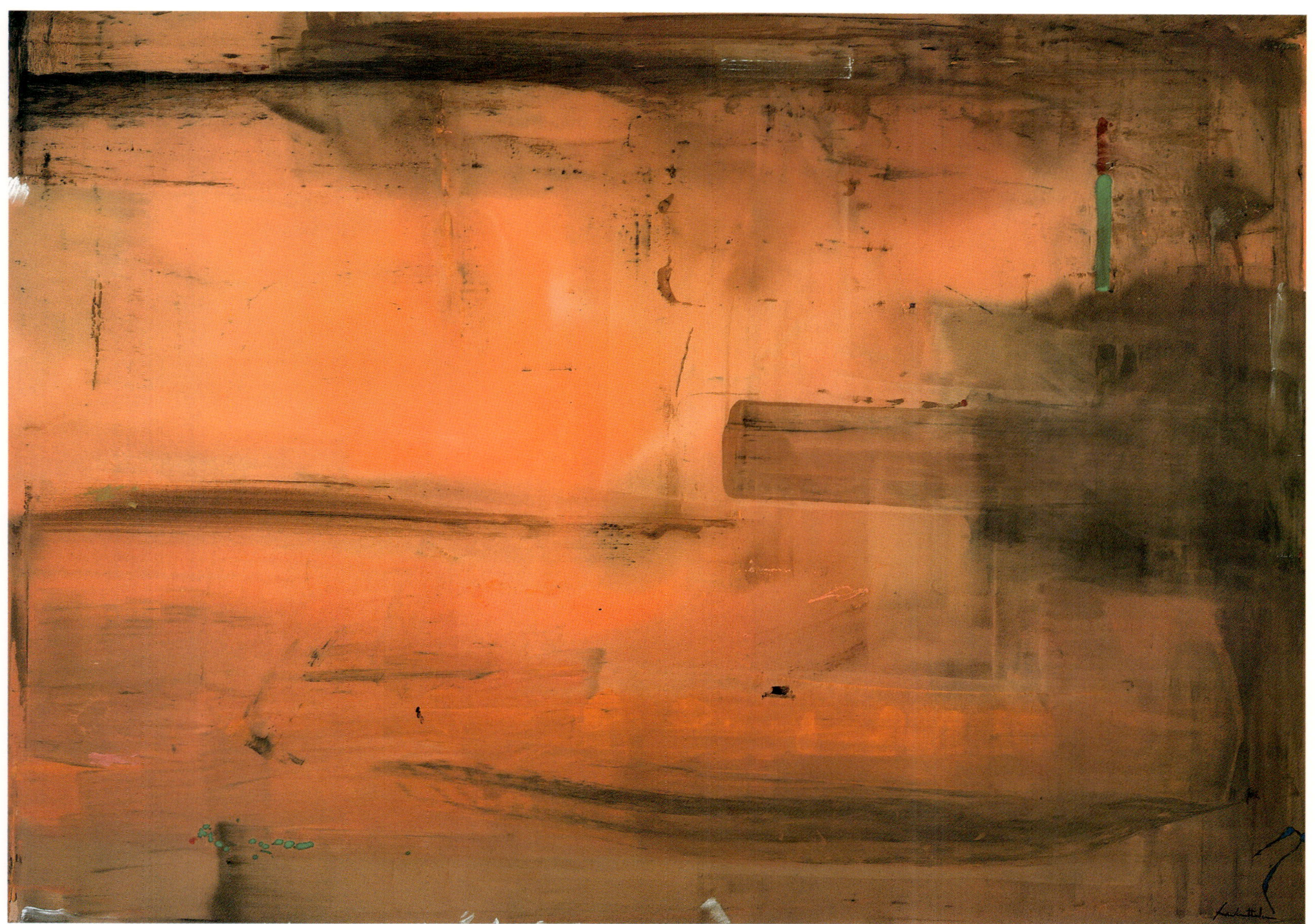

31. *M.* 1977
   Acrylic on canvas
   6′6″ x 9′6″ (198.1 x 289.6 cm.)
   Inscribed, recto, l.r.: Frankenthaler
      verso: Frankenthaler ′77 M   1977 acrylic on canvas
      78″ x 114″ (6′6″ x 9′6″)
   Private Collection

M, the present author wrote in 1978, "with its dark-brown ground and its washes of ghostly white, is quite different from the high-keyed color . . . we normally associate with the artist. . . . In many ways, it is at once the most poetic and most abstracted of Franken-thaler's paintings."[1]

Its making was also difficult. Like *Lush Spring* (cat. no. 27), *M* began with uniform color applied to the surface. Here, the rich, dark brown was then countered with white, applied first as pours on various sections of the surface that are distinguished by their opaqueness: most visible is the shape to the lower right. These pours of white were then extended out in thinner layers. "The white created an overall, controlled, autonomous shape," the artist says, "but it is a dialogue of light over dark and dark over light, confirmed by leaving the brown in the center, which is balanced in the lower left with the heavy white, the green, and the other necessary patches of color."

The sweeps of the brush seen in the opaque passage of white over the brown ground are articulated with smaller elements of color—as in *Natural Answer* and *Into the West* (cat. nos. 29, 30)—here in lighter brown, yellow, and blue. This blue, in turn, becomes a further tone, as a wash over the white at the lower center of the work.

"*M*," says the artist, "both celebrates and tenderly cherishes a nostalgic feeling for a specific life. It's a mourning, and an homage, of sorts."

Note:
1. E.A. Carmean, Jr., "On Five Paintings by Helen Frankenthaler," *Art International* 22 (April–May 1978): 28, 32.

Exhibition History:
New York: André Emmerich Gallery (cat. color ill. n.p.), 1977

Selected Critical References:
Stevens, *Newsweek* (5 December 1977), comm. p. 94
Frackman, *Arts Magazine* (February 1978), comm. p. 30
Carmean, *Art International* (April–May 1978), comm. pp. 28, 30; color ill. p. 24
Elderfield, 1989, comm. pp. 287, 304, 334; color ill. p. 286

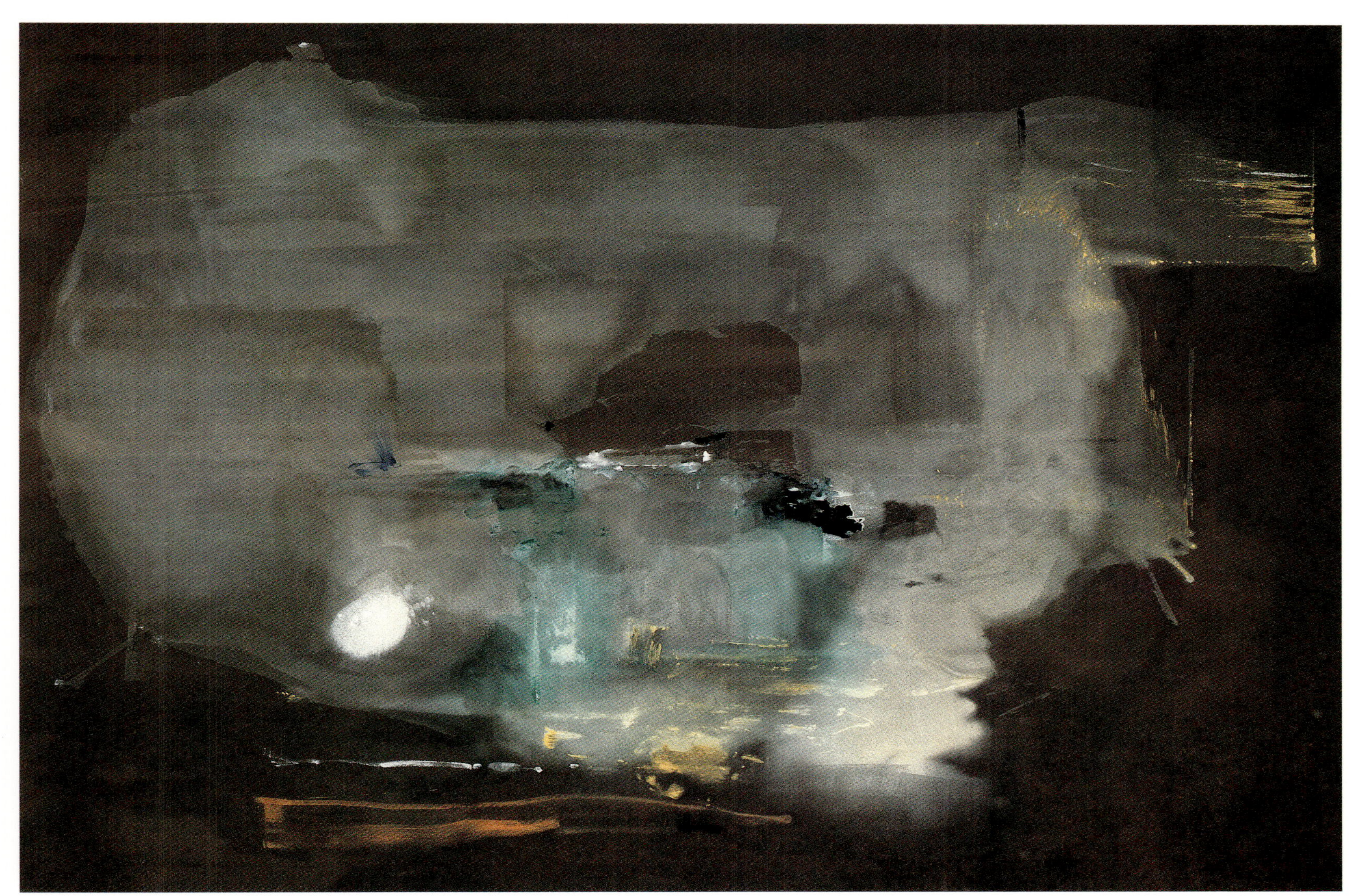

32. *Salome.* 1978
  Acrylic on canvas
  7'10" x 13'5½" (238.8 x 410.2 cm.)
  Inscribed, recto, l.l.: Frankenthaler
    verso: Frankenthaler "Salome" 1978 a/c 7'10" x 13'5½"
  Museum Moderner Kunst, Vienna, Austria. Ludwig Collection

Salome is the last of the four mid-1970s works in the present exhibition in which the artist used a dense, highly worked surface of overlapping areas of paint. The composition here is at the same time one of greater complexity—given its strident changes in color—and of increased rigidity, due to its interlocking, quasi-geometric construction. Both the large color areas and the smaller color accents seem to shift in and out spatially and to flow over and behind adjacent zones.

It is this sense of movement and transparent layering that gives the work its title of *Salome.* "It's called that," says Frankenthaler, "because it has many 'veils.' Veils on top of 'worked-into' areas of depth—like a fine curtain that covers arrangements beyond. It's a long 'dance' on a huge scale." To a degree, the picture was unexpected: "It has wonderfully strange colors—they were a surprise as I went along."

The looseness of these areas is countered by much of their shaping as in horizontal or vertical blacks—and by the drawing, which echoes the orientation of the framing edge. Frankenthaler cites these aspects as part of her "Cubism—of square after square, of planes moving in various depths yet flat on the surface. My kind of motion, which is Cubist oriented, should not be confused with action painting."

Provenance:
(Knoedler Gallery, London)

Exhibition History:
London: Knoedler Gallery (cat. color n.p.), 1978

Selected Critical References:
Maloon, *Artscribe* (December 1978), comm. p. 51
Museum moderner Kunst, 1979, color ill. n.p.
Museum moderner Kunst, 1982, comm. p. 55
Elderfield, 1989, comm. p. 288, color ill. p. 291

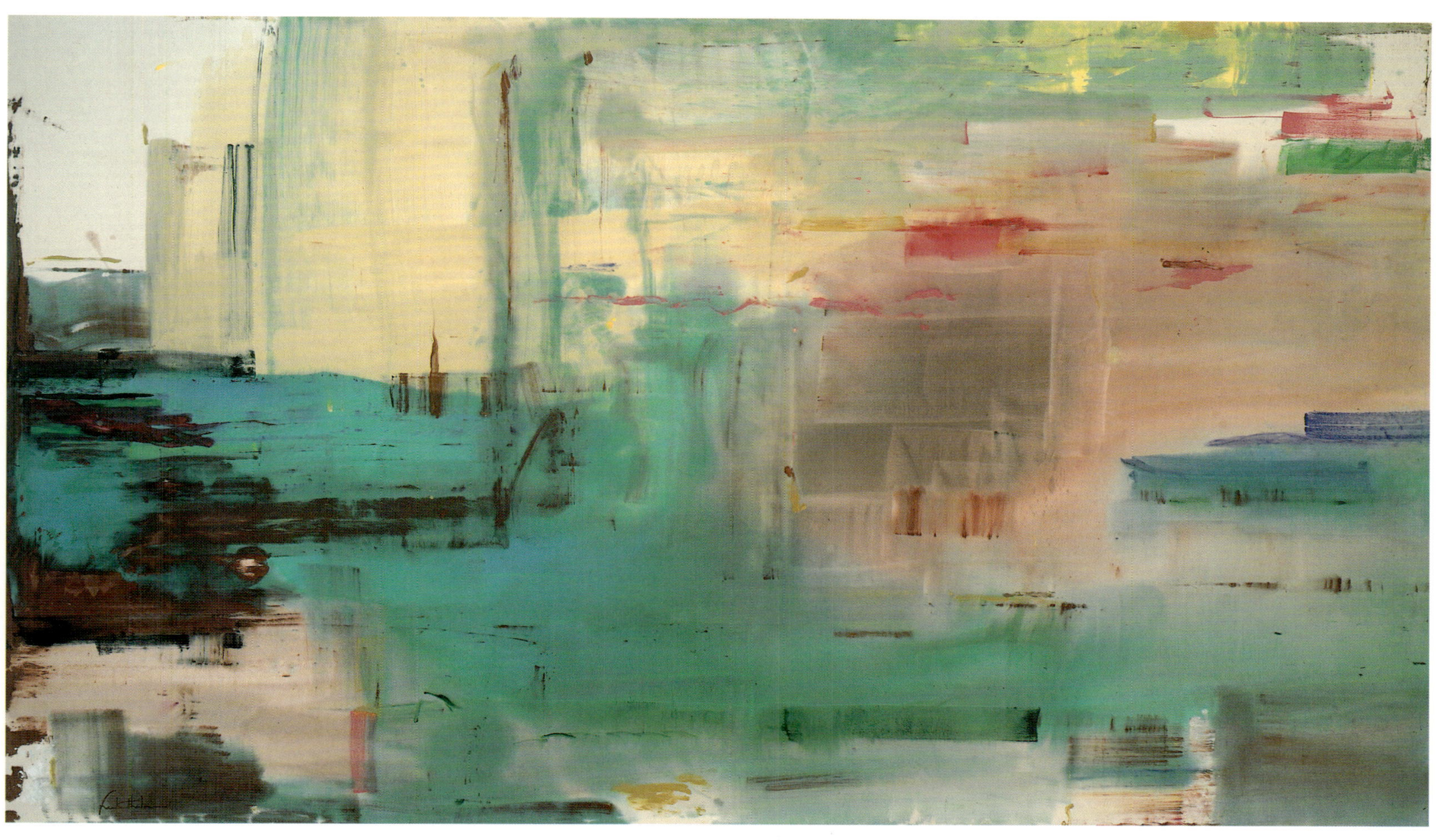

33. *Portrait of a Lady in White.* 1979
Acrylic on canvas
6'10" x 4'½" (208.9 x 123.2 cm.)
Inscribed, recto, l.r.: Frankenthaler; verso, u.l.: Frankenthaler
   '79, l.l.: "Portrait of a Lady in White" 1979 82" x 48¼"
   (6'10" x 4'¼") acrylic on canvas
Private Collection

"The one rule is—there are no rules," said Frankenthaler in a talk in 1983 at a Duke University symposium on American art of the 1950s. Stating that her own inspiration sometimes comes from postcards of works by earlier artists or seeing colors in their works, she added, "You just come up with something and then it tells you—but sometimes one doesn't listen."[1]

Fig. 5 Titian. *Portrait of a Lady in White.* c. 1535
        Oil on canvas, 40¼ x 33⅞" (102.2 x 86.1 cm.)
        Staatliche Kunstammlungen, Dresden
        Gemäldegalerie Alte Meister

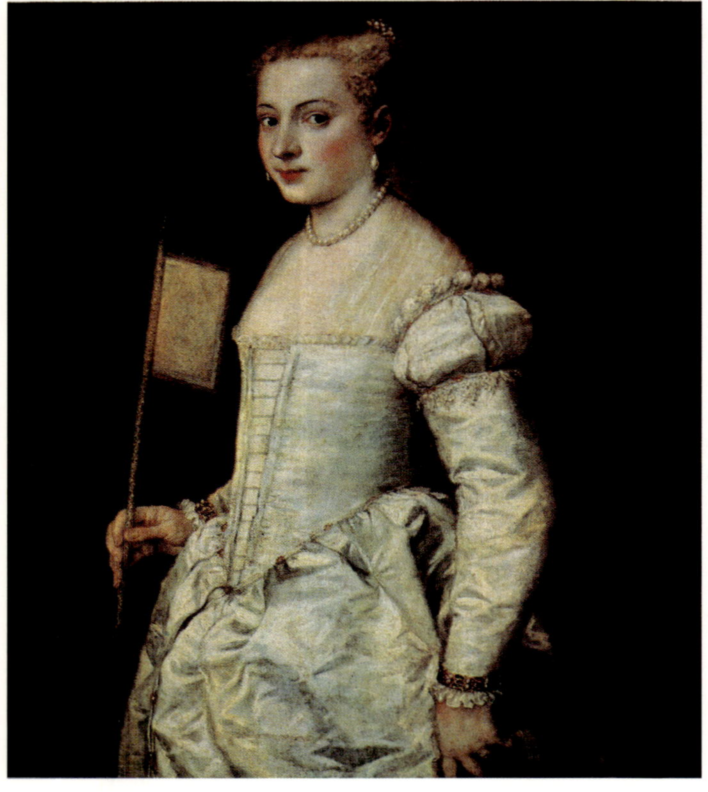

Portrait of a Lady in White, from 1979, was cited by the artist in her remarks as one of those pictures inspired by Old Master paintings, and specifically, "a work by Titian of the same name." This Titian, from 1535, is in Staatliche Kunstammlungen in Dresden (fig. 5). Frankenthaler saw the work when it was included in the *Treasures from Dresden* exhibition, shown at The Metropolitan Museum of Art in New York in 1979.

Frankenthaler used the Titian picture to create a greatly abstracted departure with a radically different composition. Where *Portrait of a Lady in White* accords with its Venetian predecessor is in the contrast of the whites against a rich brown background: Frankenthaler's thin layering of white film echoes the underpainting and glazing found in the Titian. In *Portrait of a Lady in White,* this more atmospheric surface is challenged by elements of impasto placed in the composition, tan at the left center, with bright green and pale blue to the right.

"What got to me in the Titian," Frankenthaler says of this picture, "is how much color he created using essentially black and white. I added those hints of color because the Titian painting seemed rich with similar gestures."

When *Portrait of a Lady in White* was exhibited at André Emmerich Gallery in New York in 1979, it received little critical attention. In reviewing it and other pictures in the show, Valentine Tatransky observed: "She is justly famous for her 'staining technique,' but this was only a means towards harmonizing color. However, it's not even color that she excels at. She has a sense for chiaroscuro."[2] This tendency in her pictures can be seen as early as *Yellow Caterpillar,* and it became a more prevalent aspect of her pictures in the 1980s.

Notes:
1. Melissa Clement, "Frankenthaler: America's First Lady of Abstract Art," *The Fayette Observer,* 4 November 1983.
2. Valentine Tatransky, "Helen Frankenthaler," *Flash Art,* nos. 94–95 (January–February 1980): 26.

Exhibition History:
New York: André Emmerich Gallery (cat. color n.p.), 1979

Selected Critical References:
Tatransky, *Flash Art* (January–February 1980), comm. p. 26
Clement, *The Fayette Observer,* 4 November 1983, comm.

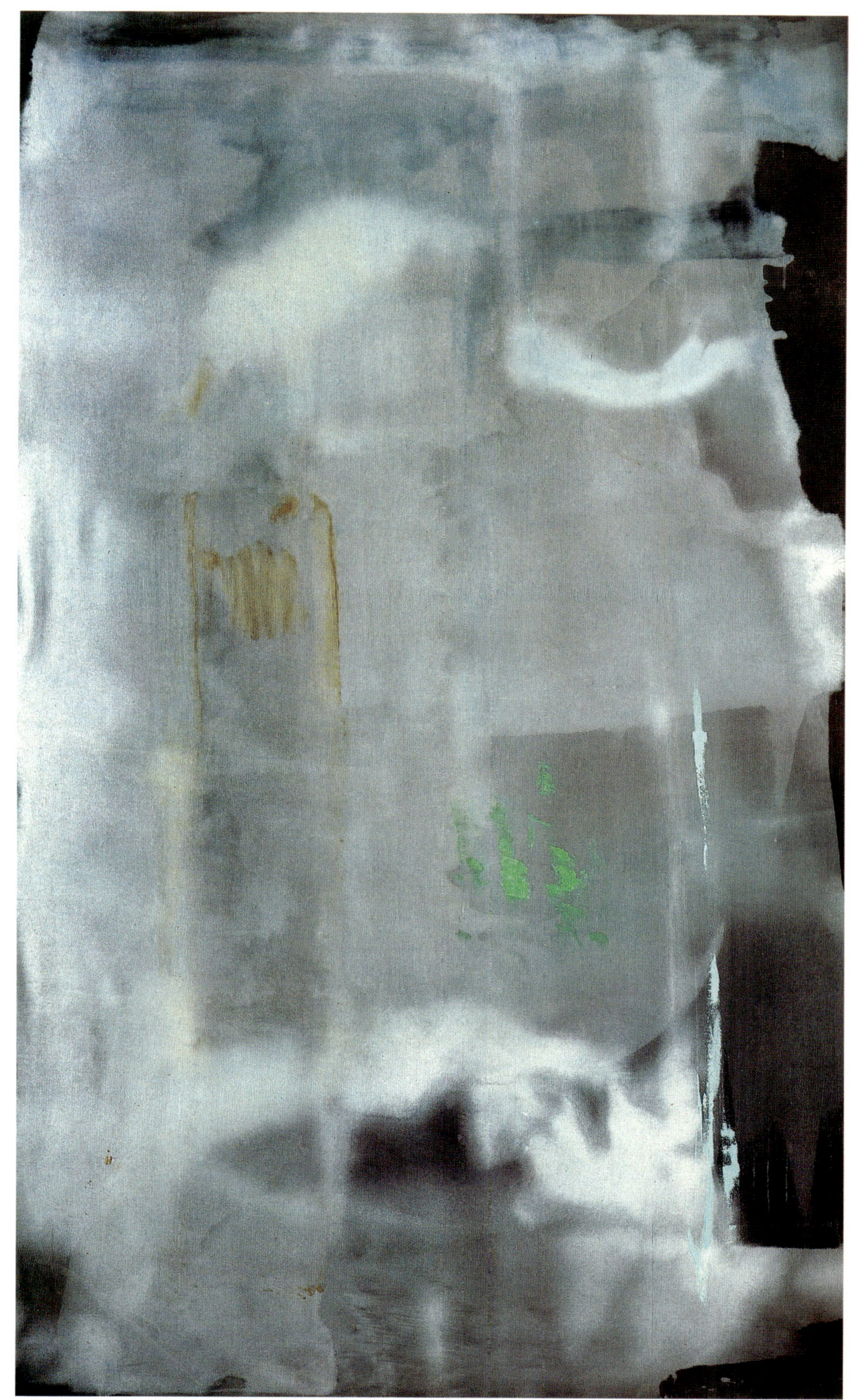

34. *For E. M.* 1981
   Acrylic on canvas
   5'11" x 9'7" (180.3 x 292.1 cm.)
   Inscribed, recto, l.r.: Frankenthaler
      verso, u.l.: Frankenthaler 1981, u.r.: "For E.M." 1981
   71" x 115" (5'11" x 9'7") a/c Frankenthaler 1981
   Private Collection

Although it was painted in 1981, *For E. M.* has not been publicly seen until the present exhibition.[1] A large, richly worked picture, this canvas is another example of Frankenthaler taking inspiration from the oeuvre of an earlier artist. In this instance her predecessor was Edouard Manet—hence the picture's title—and specifically his *Still Life With Carp* of 1864, now in the collection of The Art Institute of Chicago (fig. 6).

"Many artists make copies or variations of works by past masters," says Frankenthaler. "For me, it's usually the work of artists I admire and understand. However, this Manet painting of a carp from Chicago challenged me to find out *why* this is such a good picture. So I decided to painstakingly copy areas and colors, but there's no fish in my painting. The scale is the same but the size is very different. At times I couldn't resist ignoring the Manet to meet the needs of my own abstract canvas. Still, side by side the similarities should be obvious."

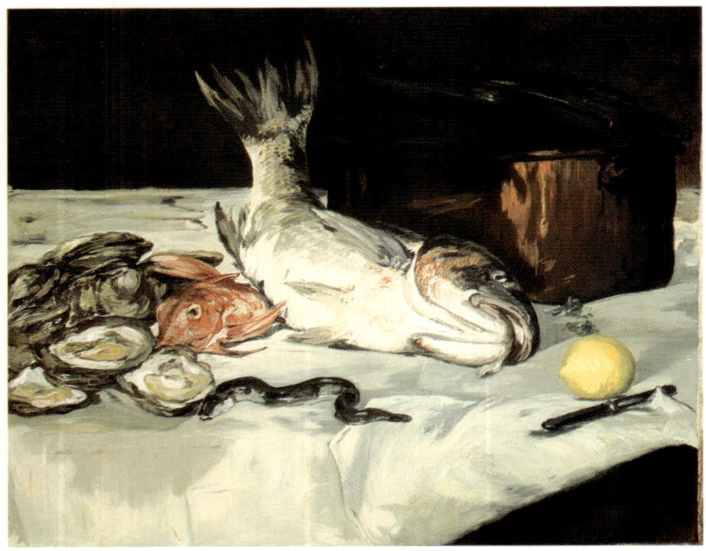

Manet's *Still Life With Carp* is centered on a large carp placed upon a diagonal white tablecloth. Behind the fish to the right is a dark copper pot, while to its left is a group of oysters and a small red gurnard. A lemon joined with a dark knife sits at the right edge of the composition, while both the horizontal background and the triangularly shaped foreground are rendered in empty dark brown.

As Frankenthaler says: "Even though *For E. M.* is abstract, when you see it with a reproduction of the Manet it is amazingly close in composition and it has the same light." Indeed, the white scumbled passages in the center of *For E. M.* do correspond loosely to the white carp in the Manet, while her dark and lighter browns at the right accord with Manet's copper pot. The greenish oysters and the red gurnard in the earlier picture are more abstractly suggested in Frankenthaler's passages of green and orange, while Manet's knife becomes in *For E. M.* a flat, dark-brown horizontal and his lemon is hinted at in yellow passages. Equally flattened but still present in the variation are the dark background and the triangular wedge of foreground space.

Other aspects of Frankenthaler's picture show greater distance from the *Still Life With Carp.* "I played around with pale green and pink, which are different from the Manet," she recalls. "I worked on the whole canvas both upright as well as on the floor. *For E. M.* is considered and formal, yet the spontaneity shines throughout."

Note:
1. The painting is also reproduced in John Elderfield, *Frankenthaler* (New York: Harry N. Abrams, Inc., 1989), 314.

Exhibition History:
This work has not been exhibited before.

Selected Critical Reference:
Elderfield, 1989, comm. pp. 306, 309, 334, 404; color ill. p. 314

Fig. 6   Edouard Manet
         Still Life with Carp. 1864
         Oil on canvas
         28⅞ x 36¼" (73.4 x 92.1 cm.)
         The Art Institute of Chicago. Mr. and Mrs. Lewis Larned
         Coburn Memorial Collection, 1942.311

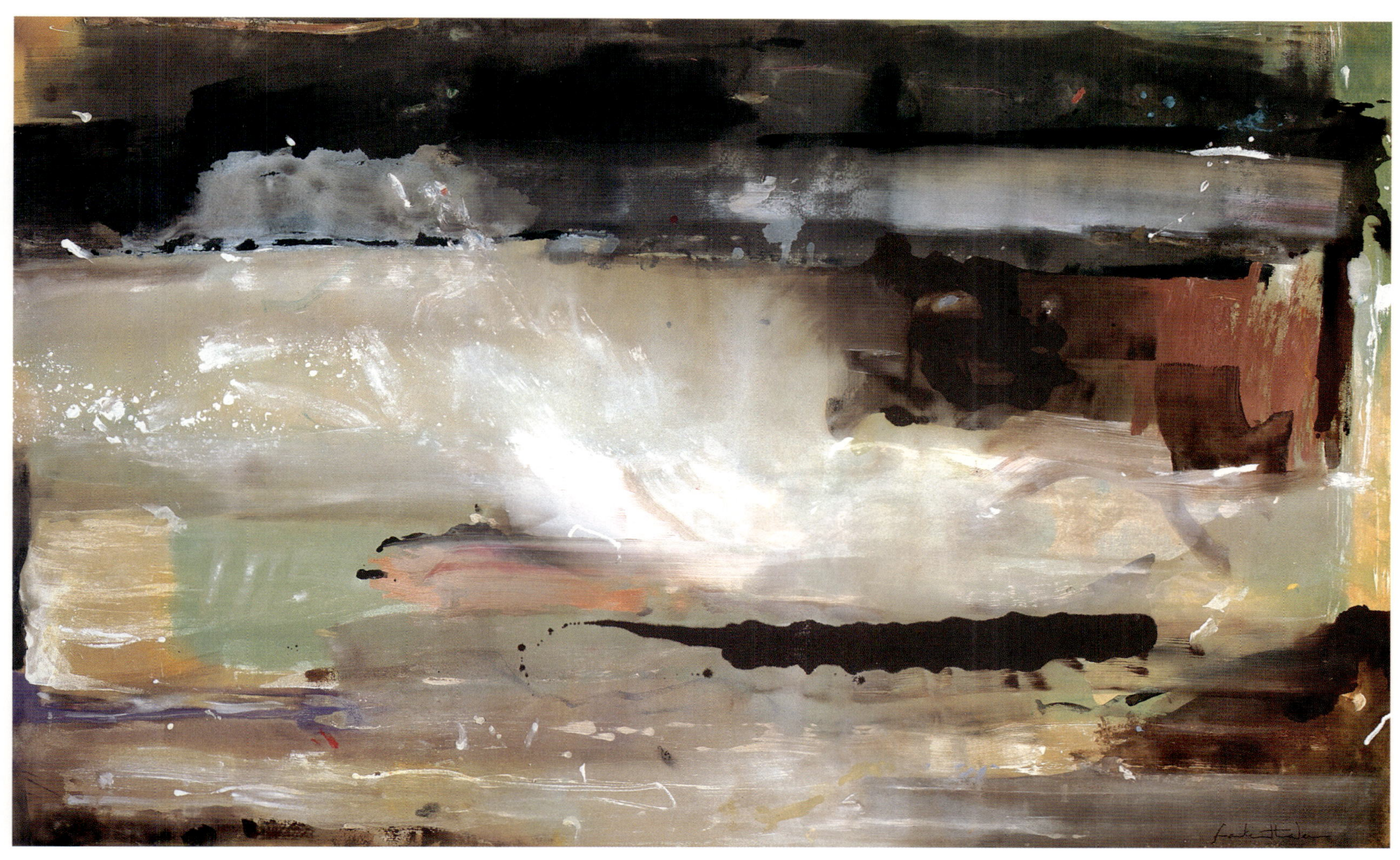

35. *Sacrifice Decision.* 1981
   Acrylic on canvas
   4′5¾″ x 9′10½″ (136.5 x 301 cm.)
   Inscribed, verso, u.l.: 1981 53¾″ x 118½″ (4′5¾″ x 9′10¾″) a/c
      Frankenthaler 1981 "Sacrifice Decision"
   Private Collection

"Flood and flow are as seductive as ever," John Russell wrote of the paintings in a 1981 Frankenthaler exhibition, "but they are joined by passages of paint that sit in high relief on the crest of the canvas."[1] Indeed, as Russell pointed out, it was the counterpoint of the two formal traits that determined the thrust of the works. "These raised areas could function primarily as road marks or an alternate system of notation, but in point of fact, they and the stained areas make music together. *Sacrifice Decision* shows exactly how this is done, and it would be a heart of stone that was not touched by its tonalities of pale mauve and pigeon-breast gray."[2]

Interestingly, of the paintings in the present exhibition, *Sacrifice Decision* is the most revealing of how the artist proceeds in her work, and of how these sequential choices determine the character of her aesthetic. As with other pictures from this period, *Sacrifice Decision* began with a large canvas spread on the studio floor, the entire fabric wet with water. The long, curving horizontal was the first step. "I took a heavy pail of gray paint and tossed all of the paint to a selected area on the canvas—pouring it with real force. The end of the pouring gesture is manifested in the thinner, whiplike line that curves and trails off. The 'whip' of this original pour was too insistent, so I flooded it with water, brushed over it, leaving its shape, with veils of tint created by it." These veils were then worked into the wet canvas, giving it its subtle modeling and overall gray tonality, with deeper tones at the left and top margins and at the right. This brushing outward is especially apparent in the stroking lines that radiate from this curving passage.

The additions of thicker paint were applied at this stage. "I then left it," recalls the artist; "the surface looked weird—bold clumps on a tissue-thin wash. Returning, I thought, should I blend in the clumps while they're still wet? Yet, the picture dictated not to touch it. I said to myself, decide, can't have it all ways. I suppose that's why it's called *Sacrifice Decision.* In the end, it was no sacrifice."

The canvas, still on the studio floor, was not yet completed and would undergo further additions when Frankenthaler began to decide how to crop the work—what parts to eliminate from its original, large size (the left and top margins were cut down, for example). "At the shaping stage, I thought it needed something, with the shadow of the splash and the five tossed shapes. It was placid and yet explosive. The next day I added the—surprising to me—black shape at the center bottom edge. Originally, that black shape was more rounded, like the tossed shapes, but I had to change it to make it more of a semicircle that both anchors and echoes the vocabulary above. Then I thought, leave the painting alone."

Notes:
1. John Russell, "Recent Paintings by Helen Frankenthaler," *The New York Times,* 13 November 1981, p. C26.
2. Ibid.

Exhibition History:
New York: André Emmerich Gallery (cat. color ill. n.p.), 1981

Selected Critical References:
Russell, *The New York Times,* 13 November 1981, comm. p. C26
Elderfield, 1989, comm. pp. 306, 321, 334; color ill. p. 318

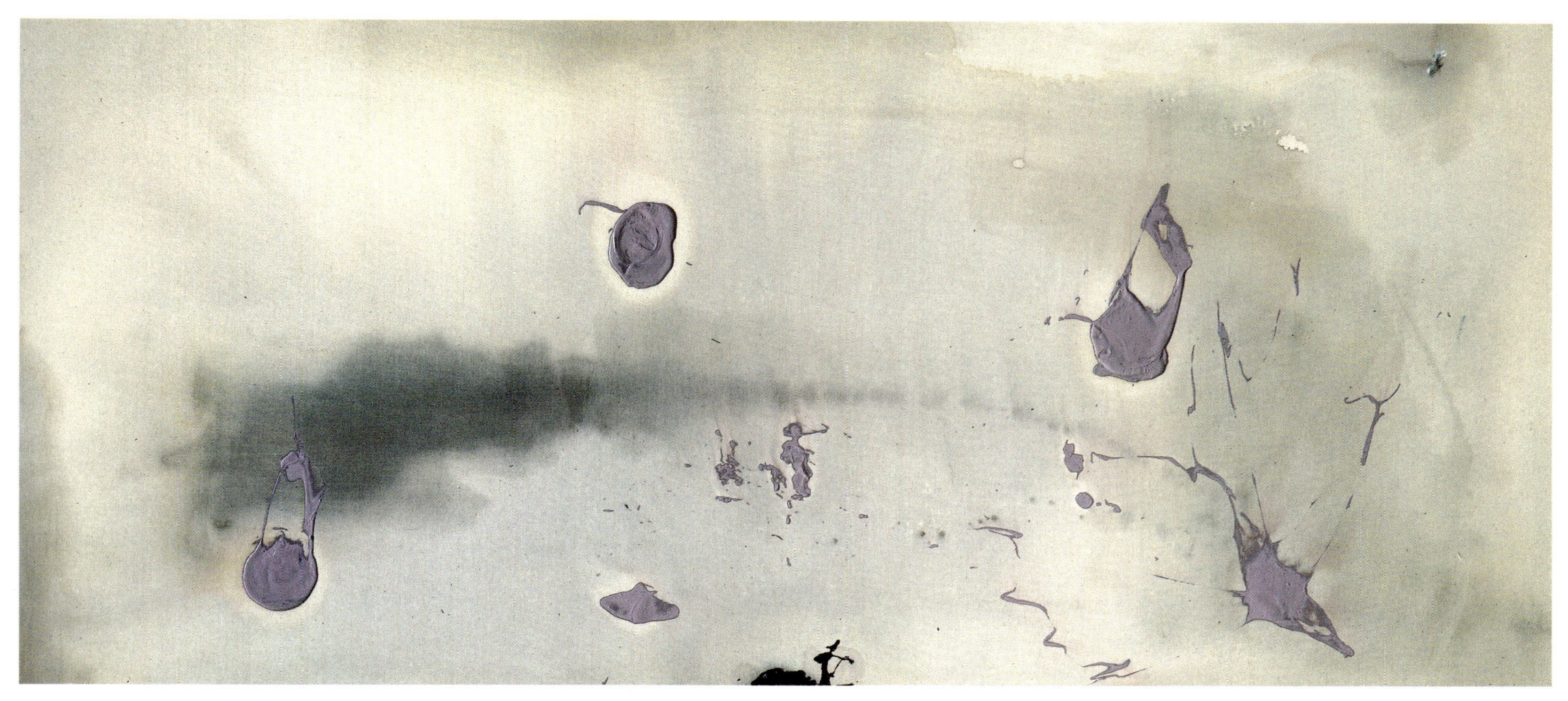

36. *Grey Fireworks.* 1982
Acrylic on canvas
6′ x 9′10½″ (182.9 x 301 cm.)
Inscribed, recto, l.r.: Frankenthaler
   verso, u.r.: "Grey Fireworks" 1982 72″ x 118″ (6′ x 9′10″)
Private Collection

"Grey Fireworks," wrote Patricia Johnson in 1982, "is a dove gray slip of background upon which bursts of color are applied. . . . Pastel washes blend happily, some disappearing like a sigh, others seeming to congeal into energized gestures."[1] Indeed, it is this range of pictorial characters—the neutral gray underground, the disappearing pale washes, and the jolt of the sharp colors— that accords with the painting's apt metaphorical title. "It's called that" says the artist, because it is "explosive. It's not gray dismal— it's gray celebrative."[1]

Like *Lush Spring* and *M* (cat. nos. 27, 31), *Grey Fireworks* began with a solidly colored surface, here a rich blue gray. Color washes of darker tones were then added, giving the picture its "real construction." These were followed by the "clumps" of pink and white, distinct shapes set apart from the more diaphanous field, "accents in the shadowy ground," as Frankenthaler calls them. "I was choosing what seemed like every conceivable color accent to play against gray. But it was important to place specific colors in exact positions to make it all successful." It is also, she notes, "what might have happened to *Sacrifice Decision* if I had not stopped."

Note:
1. Patricia C. Johnson, "Frankenthaler Poetry on Canvas," *Houston Chronicle,* 13 May 1982, sec. 4, p. 18.

Exhibition History:
Houston: Janie C. Lee Gallery (cat. color ill. n.p.), 1982

Selected Critical References:
Johnson, *Houston Chronicle,* 13 May 1982, comm. and ill. sec. 2,
   p. 18
Elderfield, 1989, comm. p. 335, color ill. p. 329

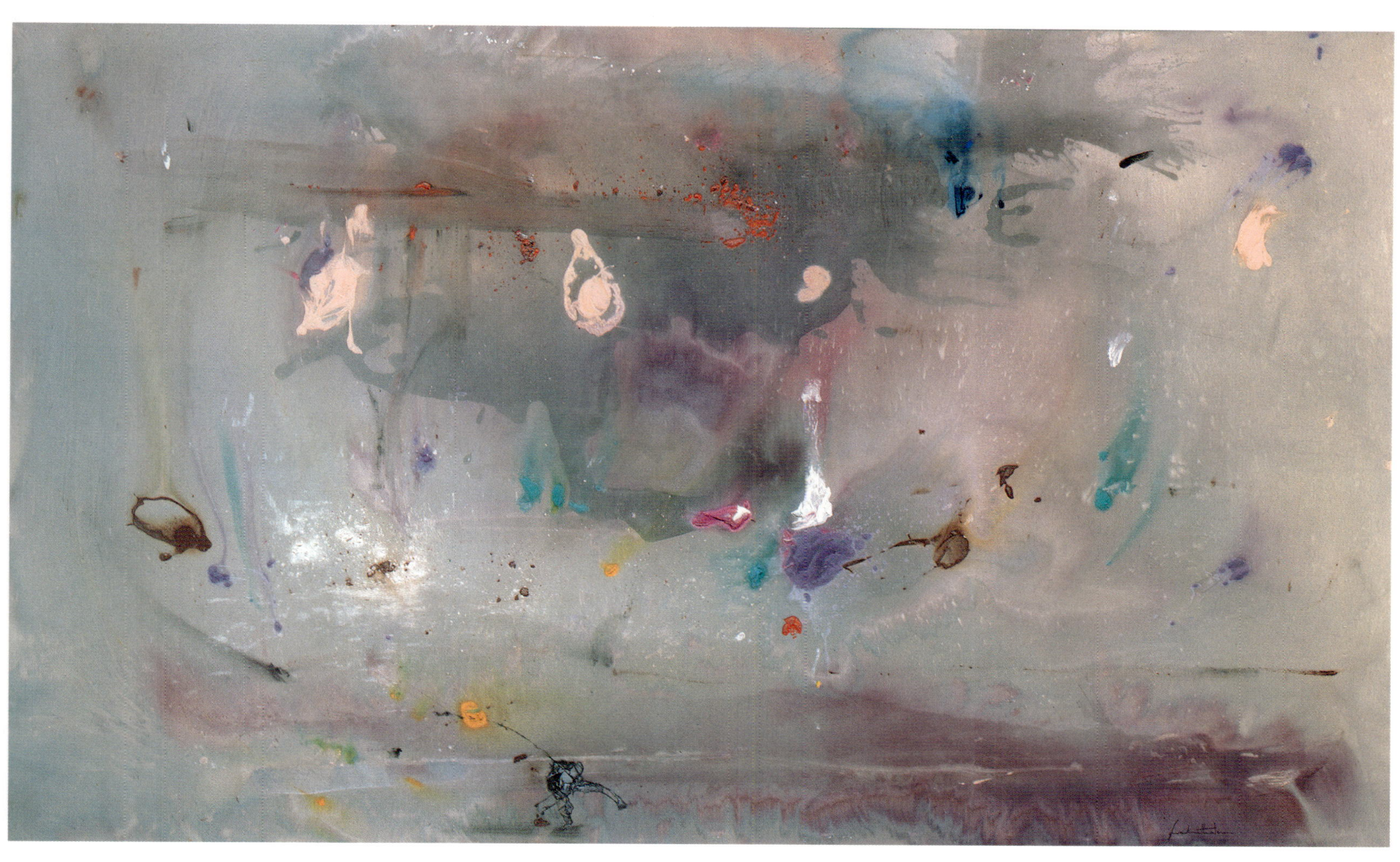

37. *On the Cusp.* 1985
Acrylic on canvas
6′8½″ x 4′1⅜″ (204.5 x 125.4 cm.)
Inscribed, recto, l.r.: Frankenthaler
    verso: Frankenthaler On the Cusp 1985 a/c 6′8″ x 4′1⅜″
Collection Lois and Georges de Menil

Frankenthaler's art is essentially a dialogue between drawing and color. Whether it takes place in the form of nuance passages or boldly shaped elements, this visual conversation is always one where the elements are either interwoven or placed in reciprocity. *On the Cusp* is one of her few works in which drawing and color are kept at some distance from each other, here with the many different linear passages seeming to float or move over a field of intense green.

"It's a play on the green, with lines and shapes balanced in a kind of shorthand," she comments on this work. "Putting the pink area on the green in that specific way, I might have felt lightheartedness seep into my wrist. I thought—I'm going to do it anyway, because it works. The picture has a certain weight, but also a feeling of immediacy. Every inch of surface and every stroke was a matter of careful choice and placement. There might also be a quality of the perverse, in that scumbled complementary pink surprise dancing at the bottom. That pink was a vital, last-minute gesture. I hesitated for a moment at the incongruity of it, but I had to do it."

On the Cusp does have elements of restraint: the blue vertical border at the right, the long black passage at the left, the crossing horizontal at the bottom, and the blue and black inverted V at the left center. But other elements seem to move around in the work. Across the center, from left to right, painted passages seem to hop up and over the blue-black angle, while the deep pink at the bottom jumps over the greenish line. Even the oval at the top seems to rotate within the light passages of pink around its lower edge, or "on the cusp." Taken together, they create another form of the abstract "cartoon" motions seen in the earlier *Eden* (cat. no. 2).

Provenance:
(André Emmerich Gallery, New York)

Exhibition History:
New York: André Emmerich Gallery (cat. no. 9, color n.p.), 1986

Selected Critical Reference:
Elderfield, 1989, comm. p. 354, color ill. p. 367

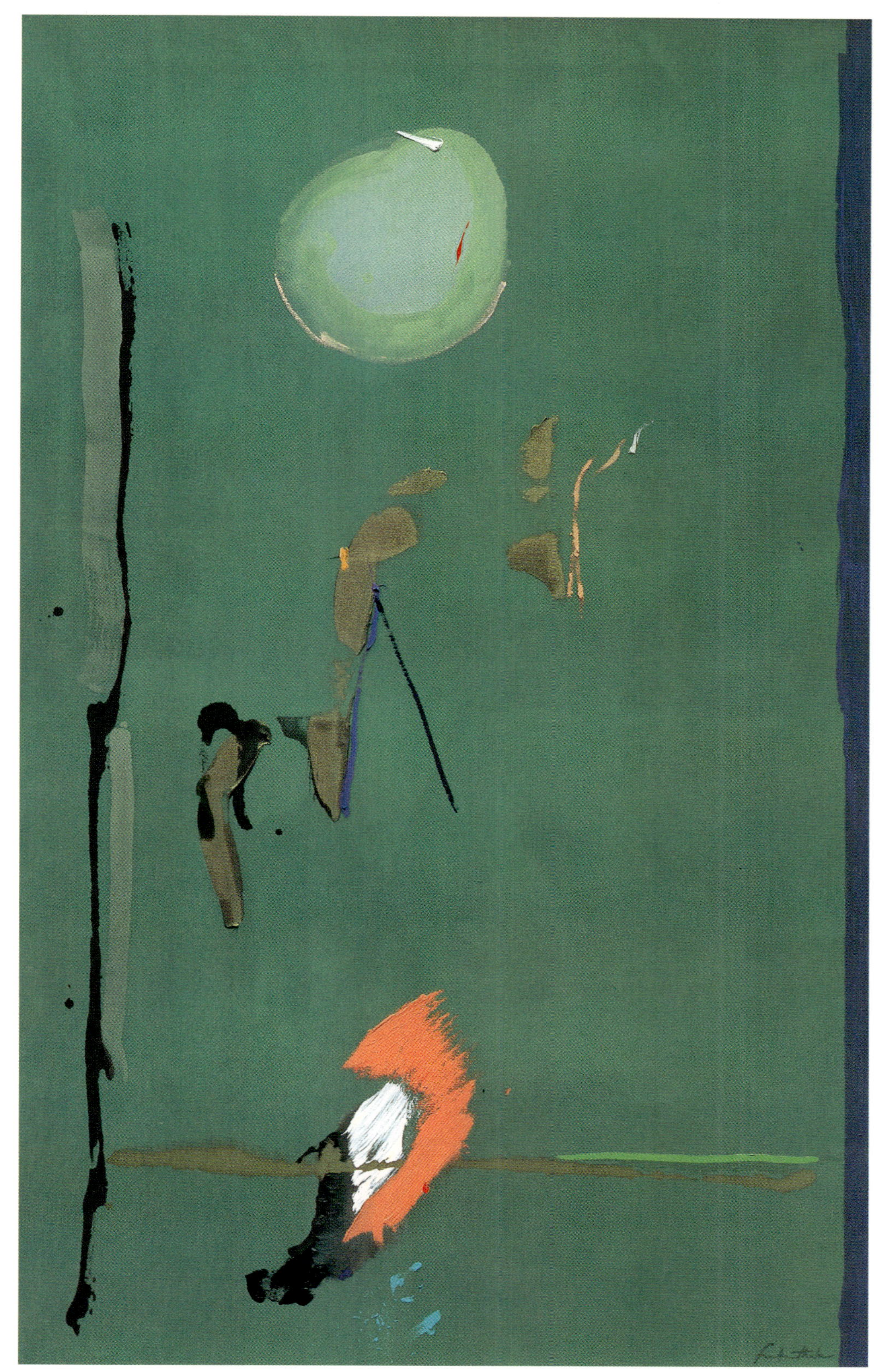

38. *Snow Queen.* 1986
  Acrylic on canvas
  8'8¾' x 5'4" (266.1 x 162.6 cm.)
  Inscribed, verso, stretcher: "Snow Queen" 1986 104¾" x 64",
    u.l.: Frankenthaler 1986
  Private Collection

Exhibition History:
San Francisco: John Berggruen Gallery (cat. color ill. p. 19), 1987

Selected Critical References:
Goldberg, *Artweek*, 9 May 1987, comm. p. 3
Elderfield, 1989, comm. p. 372, color ill. p. 372

In many of her paintings from the later 1980s, Frankenthaler introduces a dialogue between an implied gridlike structure and more amorphous areas of color. *Snow Queen*, from 1986, is a premier example of this direction, with its meandering white central shape surrounded by vertical and horizontal passages and an overall encasing band of rigid gray on three sides.

"In all my work there are notes of my aesthetic signature repeated over decades, that come back in new forms. In that sense, *Snow Queen* might have *The Bay* as a precursor," Frankenthaler comments, referring to the 1963 picture (cat. no. 12), "in the way in which the white billows in the center against a harder edge. And as with the play of blues in *The Bay, Snow Queen* is a play of grays, although in *Snow Queen* there appears to be more of an impression of chiaroscuro and scumbled paint, as opposed to the blending and fusing of the blues in *The Bay*." This latter quality—the sense of more modeling in the passages—extends to the gridlike elements as well, where paint has been only roughly applied.

This composition's tension between the Cubist-like grid and the spontaneous white center was recognized by Beth Goldberg when *Snow Queen* was first exhibited at the John Berggruen Gallery in San Francisco in 1987. Goldberg described *Snow Queen* as a picture "marking a substantial departure from [Frankenthaler's] softer, more lyrical previous style. Vertical salmon-colored bands punctuate and ground the canvas and, in fact, create a gridlike structure that threatens to achieve — and almost succeeds in achieving — a static effect, prevented only by the ghostlike dynamic forms in the center."[1]

Note:
1. Beth Goldberg, "An Evolving Gesture," *Artweek* 18 (9 May 1987): 3.

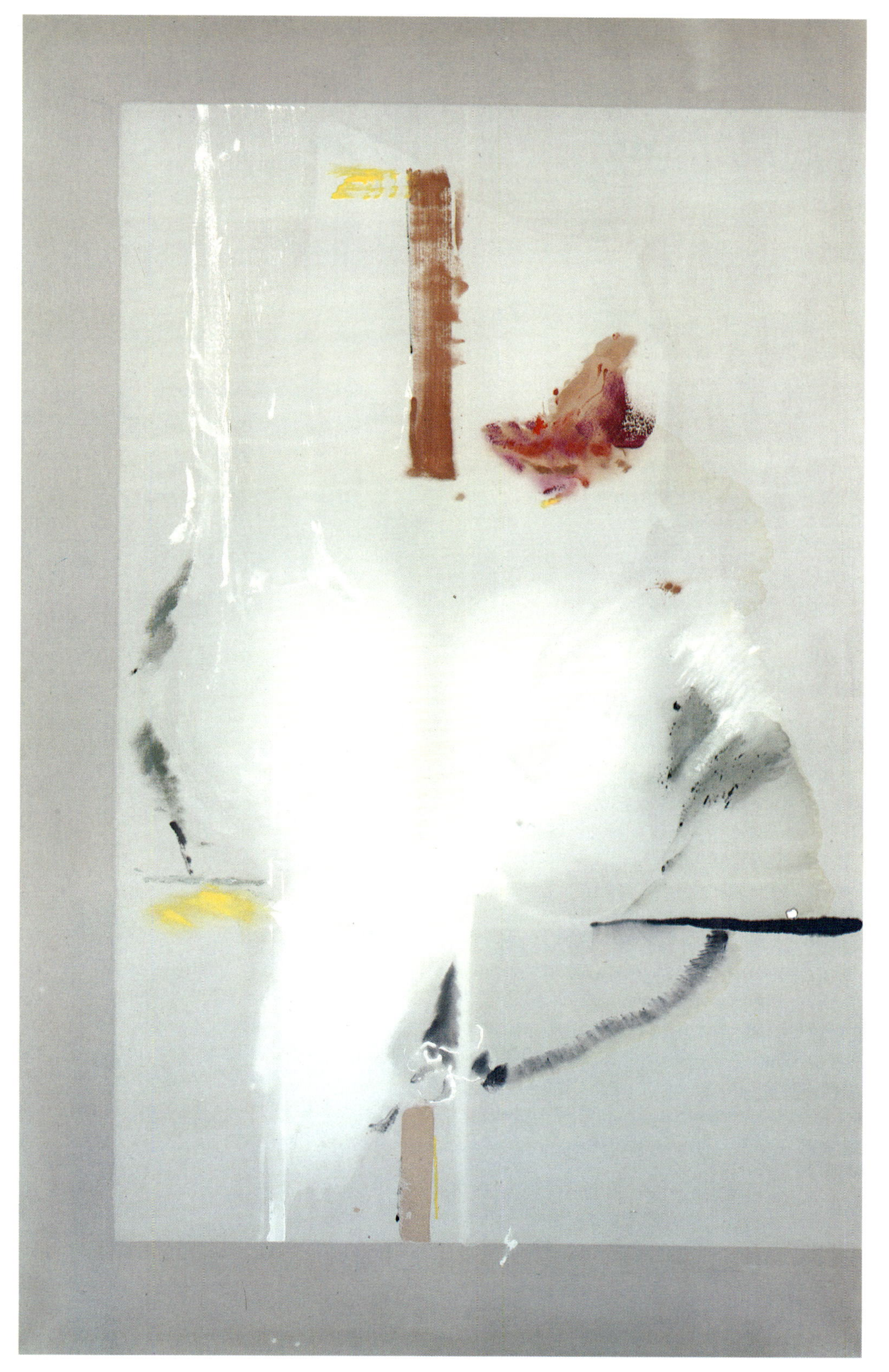

39. *Scarlatti.* 1987
Acrylic on canvas
7'4⅛" x 9'5¾" (224 x 289 cm.)
Inscribed, recto, l.r.: Frankenthaler
    verso, Frankenthaler Scarlatti 1987 a/c 7'4⅛" x 9'5¾"
Collection Robert and Linda Schmier

When *Scarlatti* and other works of 1987 were exhibited that year at the André Emmerich Gallery, it was observed that "Frankenthaler's new dependence upon geometric devices suggests a struggle for structural definition that contrasts with her signature improvisatory style."[1] A reason for this reaction may be that sometimes early critical perceptions of an artist come to form a mold by which later work is measured or compared. Frankenthaler's earlier paintings, seen in the context of Abstract Expressionism and described as spontaneous pourings of color, left the lingering impression of her art as being automatic and uncontrolled rather than composed and considered. Thus, when she began to use a gridlike structure in a more obvious way in the later 1980s, the response was one of surprise, despite the fact that previous paintings had used similar devices, albeit less directly.

Scarlatti is composed around the contrast between the diaphanous white passages in the center and the more firmly established straight lines that are placed near or tangent to the painting's exterior. Within these larger counterpoints are smaller details that reinforce or challenge the overall rhythm, such as the numerous horizontal or vertical white passages, or the long meandering green line across the bottom. Tying all of these disparate elements together is the intense blue of the picture's internal field.

Given its range of different passages and touches and its pairing of lyricism with dissonance, the picture is aptly named for the eighteenth-century Italian composer Domenico Scarlatti. "Actually it came about because one day the [Vladimir] Horowitz recording of Scarlatti was playing in the background and I happened to write down the name. A couple of weeks later I was working on this picture. It was a brilliant summer day, one that matched the sparkling mood of the Horowitz recording, so I called the painting *Scarlatti.*"

Note:
1. Susan Kandel and Elizabeth Hayt-Atkins, "Helen Frankenthaler," *Artnews* 87 (March 1987): 89.

Provenance:
(André Emmerich Gallery, New York)

Exhibition History:
New York, André Emmerich Gallery (cat. no. 2, color ill. n.p.), 1987

Selected Critical Reference:
Kandel and Hayt-Atkins, *Artnews* (March 1988), ill. p. 190

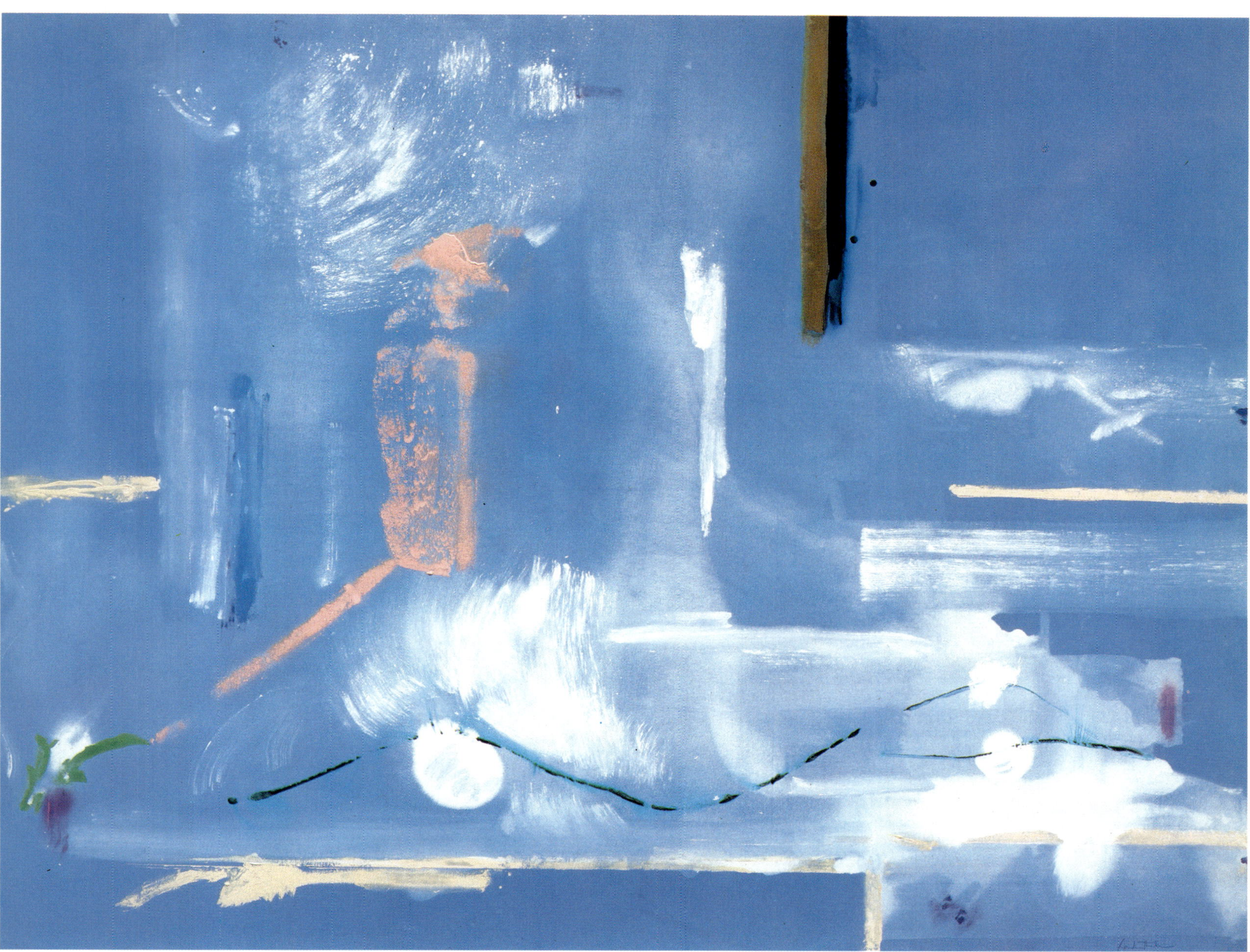

40. *Casanova.* 1988
  Acrylic on canvas
  5'11" x 11'9½" (180.3 x 359.4 cm.)
  Inscribed, l.r.: Frankenthaler
    verso: "Casanova" 1988 a/c 71" x 141½" (5'11" x 11'9½")
  Frankenthaler '88
  Private Collection

Exhibition History:
New York: André Emmerich Gallery (color ill. n.p.), 1989

Selected Critical References:
This work has not been discussed before.

"I realize," says Frankenthaler, "a different format, a shift in the shape of the canvas, often means a different kind of picture, a different attitude. I have noticed an important development in my work of the past three or four years. I often find myself making a new kind of picture that appears as a 'vertical landscape,' as opposed to all my previous horizontal landscapes." Within the forty pictures in this exhibition, certain general traits are present: the tall, vertical canvas is often more figural in character, as in *Nude, Las Mayas,* and *Portrait of a Lady in White,* while the nearly square surface leads to symmetry and a more centralized focus, as in *Swan Lake I, Buddha's Court,* or *Lush Spring.* Horizontal formats suggest the landscape, from *Eden* to *Into the West,* while more laterally extended compositions often effect bravura, as in *Chairman of the Board* or *Hint from Bassano.*

Casanova, a canvas twice as wide as its height, falls within this last category and maintains this general sense of grandeur. Here a massive black shape flows across the top of and downward into the lighter ground, a dramatic form not unlike that found in the upper region of *The Bay* (cat. no. 12). Frankenthaler notes that "here the black has the feel of a massive curtain lifting." The monumentality is checked by dense shapes of white and by smaller elements of color scattered across the surface, recalling those in *Sacrifice Decision* and *Grey Fireworks* (cat. nos. 35, 36). Arresting the downward pressure of the whole composition is the intense horizontal yellow passage across the lower edge, an element found in numerous works in this show.

Yet, despite these affinities to earlier works, *Casanova* also stands apart from them, chiefly for its palette. Frankenthaler's colors are often subtle shifts from seemingly standard ones into mauves, pinks, and pale greens. Here the hues are the basics, red, yellow, and blue, combined with white, gray, and black-brown.

(Continued from page 16)

Exhibition History:
Minneapolis, Minnesota: Minneapolis Institute of Arts (cat. no. 41),
    1957
New York: Tibor de Nagy Gallery, 1957
Osaka, Japan: Osaka International Festival (ill. p. 32), 1958
New York: The Jewish Museum (cat. no. 6, ill.), 1960
Bennington, Vermont: Bennington College (checklist no. 7), 1962
New York: Solomon R. Guggenheim Museum (checklist no. 3),
    1965
New York: Whitney Museum of American Art (traveling exhibi-
    tion, cat. no. 9, comm. p. 10, color ill. p. 23), 1969
Des Moines, Iowa: Des Moines Art Center (cat. no. 11, ill.), 1973
Waltham, Massachusetts: Rose Art Museum, Brandeis University
    (cat. no. 30, ill. p. 38), 1981

Selected Critical References:
Pollet, *Arts Magazine* (March 1957), comm. p. 54
Judd, *Arts Magazine* (March 1960), comm. p. 55
Goossen, *Art International* (20 October 1961), comm. p. 79
Berkson, *Arts Magazine* (May–June 1965), comm. p. 50
Goldin, *Arts Magazine* (February 1966), comm. p. 54
Friedman, *Artnews* (Summer 1966), comm. p. 67, ill. p. 31
Baro, *Art International* (September 1967), comm. and ill. p. 35
Rosenstein, *Artnews* (March 1969), comm. p. 31
K., H., *Berliner Morgenpost*, 4 October 1969, comm.
K., D., *Spandauer Volksblatt*, 12 October 1969, comm.
Alloway, *Artnews* (November 1971), comm. p. 89
Rose, 1972, comm. pp. 48, 50, 86; colorpl. 17
O'Hara, 1975, comm. p. 127, ill. p. 125
Guest, *Arts Magazine* (April 1975), comm. p. 59
Sandler, 1978, ill. p. 66
Munro, 1979, comm. p. 208
Belz, *Artnews* (May 1981), comm. p. 157, color ill. p. 156
Allara, *Artnews* (September 1981), comm. p. 184
Rubinstein, 1982, comm. p. 329
Elderfield, *Art in America* (February 1982), comm. p. 106, color ill.
    p. 102
———, 1989, comm. pp. 81, 103, 125, 126, 137, 337, 396; color ill.
    p. 105

(Continued from page 26)

Provenance:
(André Emmerich Gallery, New York)
Sydney and Frances Lewis, Richmond, Virginia

Exhibition History:
New York: André Emmerich Gallery, 1960
New York: The Jewish Museum (cat. no. 18, comm. p. 7, ill. p. 19),
    1960
New York: Decorative Arts Center (cat.), 1961
Bennington, Vermont: Bennington College (checklist no. 8), 1962
Waltham, Massachusetts: Rose Art Museum, Brandeis University
    (cat. no. 44, ill. p. 52), 1981
Greenville, South Carolina: The Greenville County Museum of
    Art (color ill. p. 17), 1984
Los Angeles: Museum of Contemporary Art (cat., comm. p. 47),
    1986–88

Selected Critical References:
Coates, *The New Yorker* (9 April 1960), comm. p. 159
Berkson, *Arts Magazine* (May–June 1965), comm. p. 50
Ashton, *Studio International* (August 1965), comm. p. 54
Friedman, *Artnews* (Summer 1966), comm. p. 67
Alloway, *Artnews* (November 1971), comm. p. 89
Rose, 1972, comm. p. 22, colorpl. 4
O'Hara, 1975, comm. p. 127
Taylor, *Boston Globe*, 10 May 1981, comm. p. A33
Elderfield, *Art in America* (February 1982), comm. p. 106, color ill.
    p. 104
Brandt, 1985, ill. p. 67
———, *Apollo* (December 1985), ill. p. 487
Scala, *New Art Examiner* (June 1986), ill. p. 28
Elderfield, 1989, comm. pp. 11–12, 13, 81, 137, 141, 144; color ill.
    p. 10

(Continued from page 62)
Guest, *Arts Magazine* (April 1975), comm. and color ill. p. 59
Russell, *The New York Times*, 2 May 1975, comm. p. 20
Holmes, *Houston Chronicle*, 21 October 1975, comm. sec. 1, p. 12
Elderfield, 1989, comm. p. 235, color ill. p. 212

Selected Chronology

Derived by Cathy Craft from Barbara Rose's monograph *Frankenthaler* (New York, 1972); Maureen St. Onge's version in Karen Wilkin, *Frankenthaler: Works on Paper 1949–84* (New York, 1984); and Heidi Colsman-Freyberger's revised and updated version in John Elderfield, *Frankenthaler* (New York, 1989). Travels are cited when relative to any of the forty paintings.

1928

Born December 12 in New York City to New York State Supreme Court Justice Alfred Frankenthaler and his wife, Martha (née Lowenstein); she is their third child, having been preceded by two sisters, now Mrs. Marjorie Iseman and Gloria F. Ross.

1940

Father dies January 7.

1945

After previous attendance at Horace Mann and Brearley, graduates from Dalton school. In the autumn continues to study painting, privately, with Rufino Tamayo, former art instructor at Dalton.

1946

Enters Bennington College in the spring and studies painting with Paul Feeley. The literary milieu includes Kenneth Burke, Erich Fromm, W. H. Auden, Stanley Edgar Hyman, Ralph Ellison, and schoolmate Sonya Rudikoff.

1947

Works for *MKR's Art Outlook,* a magazine review, and studies at the Art Students League with Vaclav Vytlacil during a nonresident term.

1948

Teaches art at Hale House, Boston, and works as a writer for *The Cambridge Courier* during spring nonresident term. In the summer travels with Gaby Rodgers to London, Amsterdam, Brussels, Switzerland, and Paris. In the fall shares studio on Twenty-first Street with Sonya Rudikoff in New York for one year; keeps same studio alone through winter 1951.

1949

Studies with painter Wallace Harrison at his Fourteenth Street school in New York during a nonresident term. In July graduates, with a B.A., from Bennington. In the autumn takes courses at the Graduate School of Fine Arts at Columbia University, including one with Meyer Schapiro.

1950

In New York shares an apartment with Gaby Rodgers on West Twenty-fourth Street, while painting at studio on Twenty-first Street. Organizes *Bennington College Alumnae Paintings* at Jacques Seligmann & Company in May. Meets critic Clement Greenberg and, through him, David Smith, Lee Krasner, Jackson Pollock, Willem and Elaine de Kooning, Franz Kline, Adolph Gottlieb, Barnett Newman, and other members of the first generation of the New York School. Studies for three weeks during the summer with Hans Hofmann in Provincetown, Massachusetts. Later in the summer visits Black Mountain College, North Carolina. In the autumn sees first Jackson Pollock exhibition, at Betty Parsons Gallery, New York. Adolph Gottlieb selects her work for inclusion in *Fifteen Unknowns,* an exhibition held in December at Kootz Gallery, New York.

1951

In January sees the Gorky retrospective at the Whitney Museum of American Art, New York. Moves to own apartment on West Twenty-third Street and continues to paint at the Twenty-first Street studio. Includes among her friends poets John Ashbery and Frank O'Hara, introduced to her through John Bernard Myers, and artists such as Harry Jackson, Grace Hartigan, Larry Rivers, and Alfred Leslie who are, like herself, associated with the recently started Tibor de Nagy Gallery. Begins visits to David Smith's in Bolton Landing, New York, as well as to Lee Krasner's and Jackson Pollock's in Springs, East Hampton, New York. In May participates in *9th Street: Exhibition of Paintings and Sculpture* at 60 East Ninth Street. In November has first solo exhibition at Tibor de Nagy Gallery, where she will exhibit through 1958.

1952

Included in *First Annual Exhibition of Painting and Sculpture,* held in
January at Stable Gallery, New York, and will continue to show
in the Stable Annuals through 1956. Shares studio with Friedel
Dzubas on Twenty-third Street. After summer travels through-
out Nova Scotia and Cape Breton, paints *Mountains and Sea* on
October 26.

1953

In January shows *Mountains and Sea* in second solo exhibition at
Tibor de Nagy Gallery. Visits to her studio by painters Kenneth
Noland and Morris Louis, who are impressed by her work, set
off an exchange of studio visits with the artists between New
York and Washington, D.C. During the summer travels in Spain
and France; visits the caves at Altamira and The Prado in
Madrid.

1954

Mother dies in April. In the summer travels to Spain, the hill
towns of Italy, Florence, Rome, and London and continues her
studies of Quattrocento and Old Master art. Meets Anthony
Caro. Moves to West End Avenue at Ninety-fourth Street,
where she lives and works through 1957.

1955

Rents Marca-Relli's house and studio in Springs, Long Island, during the summer. In the autumn included in *U.S. Painting: Some
Recent Directions* at Stable Gallery.

1956

During the summer travels to Paris, Germany, The Netherlands,
and Austria.

1957

In the spring is represented in several group exhibitions in New
York. In the summer visits Bolton Landing, East Hampton,
Long Island, Martha's Vineyard, and Provincetown.

1958

Marries Robert Motherwell in April. Travels extensively on hon-
eymoon during the spring and summer in Spain and France,
including trips to Altamira and Lascaux. Paints on board ship,
in Madrid, and in rented villa in Saint-Jean-de-Luz, France.
Upon return moves studio to vacant store on Ninety-fourth
Street at Third Avenue. Teaches painting in an adult education
program at Great Neck, Long Island, with other members of the
Tibor de Nagy Gallery.

1959

In the spring has first solo exhibition at André Emmerich Gallery,
New York, where she continues to exhibit. During summer
rents house in Falmouth, Massachusetts. Teaches painting and
drawing part-time at the School of Education, New York University, through 1961. Included in *School of New York: Some Younger Artists,* edited by B. H. Friedman, with an essay on the artist
by Sonya Rudikoff. Exhibits works in *Documenta II,* Kassel, West
Germany, and *V Bienal,* São Paulo, Brazil. Wins First Prize, *Pre-
mière Biennale de Paris,* Musée d'Art Moderne de la Ville de Paris,
for *Jacob's Ladder.*

1960

In January has first retrospective exhibition, organized and with
catalogue essay by Frank O'Hara, at The Jewish Museum.
Moves studio to Eighty-third Street and Third Avenue. During
the summer rents house on the Italian Riviera, in Alassio.

1961

In March has first exhibition in Los Angeles, at Everett Ellin Gallery. Establishes summer studio at Provincetown, where she
will paint during the summers, through 1969. In the autumn
has first of two solo shows at Galerie Lawrence, Paris, and is
included in *American Abstract Expressionists and Imagists* at the
Solomon R. Guggenheim Museum, New York. Executes Swan
Lake series. Appears with interviewer David Sylvester on BBC,
London. Visits Paris and London, as she will frequently during
the forthcoming years.

1962

In the spring has solo exhibition in Milan, at the Galleria
dell'Ariete, and a retrospective at Bennington College. Teaches
class for ailing William Baziotes at Hunter College, New York.
Begins to experiment with acrylic paint.

1963
Serves on Fulbright Selection Committee through 1965.

1964
In the spring has solo exhibition in London, at Kasmin Limited. Included in *Post-Painterly Abstraction* at the Los Angeles County Museum of Art. Moves Provincetown studio to residence, which overlooks the bay.

1965
David Smith dies in May. During the summer travels to Paris, Venice, Dubrovnik, Athens, the Greek Islands, and London. In December has first solo exhibition in Toronto, at David Mirvish Gallery, where she exhibits through 1976. Teaches for a short period at School of Fine Arts, University of Pennsylvania.

1966
Selected, along with Ellsworth Kelly, Roy Lichtenstein, and Jules Olitski, to represent the U.S. at the *XXXIII International Exhibition of Art* in Venice; in June travels to Italy for Biennial exhibition. Frank O'Hara dies in July. Teaches at the School of Visual Arts, New York, and at the School of Art and Architecture, Yale University, New Haven, Connecticut.

1967
In the spring has solo exhibitions at Nicholas Wilder Gallery, Los Angeles, and Gertrude Kasle Gallery, Detroit. Included in *American Art Now* in Montreal at Expo '67. Elected trustee at Bennington College, serving on the board until 1982. Moves Provincetown studio to wooded area away from the bay.

1968
Awarded the Joseph E. Temple Gold Medal by the Pennsylvania Academy of Fine Arts in Philadelphia. Appointed first woman fellow of Calhoun College, Yale University.

1969
In February touring retrospective exhibition, curated and with a catalogue essay by E. C. Goossen, opens at the Whitney Museum of American Art, New York. In the spring visits Paris, Ireland, and London. On the occasion of her retrospective, visits Berlin, Hanover, and London. Receives Honorary Degree, Doctor of Humane Letters, from Skidmore College, Saratoga Springs, New York.

1970
Moves New York studio to former carriage house on East Eighty-third Street. Teaches seminar in the spring at Yale University. In June visits Morocco and France. Teaches seminar at Hunter College, New York, in the autumn. Receives Spirit of Achievement Award from the Albert Einstein School of Medicine of Yeshiva University, New York.

1971
In the winter teaches seminar at Princeton University. Has solo exhibitions at Galerie Godard Lefort, Montreal, Heath Gallery, Atlanta, and Carl Solway Gallery, Cincinnati. Rents house for the summer in Cornwall Bridge, Connecticut. Is divorced from Robert Motherwell in July.

1972
In the spring has first solo exhibition in San Francisco, at John Berggruen Gallery, where she continues to exhibit, and at Fendrick Gallery, Washington, D.C. Included in Emile de Antonio's film *Painters Painting*. Barbara Rose's monograph on the artist is published in March. In June receives the Garrett Award at 70th American Exhibition, The Art Institute of Chicago. During the summer visits Ischia, Italy; makes sculptures at Anthony Caro's studio in London.

1973
In the spring has first solo exhibition in Dallas at Janie C. Lee Gallery, which later moves to Houston, where she continues to exhibit, and at Waddington Galleries II, London. Included in Barbara Rose's film, *American Art in the '60s*. Receives Honorary Degree, Doctor of Fine Arts, Smith College, Northampton, Massachusetts. Exhibits book-cover designs at The Metropolitan Museum of Art, New York. Elected to the Board of the Corporation of Yaddo, Saratoga Springs, New York, on which she serves through 1978.

1974

In the summer has first solo exhibition in Zurich at Galerie André
    Emmerich. Visits Strasbourg, Colmar, Basel, Ronchamps, and
    Paris. Receives Honorary Degree, Doctor of Fine Arts, Moore
    College of Art, Philadelphia. Elected Member, American Acad-
    emy and Institute of Arts and Letters. Leases house with studio
    space for two years on Ocean Drive West, Shippan Point, Stam-
    ford, Connecticut.

1975

Solo exhibition of paintings from 1969 through 1974 opens in April
    at the Corcoran Gallery of Art, Washington. Organized and
    with catalogue essay by Gene Baro, it travels to Seattle Art
    Museum and The Museum of Fine Arts, Houston. In the winter
    makes clay sculptures at Continental Can Company, Syracuse
    University. Summers in Stamford. Exhibits ceramic tiles in New
    York at both Solomon R. Guggenheim Museum and Rosa
    Esman Gallery.

1976

In March visits Arizona for the first time. Conducts seminar in the
    autumn at Harvard University and Radcliffe College. Receives
    Honorary Degree, Doctor of Arts, Bard College, Annandale-on-
    Hudson, New York, and the Art and Humanities Award, Yale
    University, Women's Forum. Designs Bicentennial commemo-
    rative poster commissioned by The Fort Worth Art Museum.

1977

During the year visits Arizona and Belgium; sees Rubens exhibi-
    tion in Antwerp. Has solo exhibitions at Greenberg Gallery, St.
    Louis, and Galerie Wentzel, Hamburg. In December has exhi-
    bition of works in different mediums at the Jacksonville Art
    Museum in Florida. Exhibition travels to the Fort Lauderdale
    Museum of Art and Loch Haven Art Center, Orlando, Florida.

1978

An exhibition of small paintings from 1949 through 1977, curated
    and with a catalogue essay by Andrew Forge, is organized by
    the International Communication Agency/USA. It debuts in
    January at André Emmerich Gallery, Downtown, New York,
    and tours the Far East, Australia, Mexico, and South America.

An exhibition of 1975–78 paintings, curated and with a catalogue essay by E. C. Goossen, is organized in the spring by
Bennington College, Vermont. In October buys a waterfront
house in Stamford, Shippan Point, Connecticut, and establishes
studio there. Holds solo exhibition at Knoedler Gallery, London, where she continues to exhibit. *Frankenthaler: Toward a New
Climate*, a film directed by Perry Miller Adato, appears as the
sixth program in *Thirteen Originals: Women in Art*, a seven-part
series produced by WNET/Thirteen, New York. Receives "An
Extraordinary Woman of Achievement" Award, National Con-
ference of Christians and Jews, and an Honorary Degree, Doctor of Art, Radcliffe College, Cambridge, Massachusetts.

1979

Spends the summer in Stamford working in the Shippan Point
    studio, a practice she continues in the 1980s. Receives an Hon-
    orary Degree, Doctor of Art, from Amherst College, Massachu-
    setts, and an Honorary Degree, Doctor of Fine Arts, from New
    York University. Receives Alumni Award for Outstanding
    Achievement, Bennington College.

1980

Exhibition of works from the 1970s, curated and with a catalogue
    essay by Cynthia Goodman, opens in February at the Saginaw
    Art Museum, Michigan, and travels throughout the state. Has
    solo exhibition at Galerie Ulysses, Vienna. Receives Honorary
    Degrees: Doctor of Fine Arts, Philadelphia College of Art; Doc-
    tor of Fine Arts, Williams College, Williamstown, Massachu-
    setts; Doctor of Art, Harvard University, Cambridge,
    Massachusetts.

1981

Travels in January to Paris and Bordeaux, France, to see *Depuis la
    Couleur*, an exhibition in which she is included. In May has an
    exhibition of work from the 1950s, curated and with a catalogue
    essay by Carl Belz, at the Rose Art Museum, Brandeis Univer-
    sity, Waltham, Massachusetts. In the autumn has solo exhibi-
    tion at Thomas Segal Gallery, Boston. Receives an Honorary
    Degree, Doctor of Fine Arts, Yale University, New Haven,
    Connecticut.

1982

Anthony Caro uses her New York studio to make paintings. Receives Honorary Degree, Doctor of Fine Arts, Brandeis University.

1983

Travels throughout the year to Japan, London, Paris, and Giverny. In the spring has first solo exhibition at Gallery One, Toronto, where she continues to exhibit. Receives Honorary Degree, Doctor of Fine Arts, University of Hartford, Connecticut.

1984

Visits Spain and London.

1985

Retrospective exhibition of works on paper, organized and sponsored by International Exhibitions Foundation, curated and with catalogue essay by Karen Wilkin, opens in February at the Solomon R. Guggenheim Museum, New York, and travels throughout the U.S. Designs sets and costumes for the Royal Ballet, Royal Opera House, Covent Garden production of *Number Three*, set to Prokofiev's Piano Concerto no. 3. Named member of the National Council on the Arts, National Endowment of the Arts, for a six-year term. Receives Honorary Degree, Doctor of Fine Arts, Syracuse University, New York.

1986

Teaches summer seminar at Skowhegan School of Painting and Sculpture in Maine. In July conducts master classes at the Santa Fe Institute of Fine Arts, New Mexico. Receives New York City Mayor's Award of Honor for Art and Culture.

1987

In the spring rents new studio space in warehouse area in Stamford. Travels to Barcelona in May.

1988

Work on paper by the artist is used in designs for poster and playbill to commemorate New York City Ballet's fortieth anniversary on the occasion of the American Music Festival at Lincoln Center. In June travels to Paris. Exhibits bronze screens at André Emmerich Gallery, New York, and Tyler Graphics Ltd., Mt. Kisco, New York. In November has solo exhibition at Heland Wetterling Gallery, Stockholm.

1989

Monograph on the artist by John Elderfield is published in January. Paintings retrospective, organized by Modern Art Museum of Fort Worth, curated and with catalogue essays by E.A. Carmean, Jr., opens in May at The Museum of Modern Art, New York. Scheduled to travel to Modern Art Museum of Fort Worth, Los Angeles County Museum of Art, and Detroit Institute of Arts.

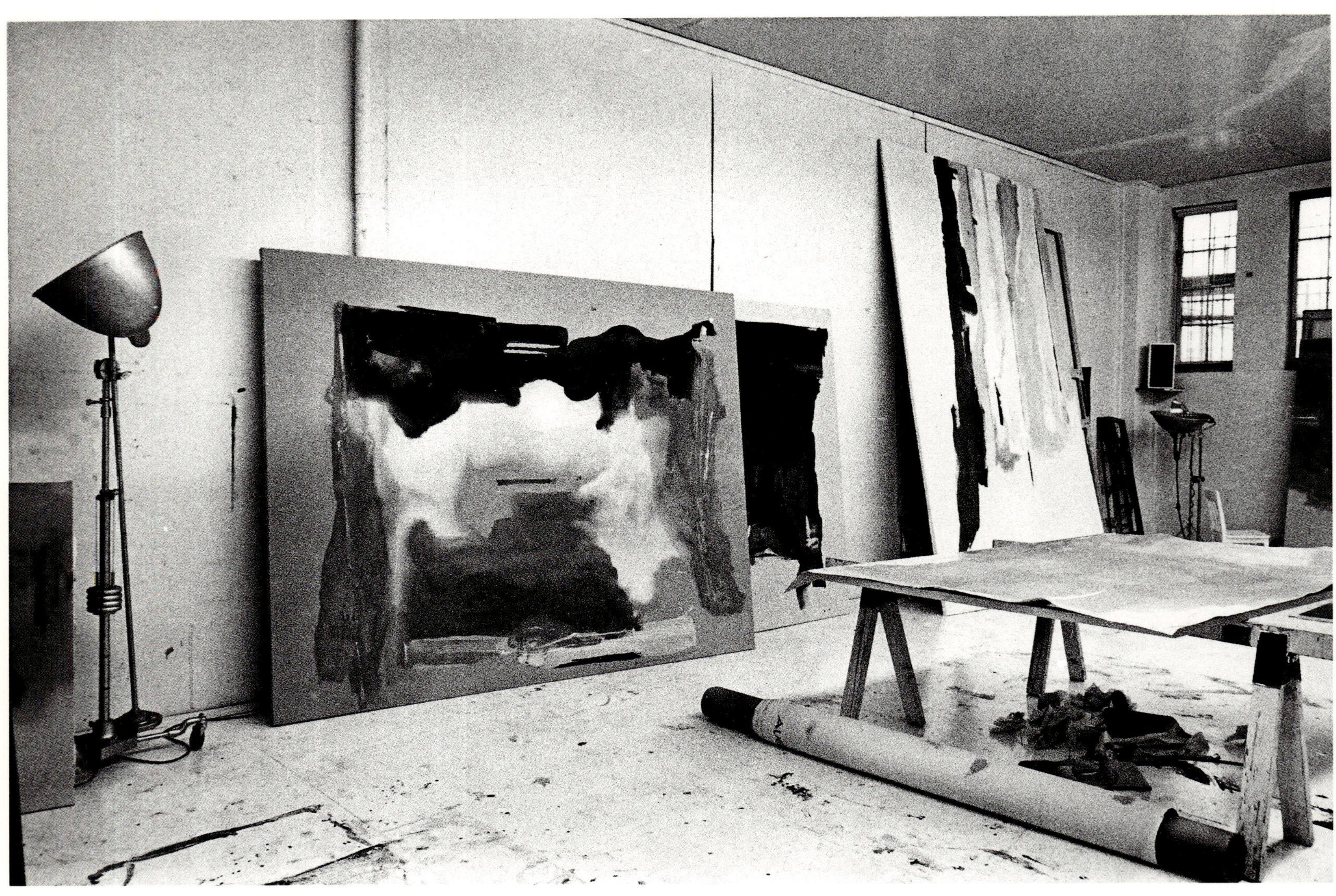

Helen Frankenthaler's New York studio, fall 1975. *Lush Spring* is seen upside down. Photograph: Edward Youklis

Selected Exhibition History

Exhibitions are listed chronologically by year and alphabetically by city within each year. Circulating exhibitions are listed under the city of the organizing institution. Catalogue information and the list of works that were shown in the exhibitions and included in this retrospective are also included. Asterisks indicate solo exhibitions. Only those exhibitions that included any of the forty paintings in this retrospective are cited in this selected exhibition history.

1953

*New York: Tibor de Nagy Gallery, *Helen Frankenthaler*, 27 January–14 February [*Mountains and Sea*]

1955

New York: Stable Gallery, *U.S. Painting: Some Recent Directions*, 29 November–23 December (checklist, foreword by Thomas B. Hess) [*Mountains and Sea*]

1957

Minneapolis, Minnesota: The Minneapolis Institute of Arts, *American Paintings: 1945–1957*, 18 June–1 September (catalogue introduction by Stanton L. Catlin) [*Eden*]

*New York: Tibor de Nagy Gallery, *Helen Frankenthaler*, 12 February–2 March [*Eden*]

1958

Buffalo, New York: Albright-Knox Art Gallery, *Contemporary Art—Acquisitions 1957–1958*, 8 December 1958–18 January 1959 (catalogue) [*Round Trip*]

*New York: Tibor de Nagy Gallery, *Helen Frankenthaler*, 6–25 January [*Round Trip*]

Osaka, Japan: Osaka International Festival, *The International Art of a New Era*, 12–20 April (catalogue essays by Michel Tapie and Jiro Yoshihara) [*Eden*]

1959

Kassel, West Germany: Museum Friedericianum, *Documenta II: Kunst nach 1945*, 11 July–11 October (catalogue with essay by Werner Haftmann) [*Mountains and Sea, Nude, Las Mayas*]

*New York: André Emmerich Gallery, *Helen Frankenthaler*, 30 March–25 April [*Nude, Las Mayas, Winter Hunt*]

São Paulo, Brazil: Museu de Arte Moderna, *V Biena!*, October; traveled to Minneapolis Institute of Arts (catalogue introduction by Sam Hunter) [*Winter Hunt*]

1960

Minneapolis, Minnesota: Walker Art Center, *60 American Painters 1960: Abstract Expressionist Paintings of the Fifties*, 3 April–8 May (catalogue essay by H. H. Arnason) [*Las Mayas*]

*New York: The Jewish Museum, *Helen Frankenthaler*, 26 January–2 March (catalogue essay by Frank O'Hara) [*Mountains and Sea, Eden, Las Mayas, Nude, Mother Goose Melody*]

*New York: André Emmerich Gallery, *Helen Frankenthaler*, 28 March–23 April [*Mother Goose Melody*]

1961

*Los Angeles: Everett Ellin Gallery, *Helen Frankenthaler: First West Coast Show*, 20 March–15 April [*Las Mayas*]

New York: Decorative Arts Center, *Art in America Show*, 7–22 December (catalogue) [*Mother Goose Melody*]

*Paris: Galerie Lawrence, *Helen Frankenthaler*, 15 October–7 November [*Las Mayas, Nude, Winter Hunt, Yellow Caterpillar*]

1962

*Bennington, Vermont: Bennington College, *Helen Frankenthaler*, May (brochure essay by Lawrence Alloway) [*Mountains and Sea, Eden, Mother Goose Melody*]

*Milan: Galleria dell'Ariete, *Helen Frankenthaler*, 8–18 March (catalogue essay by E. C. Goossen [reprinted article from *Art International* 5 (October 1961): 76–79] [*Las Mayas, Nude*]

1963

Urbana, Illinois: Krannert Art Museum, University of Illinois, *Contemporary American Painting and Sculpture: 1963*, 3 March–7 April (catalogue introduction by Allen S. Weller) [*Seascape with Dunes*]

1964

*London: Kasmin Limited, *Helen Frankenthaler*, 22 May–20 June (brochure) [*The Bay, Interior Landscape, Small's Paradise*]

1965

Detroit: Detroit Institute of Arts, *40 Key Artists of the Mid-20th Century*, 4–29 May (catalogue) [*The Bay*]

*New York: André Emmerich Gallery, *Helen Frankenthaler*, 16 March–3 April [*Buddha's Court, Tangerine*]

New York: Solomon R. Guggenheim Museum, *Word and Image*, 8 December 1965–2 January 1966 (brochure introduction by Lawrence Alloway) [*Eden*]

New York: Whitney Museum of American Art, *1965 Annual Exhibition of Contemporary American Painting*, 8 December 1965–30 January 1966 [*Tangerine*]

1966

Cleveland, Ohio: The Cleveland Museum of Art, *Fifty Years of Modern Art 1916–1966*, 15 June–31 July (catalogue by Edward B. Henning) [*Interior Landscape*]

*New York: André Emmerich Gallery, *Helen Frankenthaler*, 8–27 October (color brochure) [*Mauve District*]

Venice: *XXXIII International Biennial Exhibition of Art Venice 1966: United States of America*, 18 June–16 October; traveled to Washington, D.C.: National Collection of Fine Arts, Smithsonian Institution, 1 December 1966–15 January 1967 (catalogue introduction by Henry Geldzahler; essay by William S. Rubin) [*Mountains and Sea, Seascape with Dunes, The Bay*]

1967

Detroit: Detroit Institute of Arts, *Color, Image, and Form*, 11 April–21 May (catalogue) [*Interior Landscape*]

Grand Rapids, Michigan: Grand Rapids Art Museum, *20th Century American Painting*, 2–30 April (catalogue) [*The Bay*]

*Los Angeles: Nicholas Wilder Gallery, *Helen Frankenthaler*, 14 March–1 April [*Mauve District*]

New York: Whitney Museum of American Art, *1967 Annual Exhibition of Contemporary American Painting*, 13 December 1967–4 February 1968 (catalogue) [*Flood*]

1968

*New York: André Emmerich Gallery, *Helen Frankenthaler*, 6–25 April [*The Human Edge*]

San Francisco: San Francisco Museum of Art and San Francisco Art Institute, *Untitled 1968*, 9 November–29 December (catalogue with introduction by Wesley Chamberlain) [*Interior Landscape*]

1969

*New York: Whitney Museum of American Art, *Helen Frankenthaler*, 20 February–6 April; traveled under the auspices of the Whitney Museum of American Art and the International Council of The Museum of Modern Art with variant catalogues to London: Whitechapel Gallery, 7 May–8 June; Hanover: Orangie Herrenhausen, 21 August–21 September; Berlin: Kongresshalle, 2–21 October (catalogue essay by E. C. Goossen) [*Mountains and Sea, Eden, Round Trip, Nude, Winter Hunt, Arden, Swan Lake I, Seascape with Dunes, The Bay, Buddha's Court, Interior Landscape, Small's Paradise, Tangerine, Mauve District, Flood, The Human Edge, Summer Banner*]

New York: The Metropolitan Museum of Art, *New York Painting and Sculpture: 1940–1970*, 18 October 1969–8 February 1970 (catalogue foreword by Thomas Hoving; essay by Henry Geldzahler) [*Yellow Caterpillar*]

1971

New York: André Emmerich Gallery, 420 West Broadway, *Opening Exhibition*, September [*Sesame*]

*New York: André Emmerich Gallery, Uptown and Downtown, *Helen Frankenthaler*, 6 November–1 December (color brochure) [*Chairman of the Board*]

*Toronto: David Mirvish Gallery, *Helen Frankenthaler*, 1 May–5 June [*Sesame, Chairman of the Board*]

Yonkers, New York: The Hudson River Museum, *20th-Century Painting and Sculpture from the New York University Art Collection*, 2 October–14 November (catalogue) [*Seascape with Dunes*]

1972

Buffalo, New York: Albright-Knox Art Gallery, *Abstract-Expressionism: The First and Second Generations*, 19 January–20 February (checklist) [*Round Trip*]

1973

Des Moines, Iowa: Des Moines Art Center, *Twenty-Five Years of American Painting 1948–1973*, 6 March–22 April (catalogue introduction by Max Kozloff) [*Eden, Interior Landscape*]

*New York: André Emmerich Gallery, *Helen Frankenthaler*, 17 November–5 December (color brochure) [*Burnt Norton, Nature Abhors a Vacuum*]

*Toronto: David Mirvish Gallery, *Helen Frankenthaler*, 26 May–16 June [*Hint from Bassano*]

1974

Albany, New York: Executive Mansion, *Twentieth-Century American Painting*, September–December (catalogue) [*Round Trip*]

Houston: The Museum of Fine Arts, *The Great Decade of American Abstraction: Modernist Art 1960 to 1970*, 15 January–10 March (catalogue essay by E.A. Carmean, Jr.) [*Seascape with Dunes, Tangerine, Buddha's Court, Sesame*]

New York: National Institute of Arts and Letters, *Annual Exhibition*, Spring [*Nature Abhors a Vacuum*]

New York: Whitney Museum of American Art, *Frank O'Hara, A Poet Among Painters*, 12 February–17 March (checklist) [*Arden, Flood*]

Northampton, Massachusetts: Smith College Museum of Art, *Berenice Abbott, Helen Frankenthaler, Tatyana Grosman, Louise Nevelson*, 17 January–4 March (catalogue introduction by Charles Chetham) [*Mauve District, Nature Abhors a Vacuum*]

Richmond, Virginia: Virginia Museum of Fine Arts, *Twelve American Painters*, 30 September–27 October (catalogue essay by James M. Brown and William Gaines) [*Nature Abhors a Vacuum*]

San Francisco: Bank of America World Headquarters Building, 5 January–23 February [*Interior Landscape*]

1975

New York: André Emmerich Gallery, *Large Scale Paintings of the Sixties*, 20 September–15 October [*Buddha's Court*]

*New York: André Emmerich Gallery, *Helen Frankenthaler: New Paintings*, 8 November–2 December (color brochure) [*Lush Spring, Tulip Tint*]

New York: New York University Grey Art Gallery and Study Center, *Inaugural Exhibition, Part II*, Autumn (catalogue) [*Seascape with Dunes*]

*Washington, D.C.: Corcoran Gallery of Art, *Helen Frankenthaler: Paintings 1969–1974*, 20 April–1 June; traveled to Seattle: Seattle Art Museum, 26 June–14 September; Houston: The Museum of Fine Arts, 10 October–23 November (catalogue preface by Roy Slade; introduction by Gene Baro) [*Sesame, Burnt Norton, Hint from Bassano, Nature Abhors a Vacuum, Ocean Drive West #1*]

1976

New York: School of Visual Arts, *American Abstract Painting I: 1962–1965*, 29 March–21 April [*Buddha's Court*]

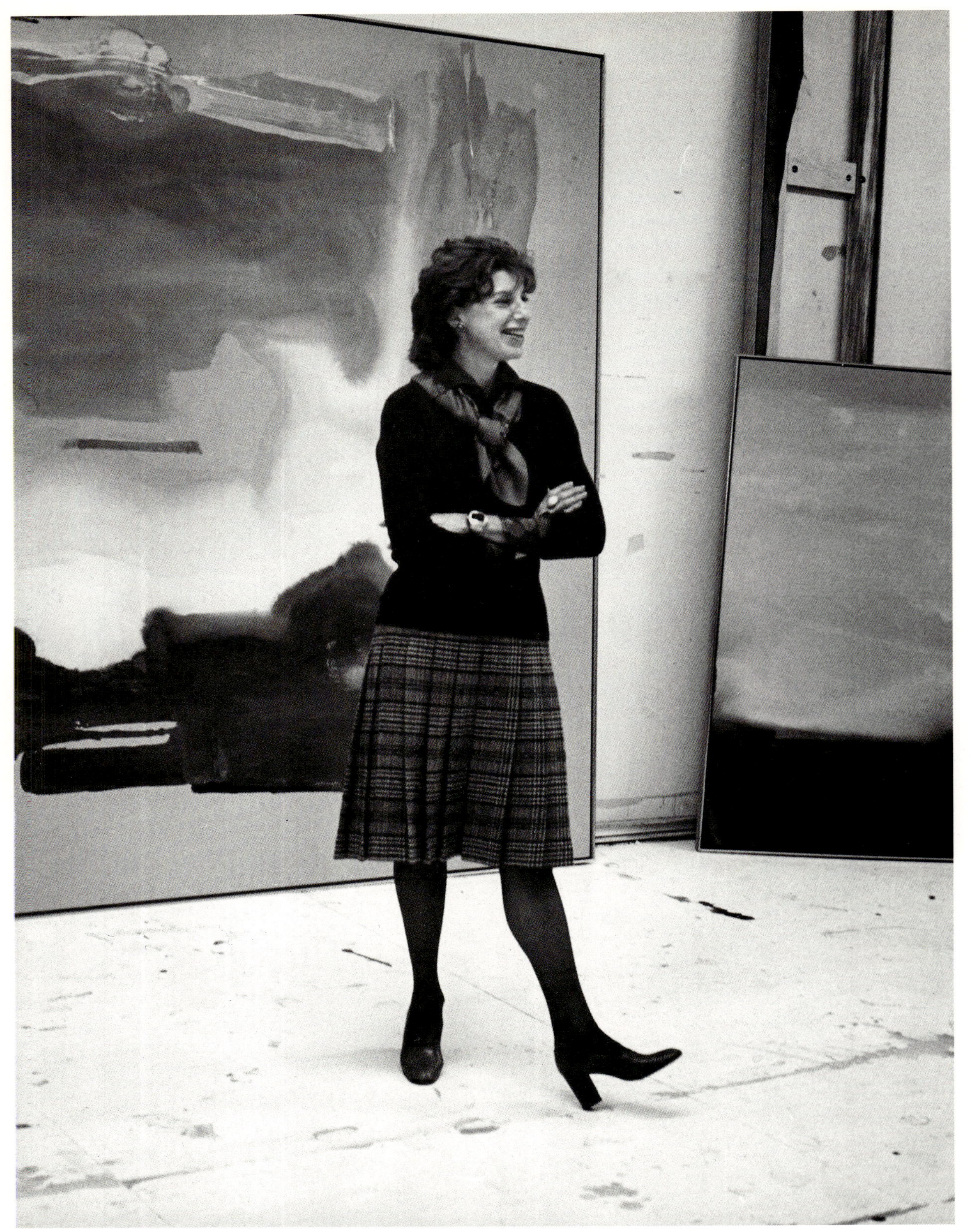

Tokyo: The Seibu Museum of Art, *Three Decades of American Art Selected by the Whitney Museum of American Art*, 18 June–20 July (catalogue essay by Thomas N. Armstrong III et al.) [*Arden*]

1977
Dallas: University Gallery, Southern Methodist University, *12 American Artists*, 15 November–18 December (checklist) [*Buddha's Court*]

Grand Rapids, Michigan: Grand Rapids Art Museum, *Themes in American Painting*, 1 October–30 November (catalogue) [*The Bay*]

*Jacksonville, Florida: Jacksonville Art Museum, *Helen Frankenthaler*, 1 December 1977–16 January 1978; traveled to Fort Lauderdale: Fort Lauderdale Museum of the Arts, 7–26 March; Orlando: Loch Haven Art Center, 18 April–4 June (catalogue essay by Christian Geelhaar [originally published in *Art International* 19 (15 October 1975): 42–49]) [*Arden, Seascape with Dunes, Small's Paradise*]

*New York: André Emmerich Gallery, *Helen Frankenthaler: New Paintings*, 19 November–8 December (color brochure) [*Natural Answer, Into the West, M*]

Paris: Salles de la Fondation Nationale des Arts Plastiques et Graphiques, *Biennale de Paris, une anthologie: 1959–1967*, 13 June–2 October; traveled to Tokyo: The Seibu Museum of Art, 3–29 March, 1978 (catalogue foreword by George Boudaille; introduction by Catherine Millet) [*Las Mayas*]

San Francisco: San Francisco Museum of Modern Art, *Collectors Collecting: American Abstract Art Since 1945*, 22 April–5 June (brochure) [*Interior Landscape*]

1978
*Bennington, Vermont: Suzanne Lemberg Usdan Gallery, Bennington College, *Helen Frankenthaler: Recent Paintings 1975–*

Helen Frankenthaler in her New York studio in fall 1975. Behind the artist is *Lush Spring* (cat. no. 27). Photograph: André Emmerich

1978, 15 April–13 May (catalogue essay by E. C. Goossen) [*Natural Answer, Into the West*]

*London: Knoedler Gallery, *Helen Frankenthaler*, opened 12 October (color brochure) [*Salome*]

1979
New York: *American Art from The Museum of Modern Art* (organized by The Museum of Modern Art); traveled to Bern, Switzerland: Kunstmuseum, 15 February–16 April; Cologne, West Germany: Museum Ludwig, 18 May–16 July; Lisbon, Portugal: Gulbenkian Foundation, 10 August–16 September; Madrid, Spain: Museo Español de Arte Contemporaneo, 8 October–18 November; Vienna, Austria: Museum des 20. Jahrhunderts, 10 December 1979–20 January 1980; Tel Aviv, Israel: Tel Aviv Museum, 18 February–12 April 1980 [*Mauve District*]

*New York: André Emmerich Gallery, *Helen Frankenthaler: New Paintings*, 3–28 November (color brochure) [*Portrait of a Lady in White*]

Reno, Nevada: Sierra Nevada Museum of Art in conjunction with Church Fine Arts Gallery, University of Nevada, *The New York School 1940–1960: The First Generation of Abstract Expressionism*, 3 February–4 March (catalogue essay by Irving Sandler) [*Winter Hunt*]

1980
Mexico City: Museo del Palacio de Bellas Artes, *La pintura de los Estados Unidos de museos de la ciudad de Washington*, 18 November 1980–4 January 1981 (catalogue essay by Milton Brown) [*Small's Paradise*]

1981
Bordeaux, France: Centre d'Arts Plastiques Contemporains de Bordeaux, *Helen Frankenthaler, Morris Louis, Kenneth Noland, Jules Olitski: Depuis la couleur 1958/1964*, 23 January–21 March (catalogue essay by Dominique Fourcade) [*Nude, Arden, Tangerine*]

Munich: Haus der Kunst, *Amerikanische Malerei: 1930–1980*, 14 November 1981–31 January 1982 (catalogue) [*Small's Paradise*]

*New York: André Emmerich Gallery, *Helen Frankenthaler: New Paintings*, 5–28 November (color brochure) [*Sacrifice Decision*]

*Waltham, Massachusetts: Rose Art Museum, Brandeis University, *Helen Frankenthaler: The 1950s*, 10 May–28 June (catalogue essay by Carl Belz) [*Eden, Winter Hunt, Mother Goose Melody*]

1982
*Houston: Janie C. Lee Gallery, *Helen Frankenthaler: New Paintings*, 30 April–May (color brochure) [*Grey Fireworks*]

Houston: Congregation Beth Israel, *Art of the 20th Century: A Revelation*, 14–24 October (catalogue essays by Carol Neuberger and Cyvia Wolff) [*Summer Banner*]

1983
Stamford, Connecticut: Whitney Museum of American Art in Fairfield County, *Live from Connecticut*, 15 September–2 November (catalogue essays by Lisa Phillips and Pamela Gruninger) [*Winter Hunt*]

1984
Greenville, South Carolina: Greenville County Museum of Art, *Andrew Wyeth: A Trojan Horse Modernist*, 9 March–15 April (catalogue essay by Thomas W. Styron) [*Mother Goose Melody*]

New York: André Emmerich Gallery, *Contemporary Classics*, 13 December 1984–5 January 1985 [*Winter Hunt*]

San Francisco: San Francisco Museum of Modern Art, *The 20th Century: The San Francisco Museum of Modern Art Collection*, 9 December 1984–17 February 1985 [*Interior Landscape*]

1985
Fort Worth: The Fort Worth Art Museum, *Grand Compositions: Selections from the Collection of David Mirvish*, 10 March–1 May (catalogue essay by Diane Upright) [*Hint from Bassano*]

1986
Fort Lauderdale, Florida: Museum of Art, *An American Renaissance, Paintings and Sculpture Since 1940*, 12 January–30 March

(catalogue introduction by Sam Hunter; essay by Robert C. Morgan) [*Nature Abhors a Vacuum*]

Los Angeles: Museum of Contemporary Art, *Individuals: A Selected History of Contemporary Art 1945–1986*, 10 December 1986–10 January 1988 (catalogue with pertinent essay by Kate Linker) [*Mother Goose Melody*]

*New York: André Emmerich Gallery, *Helen Frankenthaler: New Paintings*, 9 October–1 November (color brochure) [*On the Cusp*]

1987
*New York: André Emmerich Gallery, *Helen Frankenthaler: New Paintings*, 3–31 December (color brochure) [*Scarlatti*]

*San Francisco: John Berggruen Gallery, *Helen Frankenthaler*, 7 April–16 May (color brochure) [*Snow Queen*]

Washington, D.C.: National Museum of American Art, *Treasures from the National Museum of American Art*, 8 May–7 June 1987; traveled earlier to Seattle Art Museum, 20 February–13 April 1986; The Minneapolis Institute of Arts, 17 May–13 July; Cleveland Museum of Art, 13 August–5 October; Fort Worth: Amon Carter Museum, 7 November 1986–4 January 1987; Atlanta: The High Museum of Art, 3 February–29 March (catalogue with foreword by Charles C. Eldridge; essay by William Kloss) [*Small's Paradise*]

1988
Berlin, West Germany: Berlinische Galerie, *Stationen der Moderne*, 25 September 1988–6 January 1989 (catalogue) [*Nude*]

New York: Whitney Museum of American Art Downtown at Federal Reserve Plaza, *Made in the Sixties: Paintings and Sculpture from the Permanent Collection of the Whitney Museum of American Art*, 18 April–13 July (color brochure) [*Flood*]

1989
New York: André Emmerich Gallery, *Helen Frankenthaler*, 5–28 January (color brochure) [*Casanova*]

Selected Bibliography

This bibliography is listed chronologically and alphabetically within each year. Only those bibliographic entries that pertain to any of the forty paintings in the retrospective exhibition for which this catalogue was published have been included.

1953

F[einstein], S[am]. "Helen Frankenthaler." *Art Digest* 27 (15 February 1953): 20.

1957

P[ollet], E[lizabeth]. "Helen Frankenthaler." *Arts Magazine* 31 (March 1957): 54.

1958

G[ottlieb], E[laine]. "In the Galleries: Helen Frankenthaler." *Arts Magazine* 32 (January 1958): 55.

1959

It Is no. 3 (Winter–Spring 1959): 68.

T[illim], S[idney]. "In the Galleries: Helen Frankenthaler." *Arts Magazine* 33 (May 1959): 56.

1960

Butler, Barbara. "Movie Stars and Other Members of the Cast." *Art International* 4 (February–March 1960): 51–56.

Coates, Robert M. "The Art Galleries." *The New Yorker* 36 (9 April 1960): 155–59.

Greenberg, Clement. "Louis and Noland." *Art International* 4 (May 1960): 26–29.

J[udd], D[onald]. "In the Galleries." *Arts Magazine* 34 (March 1960): 55.

Read, Sir Herbert, and Arnason, H. Harvard. "Dialogue on Modern U.S. Painting." *Artnews* 59 (May 1960): 32–36.

S[eelye], A[nne]. "Nine Shows for Spring." *Artnews* 59 (March 1960): 39, 57–58.

1961

Ashbery, John. "Savage Splendor in Paris Persian Art Show." *New York Herald Tribune,* 18 October 1961.

———. "Paris Notes." *Art International* 5 (20 November 1961): 50.

Goossen, E. C. "Helen Frankenthaler." *Art International* 5 (20 October 1961): 76–79.

Gray, Cleve. "Art in America Show." *Art in America* 49 (1961): 94–100.

1962

Schoenberger, Gualtiero. "Les Expositions à Milan." *Art International* 6 (April 1962): 58.

1964

Bowen, Denis. "Helen Frankenthaler." *The Arts Review* 16 (May–June 1964): 2, 25.

Reichardt, Jasia. "Les expositions à l'étranger." *Aujourd'hui* 8 (October 1964): 56.

1965

Ashton, Dore. "Helen Frankenthaler." *Studio International* 170 (August 1965): 52–55.

Berkson, William. "Poet of the Surface." *Arts Magazine* 39 (May–June 1965): 45–50.

Braun, Lillian. "Often What I Want to Say Requires a Large Canvas." *Detroit Free Press,* 6 May 1965.

C[ampbell], L[awrence]. "Helen Frankenthaler." *Artnews* 64 (May 1965): 10.

Fried, Michael. "The Achievement of Morris Louis." *Artforum* 5 (February 1965): 34–40.

Geldzahler, Henry. "An Interview with Helen Frankenthaler." *Artforum* 4 (October 1965): 36–38.

Kozloff, Max. "Frankenthaler and Olitski." *The Nation* 200 (5 April 1965): 374–76.

1966

Baro, Gene. "USA at Venice." *Art and Artists* 1 (June 1966): 58–61.

Benedikt, Michael. "New York Letter." *Art International* 10 (December 1966): 64–65.

B[urton], S[cott]. "Helen Frankenthaler." *Artnews* 65 (November 1966): 11–12.

Friedman, B. H. "Towards the Total Color Image." *Artnews* 65 (Summer 1966): 31–33, 67–68.

Geldzahler, Henry. "Frankenthaler, Kelly, Lichtenstein, Olitski: A Preview of the American Selection at the 1966 Venice Biennale." *Artforum* 4 (June 1966): 32–38.

Goldin, Amy. "In the Museums: Helen Frankenthaler." *Arts Magazine* 40 (February 1966): 54.

Hudson, Andrew. "Biennale Begins Season—at Last." *The Washington Post*, 4 December 1966, p. G1.

Lowe, Harry. "In Venice: Backstage at the Biennale." *Museum News* 45 (November 1966): 11–18.

Lynton, Norbert. "Venice 1966." *Art International* 10 (15 September 1966): 80.

1967

Baro, Gene. "The Achievement of Helen Frankenthaler." *Art International* 11 (September 1967): 33–38.

Canaday, John. "Art: The Whitney Museum Annual." *The New York Times*, 13 December 1967, p. 54.

Gold, Barbara. "His, Hers Not in Towels Only." *The Sun* (Baltimore), 8 October 1967, p. D20.

Hudson, Andrew. "Business' 3c Starves Art." *The Washington Post*, 1 January 1967, p. G8.

Kramer, Hilton. "Sixties in Retrospect." *The New York Times*, 2 July 1967, sec. 2, p. D19.

Livingston, Jane. "Los Angeles Reviews." *Artforum* 5 (May 1967): 61–62.

Rose, Barbara. *American Art Since 1900.* New York: Praeger, 1967.

1968

Arnason, H. H. *History of Modern Art.* New York: Harry N. Abrams, Inc., 1968.

B[urton], S[cott]. "Helen Frankenthaler." *Artnews* 67 (May 1968): 13–14.

Mellow, James R. "New York Letter." *Art International* 12 (15 May 1968): 67–68.

Pomeroy, Ralph. "The Fall of France." *Art and Artists* 3 (June 1968): 36–37.

Rubin, William S. "New Acquisitions: Painting and Sculpture 1967–68." *The Museum of Modern Art Members Newsletter* (October 1968): n.p.

Willard, Charlotte. "In the Art Galleries." *New York Post Magazine*, 20 April 1968, p. 14.

1969

Andreae, Christopher. *Christian Science Monitor*, 19 March 1969, p. 12.

Battcock, Gregory. "Helen Frankenthaler." *Art and Artists* 4 (May 1969): 52–55.

Bowles, Jerry. "Helen Frankenthaler." *Arts Magazine* 43 (March 1969): 20, 22.

Brett, Guy. "Evolution of Frankenthaler." *The Times* (London), 26 May 1969, p. 5.

Denvir, Bernard. "London Letter." *Art International* 13 (September 1969): 66.

Gold, Barbara. "A Retrospective in Limbo." *The Sun* (Baltimore), 23 March 1969, p. D22.

Grinke, Paul. "Free Fall." *The Spectator* (London), 16 May 1969.

"Heiress to a Tradition." *Time* 93 (28 March 1969): 64–69.

K., D. "Das Vorbild läßt sich inspirieren." *Spandauer Volksblatt*, 12 October 1969.

K., H. "Ihre Heimat sind die arkadischen Gefilde." *Berliner Morgenpost*, 4 October 1969.

Kramer, Hilton. "Abstraction and the Landscape Paradigm." *The New York Times*, 2 March 1969, sec. 2, p. 31. [Reprinted in Kramer, Hilton. *The Age of the Avant-Garde.* New York: Farrar, Straus, and Giroux, 1973].

L., W. "Aus einem Guß." *Telegraf* (Berlin), 4 October 1969.

Mellow, James R. "New York Letter." *Art International* 13 (20 May 1969): 56.

Overy, Paul. "Colour Painting." *The Financial Times* (London), 20 May 1969.

Rose, Barbara. "Painting within the Tradition: The Career of Helen Frankenthaler." *Artforum* 7 (April 1969): 28–33.

Rosenberg, Harold. "In the Galleries." *The New Yorker* 45 (29 March 1969): 118, 120.

Rosenstein, Harris. "The Colorful Gesture." *Artnews* 68 (March 1969): 29–31, 68.

1970

Catalog of the Permanent Collection of Painting and Sculpture. San Francisco: San Francisco Museum of Art, 1970.

Fried, Michael. *Morris Louis.* New York: Harry N. Abrams, Inc., 1970.

Hunter, Sam. *La Pittura Americana del Dopoguerra.* Milan: Frateli Fabbri Editori, 1970.

Lucie-Smith, Edward, and White, Patricia. *Art in Britain 1969/70.* London: J. M. Dent and Sons, Ltd., 1970.

1971

Alloway, Lawrence. "Frankenthaler as Pastoral." *Artnews* 70 (November 1971): 67–68, 89–90.

Heywood, Irene. "Twenty Years toward Instant Success." *The Montreal Star,* 20 February 1971.

Leymarie, Jean. Foreword to *Art Since Mid-Century.* Vol. 1, *Abstract Art.* Greenwich, Connecticut: New York Graphic Society, 1971.

Nemser, Cindy. "Interview with Helen Frankenthaler." *Arts Magazine* 46 (November 1971): 51–55.

Pop, Happening, Hard Edge, Neo-Surrealismus, Kritischer Realismus, Minimal Arts Povera, Kinetik, Post-Painterly Abstraction, Land-Art, Electronic-Art Op, Project-Art, Process-Art, Fluxus: Revolution ohne Programm. Munich: Bertelsmann Kunstverlag, 1971.

Raphael, Shirley. "Frankenthaler — Sharing the Joy of Life." *The Gazette* (Montreal), 20 February 1971, p. 42.

———. "Un Tachiste Parmi Nous: Helen Frankenthaler." *Vie Des Arts,* no. 64 (Autumn 1971): 66–69.

Wilson, Peter. "A 'Pioneer' Artist Who Has Lasted." *Toronto Daily Star,* 8 May 1971.

1972

Champa, Kermit S. "New Work of Helen Frankenthaler." *Artforum* 10 (January 1972): 55–59.

Contemporary Art 1942–72: Collection of the Albright-Knox Art Gallery. New York: Praeger Publishers, Inc., in association with the Albright-Knox Art Gallery, 1972.

Hunter, Sam, and Jacobus, John. *American Art of the 20th Century.* New York: Harry N. Abrams, Inc., 1972.

Kingsley, April. "James Brooks: Stain into Image." *Artnews* 71 (December 1972): 48.

"Myths of Sensibility." *Time* 99, pt. 1 (20 March 1972): 72–77.

Nemser, Cindy. "Stereotypes and Women Artists." *Feminist Art Journal* 1, no. 1 (April 1972): 22–23.

Price, Vincent. *The Vincent Price Treasury of American Art.* Waukesha, Wisconsin: Country Beautiful Corp., 1972.

Rose, Barbara. *Frankenthaler.* New York: Harry N. Abrams, Inc., 1972.

1973

Kramer, Hilton. "Helen Frankenthaler." *The New York Times,* 1 December 1973, p. 27.

Loercher, Diana. "Has Modern Art Run Out of Ways to Be Abstract?" *The Christian Science Monitor,* 6 December 1973, p. 30.

Masheck, Joseph. "Reviews." *Artforum* 11 (March 1973): 87.

Rose, Barbara. "Painting Today." *Partisan Review* 1 (1973): 82–94.

Von Baron, Judith. "Helen Frankenthaler." *Arts Magazine* 48 (December 1973): 72–73.

1974

Carmean, E.A., Jr. "Modernist Art." *The Art Gallery* (January 1974): 55–58.

Kim, Whee. "A Personal Definition of Pictorial Space." *Arts Magazine* 49 (November 1974): 74–78.

1975

Baro, Gene. "Helen Frankenthaler." *Vogue* (June 1975): 104, 144.

Forgey, Benjamin. "A Frankenthaler Spring in D.C." *Washington Star-News,* 27 April 1975, pp. E1, E3.

Guest, Barbara. "Helen Frankenthaler: The Moment and the Distance." *Arts Magazine* 49 (April 1975): 58–59.

Holmes, Ann. "Frankenthaler's Canvases Soar with Buoyancy." *Houston Chronicle,* 21 October 1975, sec. 1, p. 12.

Hudson, Andrew. "Washington Letter." *Art International* 6 (15 June 1975): 97–98.

Kagan, Andrew. "Paul Klee's Influence on American Painting." *Arts Magazine* 50 (September 1975): 84–89.

Kramer, Hilton. "Art: Lyric Vein in Frankenthaler Paintings." *The New York Times,* 15 November 1975, p. 21.

Metzger, Jeanne. "Art Scene." *The Herald* (Everett, Washington) 28 June 1975.

O'Hara, Frank. *Art Chronicles: 1954–1966.* [Reprint of essay in The Jewish Museum 1960 retrospective catalogue] New York: George Braziller, 1975.

Richard, Paul. "A Painting of Influence." *The Washington Post*, 16 January 1975, p. C1.

Russell, John. "Art: Helen Frankenthaler at Corcoran." *The New York Times*, 2 May 1975, p. 20.

1976

"Americans in Paris." *The Art Gallery* 19 (August–September 1976): 44.

Carmean, E.A., Jr. "Morris Louis and the Modern Tradition I: Abstract Expressionism." *Arts Magazine* 51 (September 1976): 70–75.

Hoesterey, Ingeborg. "New York." *Art International* 20 (February–March 1976): 63.

Lorber, Richard. "Helen Frankenthaler." *Arts Magazine* 50 (February 1976): 12.

Preble, Duane. *We Create Art Creates Us.* San Francisco: Cranfield Press, 1976.

Wood, Harry. "Frankenthaler Has an Unobtrusive Presence." *Phoenix Lecture*, 11 March 1976, pp. 38–39.

1977

Arnason, H. H. *History of Modern Art.* 2d ed. New York: Harry N. Abrams, Inc., 1977.

Carmean, E.A., Jr. *Morris Louis: Major Themes and Variations.* Washington, D.C.: National Gallery of Art, 1977.

Elderfield, John. "Morris Louis and Twentieth-Century Painting." *Art International* 21 (May–June 1977): 24–32.

"La Cote des peintres, le prix des femmes." *Art Press International* (March 1977): 38.

S[tevens], M[ark]. "Sophisticated Lady." *Newsweek* 90 (5 December 1977): 94.

Touraine, Liliane. "Helen Frankenthaler: le geste et le savoir." *Art Press International* (March 1977): 22–23.

1978

Carmean, E.A., Jr. "On Five Paintings by Helen Frankenthaler." *Art International* 22 (April–May 1978): 28–32.

Forge, Andrew. "Frankenthaler: The Small Paintings." *Art International* 22 (April–May 1978): 21–25, 33.

Frackman, Noel. "Helen Frankenthaler." *Arts Magazine* 52 (February 1978): 30.

Goossen, E. C. "Helen Frankenthaler: Notes on Some Recent Paintings." *Bennington Review* (April 1978): 45–61.

Maloon, Terence. "Helen Frankenthaler at Knoedler." *Artscribe*, no. 15 (December 1978): 50–52.

Sandler, Irving. *The New York School: The Painters and Sculptors of the Fifties.* New York: Harper & Row, Publishers, 1978.

1979

Munro, Eleanor. *Originals: American Women Artists.* New York: Simon and Schuster, 1979.

Museum moderner Kunst: Kunst der Letzten 30 Jahre. Wien: Museum moderner Kunst, 1979.

1980

Goodman, Cynthia. *Helen Frankenthaler: Works of the Seventies.* Saginaw, Michigan: The Saginaw Art Museum, 1980.

Katzen, Lila. "Manifest Destiny: Mentors and Protégés." *Art Journal* (Summer 1980): 257–59.

Rose, Barbara. *American Painting.* New York: Rizzoli International Publications, 1980.

Tatransky, Valentine. "Helen Frankenthaler." *Flash Art*, nos. 94–95 (January–February 1980): 26.

1981

Allara, Pamela. "Whispers and Cries." *Artnews* 80 (September 1981): 182–84.

Belz, Carl. "Eden." *Artnews* 80 (May 1981): 156–57.

Deschamps, Madeleine. *La Peinture Americaine: Les mythes et la matière.* Paris: Editions Denoël, 1981.

Huth, Michel. "La Mémoire Future." *Connaissance des Arts* (October 1981): 83.

Kramer, Hilton. "Helen Frankenthaler's Art in the 50's." *The New York Times*, 7 June 1981, p. D31.

Mays, John Bentley. "Energy and Spirit of 1950s Keep Frankenthaler Fresh." *The Globe and Mail* (Toronto), 23 May 1981.

Russell, John. *The Meanings of Modern Art.* New York: Harper & Row, Publishers, 1981.

———. "Recent Paintings by Helen Frankenthaler." *The New York Times*, 13 November 1981, p. C26.

Taylor, Robert. "Frankenthaler Show Splendid and Revealing." *Boston Globe*, 10 May 1981, pp. A27, A33.

1982

"Art: The Tightrope Helen Frankenthaler Walks." *The New York Times,* 9 December 1982.

Carmean, E.A., Jr. "Celebrating the Birth of Stain Painting." *The Washington Post,* 26 October 1982, p. B7.

Elderfield, John. "Specific Incidents." *Art in America* 70 (February 1982): 100–106.

Fenton, Terry. "The Painting of Morris Louis." *Arts Magazine* 57 (September 1982): 66–68.

Johnson, Patricia C. "Frankenthaler Poetry on Canvas." *Houston Chronicle,* 13 May 1982, sec. 4, p. 18.

Museum moderner Kunst. Wien: Verlag Westermann, 1982.

Rubinstein, Charlotte S. *American Women Artists.* Boston: Avon Publishers, 1982.

1983

Berman, Avis. "Arena for Art High Above Manhattan." *Architectural Digest* 40, pt. 3 (September 1983): 158–65.

Clement, Melissa. "Frankenthaler: America's First Lady of Abstract Art." *The Fayette Observer* (Fayetteville, North Carolina), 4 November 1983.

Hall, Lee. "Celebrations in an Age of Anxiety." *House & Garden* (December 1983): 29.

Raynor, Vivien. "Works of State Residents Shine in 3 Shows." *The New York Times,* 20 October 1983, p. 24.

1984

Broder, Patricia Janis. *The American West: The Modern Vision.* Boston: Little, Brown & Co., 1984.

1985

Baele, Nancy. "Works Provide Glimpse of Artist's Sensibility." *Ottawa Citizen,* 2 August 1985.

Brandt, Frederick R. "Building a Collection for the Twentieth Century: The Sydney and Frances Lewis Collection of Late Twentieth-Century American Art." *Apollo* (December 1985): 484–87.

———. *Late 20th-Century Art: Selections from the Sydney and Frances Lewis Collection in the Virginia Museum of Fine Arts.* Richmond: Virginia Museum of Fine Arts, 1985.

Hunter, Sam, and Jacobus, John. *Modern Art: Painting, Sculpture, Architecture.* New York: Harry N. Abrams, Inc., 1985.

Mays, John Bentley. "Frankenthaler at Her Suburban Best." *The Globe and Mail* (Toronto), 27 July 1985.

Upright, Diane. *Morris Louis: The Complete Paintings.* New York: Harry N. Abrams, Inc., 1985.

W[eiss], P[eg]. "Collections." *Everson Museum of Art Bulletin* (January 1985): n.p.

1986

Arnason, H. H. *History of Modern Art: Painting, Sculpture, Architecture, Photography.* 3d ed. New York: Harry N. Abrams, Inc., 1986.

Elderfield, John. *Morris Louis.* New York: The Museum of Modern Art, 1986.

The Robert O. Anderson Building. Los Angeles: Los Angeles County Museum of Art, 1986.

Scala, Mark. "Virginia Museum Adds $22 Million West Wing." *New Art Examiner* (June 1986): 28–31.

1987

Goldberg, Bob. "An Evolving Gesture." *Artweek,* 9 May 1987, p. 3.

1988

Clothier, Peter. "Eli Broad, A Cool Head about Hot Art." *Artnews* 87 (January 1988): 142–45.

Kandel, Susan, and Hayt-Atkins, Elizabeth. "Helen Frankenthaler." *Artnews* 87 (March 1988): 189–90.

Sandler, Irving. *American Art of the Sixties.* New York: Harper & Row, Publishers, 1988.

Yarrow, Andrew L. "Whitney Returns to Downtown." *The New York Times,* 16 April 1988, p. 12.

1989

Elderfield, John. *Frankenthaler.* New York: Harry N. Abrams, Inc., 1989.

Notes to the catalogue

This catalogue serves as an accompaniment to Frankenthaler's 1989–90 paintings retrospective, and it takes a specific and focused look at each of the forty works included in this exhibition. Consequently, apparent "gaps" in the Selected Exhibition History, Selected Bibliography, and Chronology exist because the information did not pertain to any of the forty paintings.

Catalogue entries contain information under the following categories:

Catalogue number
Title
Date
Dimensions
Inscription
Collection
Provenance
Exhibitions
References

Information is as complete as possible through November 1988. The paintings are numbered consecutively from one to forty and are ordered chronologically.

Titles and dates are those given by the artist and are in accordance with the latest verification found in John Elderfield's 1989 monograph on the artist. Dimensions are given in feet and inches, followed by centimeters; height precedes width.

The full wording and placement is given for all inscriptions, whenever available. Since the mid-1970s, Frankenthaler's general policy is to record in china marker on a canvas's verso its title, date, medium, dimensions in feet and inches, and her signature.

The name and place of residence of each current owner are listed unless the owner restricted this information. Former owners and dealers involved in the transfer of ownership, beginning with the earliest, are listed. The André Emmerich Gallery, New York, Frankenthaler's dealer since 1959, was a major source in tracing provenance.

Exhibitions are listed chronologically by year, beginning with the earliest, and alphabetically by place within a single year. Listings include the city, museum or gallery, year, and catalogue and illustration information. Circulating exhibitions are noted under city of origin and then as "traveling exhibition." Their complete itinerary, along with complete exhibition information for all pertinent shows, can be found in the Selected Exhibition History. Catalogues with essays differ from color brochures and are noted. Catalogue information is recorded in the Selected Exhibition History and is not repeated in the Selected Bibliography.

Specific references to each painting found in books, monographs, and articles are abbreviated and listed chronologically. Since references often document reproductions, any that include comments in the text are noted with the abbreviation "comm." References are as complete as the information available to the compiler. Complete bibliographic information can be found in the Selected Bibliography.

Abbreviations:

a/c	acrylic on canvas
cat.	catalogue
cat. no.	catalogue number
c.l.	center left
c.r.	center right
color ill.	color illustration
colorpl.	colorplate
comm.	commentary
ill.	illustration
l.l.	lower left
l.r.	lower right
n.p.	no page
p., pp.	page, pages
r.c.	right center
sec.	section
u.l.	upper left
u.r.	upper right

Modern Art Museum of Fort Worth Board of Trustees